# The Rural Middle East

## Peasant Lives and Modes of Production

Edited by
Kathy & Pandeli Glavanis

Birzeit University
Zed Books Ltd
London and New Jersey

*The Rural Middle East* was first published by Zed Books Ltd,
57 Caledonian Road, London N1 9BU, UK,
and 171 First Avenue, Atlantic Highlands, New Jersey 07716, USA,
and by Birzeit University in 1990



Cover design by Andrew Corbett.

Typeset by Photosetting, Yeovil, Somerset.

Printed and bound in the United Kingdom
by Biddles Ltd, Guildford and King's Lynn.



**British Library Cataloguing in Publication Data**

The Rural Middle East : peasant lives and modes of
production.
1. Middle East. Social conditions
I. Glavanis, Kathy II. Glavanis, Pandeli
956'.06

ISBN 0-86232-770-9
ISBN 0-86232-771-7 Pbk

**Library of Congress Cataloging-in-Publication Data**

The Rural Middle East : peasant lives and modes of
production/edited by Kathy & Pandeli Glavanis :
with a preface by Norman Long.
p. cm.
Bibliography: p.
Includes index.
ISBN 0-86232-770-9 : £29.95 ($55.00 U.S.).—
ISBN 0-86232-771-7 (pbk.) : £8.95 ($16.95 U.S.)
1. Peasantry—Middle East. 2. Middle East—Rural
conditions.
I. Glavanis, Kathy R.G. II. Glavanis, Pandeli M.
D1537.3.R87 1989
305.5'633'0956—dc20

# Contents

**Tables**



**Figures**

Dedicated to the memory of
'ALI MUKHTAR
A prominent Egyptian socio-political thinker who was central in the development of many of the ideas and concepts in this book and unique among Arab intellectuals in his critical and insightful approach to the study of contemporary agrarian relations in the Middle East.

# A Note from Birzeit University

Birzeit University, an independent Palestinian university located in the Israeli-occupied West Bank, or occupied Palestine, is pleased to have hosted the 1983 and 1985 conferences on rural sociology, some of whose papers constitute the present volume. These meetings of local and international scholars and researchers embodied several facets of our core concerns: relevant research on critical questions in our area, interaction between the university and the community, and international exchange and co-operation.

Today, the university campuses where this exchange took place have been closed by military order for over 16 months, since 9 January 1988, and the university's 2,650 students, 210 faculty and 330 staff members are barred from using any of the facilities. Students and teachers are barred from classrooms, researchers from the library, and scientists and engineers from their laboratories. Faculty and students have attempted to continue education off-campus, but have been harassed by the army and classes have been banned by the authorities.

The five other Palestinian universities in the West Bank and Gaza are suffering a similar fate and all schools in the West Bank have been closed for most of this period. Schoolchildren are thus banned from learning to read and write. Israeli policy at present can be summed up in one phrase: 'Education is forbidden.' The military authorities have used the closure of schools and universities as a means to pressure and punish an entire population. To starve minds is perhaps a more sophisticated punishment than to embargo food, but it is no less a fundamental violation of a basic right. Birzeit University hopes the readers of this volume will both enjoy the fruits of the 1983 symposium and act to ensure that future academic endeavours may take place in fully functioning independent Palestinian universities.

Dr Gabi Baramki, Vice-President
Birzeit University
Ramallah

# Acknowledgements

The editors wish to thank the Department of Sociology and Social Policy and the Centre for Middle East Studies at the University of Durham, the Institute of Sociology and Social Anthropology at the University of Amsterdam and the Department of Sociology and Anthropology at the University of Birzeit for sponsoring the two conferences which generated the ideas, arguments and contributions that led to the publication of this volume. The editors also wish to thank the contributors for waiving their royalties in order that Birzeit University could undertake the role of co-publisher. Finally, the editors wish to thank the editors of *Review* who have kindly given their permission to reproduce Georg Stauth's article 'Capitalist farming and small peasant households in Egypt' which was initially presented at an earlier conference held in Durham in 1981.

Kathy Glavanis and Pandeli Glavanis
Ramallah

# Contributors

**Kathy R. G. Glavanis** Assistant Professor, Department of Sociology and Anthropology, Birzeit University, Palestine.

**Pandeli M. Glavanis** Lecturer in the sociology of the Middle East and Islamic Studies, Department of Sociology and Social Policy, University of Durham, United Kingdom.

**Nico Kielstra** Senior Lecturer in social anthropology, Department of European and Mediterranean Studies, University of Amsterdam, The Netherlands.

**Sarah Graham-Brown** Freelance writer on the Middle East, London, United Kingdom.

**Salim Tamari** Assistant Professor, Department of Sociology and Anthropology, University of Birzeit, Palestine.

**Alex Pollock** Project Co-ordinator, United Nations Association International Service, Palestine.

**Georg Stauth** Lecturer, Sociology of Development Research Centre, University of Bielefeld, Federal Republic of Germany.

**Zülküf Aydin** Lecturer, Department of Sociology and Social Policy, University of Durham, United Kingdom.

**Deniz Kandiyoti** Senior Lecturer, Social Sciences Division, Richmond College, United Kingdom.

**Annelies Moors** Lecturer, Department of European and Mediterranean Studies, University of Amsterdam, The Netherlands.

# Introduction

*Kathy and Pandeli Glavanis*

The continuing failure of capitalist relations of production to become generalized within Third World countries has in recent years prompted a re-examination of the nature of capitalism and its ability to dissolve and supplant non-capitalist forms of production. This theoretical issue has constituted one of the primary concerns of those scholars who focus on the study of underdeveloped societies and in particular of agrarian relations.

This volume reflects the recent introduction of such debates in the study of the rural Middle East and as such constitutes an important landmark in this field. Middle East studies, and in particular the study of rural society, is characterized by a paucity of any serious theoretical and conceptual debate and analysis. The predominant functionalist–orientalist paradigm and a small, but influential, number of uncritical 'Leninist' interpretations constitute virtually the sole models employed in rural social analysis.

This volume also constitutes a theoretical contribution in so far as it contains important reinterpretations of agrarian relations that are based upon a reformulation of conventional Marxism and its application to contemporary Middle Eastern social reality. The significance of the contributions derives from the fact that they employ categories originating from within the discourse of historical materialism in order to analyse and discuss such phenomena as the 'persistence' of non-wage forms of labour organization, 'traditional' and patriarchal household division of labour, and informal co-operation. Whilst conventional historical materialism tends to generalize about the effects of the expansion of capitalism on non-capitalist relations, this volume locates such relations at the centre of their analysis of capitalist expansion. In fact, the dynamic reproduction of non-capitalist relations within the historical process of capitalist expansion constitutes the major theoretical problem under consideration in this volume.

This is in distinct contrast to the functionalist–orientalist paradigm which sees such phenomena as reflecting essentialist characteristics of Arab and Islamic society, and the 'Leninist' tradition which either ignores them or views them as merely 'transitional'. Nevertheless, the contributions in this volume do not primarily engage in a debate with the conventional functionalist–orientalist paradigm or with the 'Leninist' interpretations, but focus both substantively and theoretically on the analysis of the various non-capitalist relations which tend to characterize socio-economic relations in most parts of the rural Middle East. Thus, this volume represents an important paradigm shift within rural Middle East studies. The contributions, however, do not reflect a single elaborated theoretical framework, but instead explore several issues and problematics which together, we would argue, constitute a sound basis for the further development of rural social theory.

The focus of the empirical investigations in the attempt to reconceptualize agrarian relations is at the level of the productive unit, which is usually household-centred. Particular attention is given to analysis of the internal organization of these household-based units of production, with the nature of the labour process and gender-related issues constituting the primary concerns. Similarly, an analysis of the various factors affecting decision-making by peasants in their struggle to guarantee their livelihood is an important concern of the research. This is premised on a theoretical assumption that the reproduction of these household-based units of production does not derive from capitalist calculations, but from a form of calculation which attempts to realise a certain level of income in cash and kind, the specifics of which depend upon the changing socio-economic circumstances within which the peasant producers are located.

The household, while it may be the basic unit around which production and reproduction revolves, is differentiated internally with regard to the production process and the distribution of the product according to gender and age criteria. The specific nature of such differentiation is seen to constitute a central aspect in the reproduction of these social units and an important object of research. Once more, the structuration of these relations is assumed to be dynamic rather than essentialist and thus concern is shown for an understanding of processes such as the changing relationship between the sexes. For example, the absence of males from the household, due to labour migration, is likely to alter significantly the status and role of females in the reproduction cycle of the unit of production.

Despite the centrality of the household as the predominant axis around which these interpretations revolve, it is recognized that household units are not autonomous nor isolated. Individual peasant households are invariably enmeshed in a whole series of relationships with other units of production, individuals and institutions, which are central to the process of reproduction of the households themselves. It is necessary to delineate the nature of these relationships which may be based, for instance, on kinship, on living in the same neighbourhood or on cultivating plots of land in close proximity. Such relationships may be within the geographic confines of the village, or the larger rural locality (a neighbouring village), or they may reach beyond to the national capital or even outside the boundaries of the nation state. Typical examples are a son or daughter living in the city or a relative sending remittances from abroad. Once more, the nature of such relationships is assumed to be dynamic and hence their effect upon the reproduction of the household-based unit of production to be *variant*. They may at times enhance its ability to realize its livelihood; at other times they may increase its vulnerability or they may do both at the same time.

Peasant household units of production are also located within a global economic structure characterized by the dominance of capitalist relations which condition the process of their reproduction, even if they are mediated by the specific location of a particular nation state in the international division of labour. Thus, any analysis of the dynamics of agrarian transformation in the Middle East necessitates an analysis of such relations and the manner in which they constitute an important force in the reproduction process at the household level. Such relationships are also assumed to be variant. World trends in primary commodity prices, the structure and role of multinational companies, international agencies and organizations, national economic policies, etc. must be examined inasmuch as they constitute conditioning factors for the reproduction of the household.

This approach to the study of rural society makes no attempt to reduce or purify the *variant* data into idealized theoretical categories such as the bourgeoisie or the proletariat. Equally, it rejects the empiricist model whereby each case is studied independently and is seen to increase in geometric fashion our knowledge of the reality we are seeking to interpret. On the contrary, this new problematic provides the basis for the further elaboration of conceptual categories that are essential to the study of social reality in the rural Middle East. In order to highlight the manner in which these interpretations contribute to theoretical debates in the field of rural sociology, and thus differ from the conventional functionalist–orientalist paradigm and the 'Leninist' interpretations, each will be discussed in some detail below.

## The functionalist–orientalist paradigm[1]

Most studies of the rural Middle East have taken the form of the traditional functionalist ethnography which tends to characterize rural society as static and resistant to social change.[2] When portraying peasant and village life, such studies have tended to focus on the existence of cultural barriers and normative values for an account of the apparent absence of social change. Thus, peasants are often seen as resenting any intrusion from the outside world and all changes which challenge traditionally accepted norms. Such accounts of peasant life rely on the presentation of ethnographic data which emphasize the contempt held for those who acquire new values. Ideas, concepts and behaviour which relate to a change in gender relations, class relations, rationalization of the productive process, etc. are invariably rejected. Change, therefore, is always attributed to external forces, and quite often this takes the form of peasants who have emigrated and then returned to influence village life. Such studies tend to focus on emigration as constituting one of the most significant factors in bringing about transformation in the village.[3] In this paradigm the social structure of the village itself is seen as constituting an additional factor hindering any form of social change. Lineage, kinship structures, religious sects, gender inequalities, etc. are seen to be integrated and interlocked, hence forming a configuration which is particularly resistant to any form of socio-economic transformation. Low productivity in agriculture and the absence of modern agro-technical methods of production are seen to be the result of the persistence of such socio-cultural structures.[4]

This type of portrayal of the rural Middle East is paralleled in the studies produced by 'sociologists and political scientists [who] offer a series of stereotypes of rural life in the Middle East and [who] carry the ethnographic approach to social change to an extreme'.[5] In these studies the peasantry is often stereotyped as so ignorant, diseased and tradition-bound that it must wait to be organized and led by the new urban middle classes.[6] Given such an account of rural society, it is not surprising that the role of communications and the media are isolated as being central to any potential for change. In fact, these diffusion-oriented studies take communications as the only major force that is capable of bringing about transformations in the rural Middle East.[7] Despite the fact that such an approach has been radically re-examined and often rejected in the fields of underdevelopment and rural sociology, starting with the seminal work of André Gunder Frank, *The Sociology of Development and the Underdevelopment of Sociology*,[8] it still constitutes a predominant framework for the study of the rural Middle East.

The central conceptual schema underlying the above interpretations of rural Middle East society is that of functionalism as exemplified in the British social anthropology of the first half of the 20th century,[9] which was born and developed within the context of British colonial expansion in the Third World. This functionalism perceives society as a self-contained organism maintaining an internal equilibrium and hence lacking any historical dimension. The limitations of using such a conceptual framework in understanding rural society in the Middle East are discussed in some detail by a number of scholars and in particular by Dale Eickelman in his work *The Middle East: An Anthropological Approach*.[10] The ideological and political dimensions inherent in this theoretical framework are explored in the pioneering volume *Anthropology and the Colonial Encounter*, edited by Talal Asad.[11]

Such limitations are highlighted through a comparison of two classic studies of Lebanese rural society by a leading social anthropologist and Middle East scholar, Emrys Peters.[12] In his first study, which is characterized by the functionalist paradigm, he relies upon global social categories used by the peasants themselves in order to describe the village social structure. These categories deny the existence of any form of social conflict. As a result, Peters's attention was directed 'away from certain major economic and status transformations which were then occurring',[13] and thus he was unable to predict the results of the village elections that completely invalidated the equilibrium model of the village social structure he had adopted.[14] Returning to the same village a number of years later for a re-study, he totally rejected his previous framework and adopted a transactionalist approach in order to account for the changes experienced in rural Lebanese society. This latter approach dissolved any concept of structure in favour of a focus on individual capabilities in the maximization and use of existing resources. The limitations of transactionalism have been discussed in some detail by Talal Asad in his critique of the work of Frederick Barth, another leading figure in the social anthropology of the Middle East.[15] The dissolution of structure, of course, prevents any attempt at relating transformations occurring at the village level to the expansion of capitalism in the region and also detracts from a concern with internal differentiation along class and gender lines.

In the functionalist–orientalist paradigm, Islam constitutes a central explanatory category accounting for most aspects of socio-cultural reality and hence plays an important role in the interpretation of rural Middle East society. This particular conceptualization of Islam derives from the Orientalist tradition and constitutes the common element that binds functionalist social anthropology and Orientalism. This shared characteristic is highlighted by Talal Asad in his article 'Two European images of non-European rule', in which he notes that the Orientalist,

> in his desire to characterize a distinctive 'Islamic society', on the basis of a considerable body of textual material relating to many eventful centuries ... is led to adopt a partly functionalist perspective; for the emphasis on the integrative role of Islam as a religion is reminiscent of the social anthropologist's treatment of the integrative function of 'tribal' religious values in many African political systems. Islamic history thus collapses into an essentialist synchrony, for much the same reasons as African history does in the hands of the functional anthropologist.[16]

Thus, it is not surprising that most social scientists writing on the rural Middle East adopt the essentialist characterization of society employed by the Orientalists. This characterization defines a priori the essential character of Middle Eastern societies in terms of Islamic traditions which are by definition traditional and decadent as compared to Western 'Graeco-Roman humanism' which is seen as modern and progressive. Continuity is thus contained by definition in this idealist conception of Islamic society.[17] This fusion of functionalist social anthropology and Orientalism constitutes the framework of most conventional studies on the rural Middle East, and this framework presents a uniquely conservative portrayal of the peasantry in one part of the Third World.

This portrayal of the peasantry is paralleled by the writings of scholars who examine other aspects of Middle Eastern society. This is primarily because modern Middle East studies trace its intellectual origins to Orientalism and construct its analytical frameworks on similar foundations. Contemporary, problem-oriented social science research and scholarship remain underdeveloped in Middle East studies due to the continuing dominance of the philological tradition of Orientalism. This tradition emphasizes the study of language and religion as the primary components in the analysis of Middle Eastern society. It is the combination of such a methodology with the essentialist characterization of society that inhibits Middle East studies, and rural Middle East studies in particular, from generating any form of competent scholarship. Even Leonard Binder, one of the leading proponents of the above framework, notes that 'Middle Eastern studies contain a "great deal of incompetent scholarship"'.[18]

> Others would go even further and argue that for sloppiness of construction, for weakness of argument, and for the sheer undisguised shoddiness of the work of some of its most eminent practitioners it has no rival among academic studies devoted to the various regions of the non-European world.[19]

Incompetent scholarship is not the sole failing of Middle East studies. In fact, the ideological nature of the interpretations represents by far the most significant limitation of the use of such a framework. For we would suggest that the underlying concern of Middle Eastern scholarship has been to contrast its a priori, essentialist, and ahistorical characterization of the region with Western progress and development. Consequently the static account of rural society is continuously reproduced.

Such an ideological approach to the study of the Middle East conceptually precludes any consideration of the changing relations of power and ability to exploit that has continuously transformed the political–economic structures and systems of classes in the region. What is lacking is the location of scholarly work within an analytical framework that posits the international division of labour and the unequal relationship between the Middle East and Western capitalism as central problematics for analysis. Given the historical origins of the two primary components whose fusion constitutes the predominant paradigm in rural Middle East studies, functionalist social anthropology and Orientalism, it is not surprising that such an analytical framework has failed to emerge. For, as Talal Asad notes with regard to one of these components:

> It is not a matter of dispute that [functionalist] social anthropology emerged as a distinctive discipline at the beginning of the colonial era, that it became a flourishing academic profession towards its close, or that throughout this period its efforts were devoted to description and analysis – carried out by Europeans, for a European audience – of non-European societies dominated by European power. And yet there is a strange reluctance on the part of most professional anthropologists to

> consider seriously the power structure within which their discipline has taken shape.[20]

The colonial context within which the predominant paradigm of rural Middle East studies was first nurtured structured its perspective and characterization of rural society. The conventional and essentialist paradigm was elaborated during the era of imperialism in the Middle East, namely from the turn of this century to the 1950s. During this period 'the whole Arab world was definitely brought into the capitalist system as a dominated periphery'.[21] With the rise of radical nationalism (Nasserism) in the 1950s and the ensuing struggles for independence, there emerged an indigenous scholarship that made the first attempt to challenge the predominant conceptualization of rural society in the Middle East. This scholarship constitutes the 'Leninist' interpretations of rural Middle East society.

## The 'Leninist' interpretations[22]

The two decades of the 1950s and 1960s in the Middle East were characterized by a rapid movement towards independence in all the Arab states, except for Palestine, and by three fundamental features which structured social, political and economic realities in the region:

> Firstly, the bankruptcy of the Arab bourgeoisie and . . . the rise of the nationalist petit-bourgeoisie; secondly, the end of Britain's influence in the area, the growing role of the two superpowers, the US and USSR . . . thirdly, the affirmation of Zionist Colonialism's expansionist character. The interaction between these three features was to determine the history of the period.[23]

The most significant event during these two decades was the emergence of Nasserism as a major socio-political force in the region. Nasserism was not only a form of radical Arab nationalism, but furthermore it helped bring about a major restructuring of the socio-political and economic structures within Egypt and the region as a whole. It accomplished this by challenging both Western capitalist hegemony in the region and its indigenous allies. New social classes entered the political arena, and within a decade of Nasser coming to power, various forms of state capitalism emerged in several Arab countries, reflecting the emergence of the *petite bourgeoisie* as the new major political force. An essential aspect of these transformations was the centrality of agrarian policies that consisted primarily of a series of agrarian reforms. In Egypt the first agrarian reform law was promulgated only six weeks after the July 1952 revolution and within the next two decades most Middle Eastern countries had followed along the same path.

The series of agrarian reforms, despite their inherent limitations, seriously challenged the socio-economic and political power of the landed aristocracies that had dominated most of the Middle East since their emergence in the latter half of the 19th century, albeit under the hegemony of Europeans.[24] This significant dislocation of the agrarian structures in predominantly rural societies was the impetus for the emergence of new interpretations of the nature of agrarian relations. These new interpretations were politically influenced by radical nationalism and theoretically inspired by a particular reading of Lenin's seminal work *The Development of Capitalism in Russia*.[25]

Lenin argued that the path of development in agriculture would follow that of industry. He attempted to demonstrate that as the means of production became increasingly concentrated in the hands of a few capitalist farmers, the majority of the peasantry would become less able to provide their own subsistence and would thus migrate to the cities to join the urban proletariat. This thesis was based on a re-examination of *zemstvo* aggregate statistics, which highlighted the process of concentration and differentiation occurring in the Russian rural areas at the turn of the 20th century. Specifically, Lenin re-examined the statistics relating to landholdings, livestock, type of crops cultivated, peasant household budgets and the occurrence of wage labour. While Lenin clearly demonstrated from these statistics the socio-economic inequalities at a given moment in time, he was less successful in substantiating the specific nature and pace of the transition. Lenin did recognize a variety of non-capitalist production relations which seemed to impede the complete dissolution of the peasantry as a social category. Nevertheless, his thesis asserted the inevitability and desirability of the destruction of these non-capitalist relations for the progressive development of the country.

Lenin's analysis of the development of capitalism in Russian agriculture has been accepted uncritically by many social scientists as a model for the process of the transformation of agriculture. Many writers seem too intent, regardless of their data, to insist that the days of the peasantry are limited or that peasant household producers have the appearance of being peasants but are really not, thereby creating new analytical categories such as the 'disguised proletariat'.

Lenin's thesis and methodology have been reproduced by a significant number of Middle East scholars examining agrarian relations. Ibrahim 'Amir's *al-Ard wa'l Fallah. al-Mas'ala al-zira'iyya fi Misr* ('Land and the peasant. The agrarian question in Egypt'),[26] published in 1958, was one of the most influential studies to emerge during this period. 'Amir examines the transformation experienced by Egyptian agriculture from the 19th to the middle of the 20th century, which he characterizes as a transition from feudalism to capitalism. Within this general schema, 'Amir discusses on the one hand the development of private property, landlordism and the intensification of commercial agriculture, and on the other the concomitant increasing exploitation, marginalization and proletarianization of the Egyptian peasantry. His portrayal of developments in agrarian relations is primarily based upon an examination of changes in the pattern and differentiation of landownership by reference to aggregate statistics. He also emphasizes the centrality of increasing influence of land and credit banks and the production of cotton as a major commercial crop. 'Amir derives this framework from a particularistic reading of Lenin and applies the Leninist categories in a static manner. For example, by concentrating on landownership he neglects to consider the variety of forms of access to land available to the peasants that do not derive from direct ownership, such as sharecropping, labour–rent agreements, and other forms of tenancy, all of which are used by Lenin in his analysis.

'Amir's study of the transformation of agrarian relations in Egypt, during the peak period of radical nationalism in the Arab world, provided the major impetus for an extensive use of the Leninist model throughout the region. Ra'uf 'Abbas Hamid in his study *al-Nizam al-ijtima'i fi Misr fi Zill al-Milkiyyat al-zira'iyya al-kabira, 1837–1914* ('The social system in Egypt under the influence of the large landowners, 1837–1914')[27]

> sets out to impress on the reader the importance of a relational concept of class. But, as he writes, because of the complexity of the land system and the different values of different types of land, this concept became very hard to employ. With reluctance, therefore, he accepted Cromer's definition (formulated in 1894) of a large landowner as someone who owned more than fifty feddans.[28]

Cromer, of course, was the British consul-general who effectively ruled Egypt from 1883 to 1908 and formulated his definitions for the purposes of tax collection and control. Hamid's acceptance of such a picture of class structure highlights the problematic application of the Leninist methodology. In other words, his concern to follow Lenin in the use of aggregate quantitative data relating to landholdings, in a situation where the historical archives do not provide the necessary material, forced Hamid to adopt categories and data which pre-empt any discussion of the social relations of production, which is fundamental to a class analysis. Thus Hamid, although claiming to rely upon the Leninist approach, in fact provides a descriptive account of the stratification of landownership rather than a class analysis of agrarian relations.

It should be acknowledged, of course, that the Egyptian archives for the 19th century do not contain the wealth of data that was available to Lenin. Thus, adopting a methodology which requires reliance upon aggregate statistical data is necessarily going to generate major problems in any attempt to provide a class analysis of agrarian relations. A class analysis of Egypt during this period should take into account her dependent position in an international division of labour and the influence of powerful British interests in her economic and political affairs. Agrarian relations should be examined in the context of the preponderant cultivation of cotton as a commercial export crop and of the domination by non-Egyptian capital by virtue of an almost exclusive control over the marketing and pricing of the commodity. Sole reference to aggregate statistical data on landownership is an inadequate indicator of the changing nature of class relations that obtained in Egypt during this period. The power which conditioned Egyptian agrarian class relations lay beyond her political borders.[29] Hamid does discuss Egypt's dependent status and the significance of cotton, but he fails to use such factors in his 'class' analysis because of his rigid application of the Leninist methodology.

The Arab–Israeli war of 1967, and especially the Zionist occupation of the rest of Palestine, sent massive shockwaves throughout the Middle East and posed a serious challenge to the influence of Nasserism in the region. Western powers seized the opportunity to re-establish their hegemony and within a short period of time the Middle East witnessed the rapid dissolution of the radical socio-economic, political and intellectual trends that had dominated the region since 1952. This clearly highlighted the limitations of this form of radical nationalism when used as a basis to bring about a radical transformation of dependent societies. These limitations were seen to derive primarily from the particular political and economic form that Nasserism had advocated, namely state capitalism. One of the major implications of the reliance upon state capitalism was that, in spite of the implementation of radical and extensive agrarian reforms, the agrarian sector was invariably made to carry the burden of the intensive programmes of industrialization. Through the manipulation of prices of agricultural commodities, imports, control of markets, centralization of all investment institutions and decisions over choice of crop cultivation, the state was able to divert surplus from one sector to the other. Thus peasant production was further integrated into the national, and therefore, international economy as a dependent and dominated socio-economic sector. The effect of these state agrarian policies was the further consolidation and expansion of small peasant holdings and increased reliance by peasants upon the household as a mechanism for survival, albeit in the context of their subordinate position in the international division of labour.

The limitations of radical nationalism, in its Nasserist form, and the implications of reliance upon state capitalism were reflected in the writings of Middle Eastern intellectuals. Many of those intellectuals who had espoused Nasserism sought new analytical frameworks that would allow them to account for the demise of radical nationalism and the failure of state capitalism to bring about social transformation. Amongst those intellectuals there emerged another attempt to re-examine agrarian relations which, it was argued, had been inadequately interpreted during the height of Nasserism. This new attempt to re-interpret agrarian relations still relied heavily on the Leninist model of agrarian transformation, but sought to incorporate the effects of integration into the world economy in their attempts to account for the continuing underdevelopment of rural society in the Middle East.

In fact, during the 1950s and 1960s rural society in the Middle East was further integrated as a dependent region in the capitalist international division of labour. Such a process of integration posed a challenge to the survival capabilities of the former subsistence-oriented peasant communities, but did not result in the emergence of homogeneous forms of peasant production and social organization. Instead, earlier social structures mediated the increased integration of the peasantry into the world economy, so that paths of integration exhibited a variety of outcomes ranging from full proletarianization to partial proletarianization or independent commodity production.

The impact of these new socio-political and economic realities is most evident in the work of Salih Muhammad Salih, *al-Iqta' wa'l-Ra'smaliyya al-zira'iyya fi Misr min 'Ahd Muhammad 'Ali ila 'Ahd 'Abd al-Nasir*[30] ('Feudalism and Agricultural Capitalism in Egypt from the Era of Muhammad Ali to the Era of Abd al-Nasir'), published in 1979. The book was written as a specific critique of Ibrahim 'Amir's influential work. Salih emphasizes the need for and importance of a critique of the mode of analysis employed by 'Amir, particularly in the light of the political implications which followed from it. For 'Amir assumed that Egypt had undergone its transition to capitalism within the agrarian sector during Muhammad Ali's reign at the beginning of the 19th century. Salih argues that 'Amir utilized incorrect indicators in evaluating the extent of capitalist development in rural Egypt, for instance landownership statistics, land and credit bank activities, and the unification of the taxation system. All of these he criticizes and dismisses as being inadequate. Essentially, Salih argues that none of these reveal the transformation of the relations of production into capitalism, and that 'Amir thus underestimates the extent of feudal relations existing in Egyptian agrarian society. Likewise, Salih emphasizes the international dimension, something absent in 'Amir's work, stressing the forced integration of Egypt into the world market and the consequent disarticulation of the Egyptian social formation.

Nevertheless, Salih's alternative remains within the Leninist thesis of the inevitability of capitalism in agriculture, as is made blatantly clear to the reader by the myriad quotations from Lenin's work. He argues that the extent of the development of the capitalist mode of production must be measured by reference to three indicators: 1) the extent of use of large-scale machinery; 2) the extent of commodity production; and 3) the extent of wage labour. He places the emphasis on the first two factors, the development of the productive forces and the market economy, as does Lenin. The third factor, which in our view is the most crucial, receives limited attention. He thus fails to focus on relations of production. Likewise, he does not examine the phenomenon of wage labour within the peasant household unit of production, where wage labour may play the role of reinforcing rather than dissolving non-capitalist forms of production. Salih simply concludes that the essential parameters of transformation in Egyptian agriculture are capitalist.

Samir Radwan in his study *Capital Formation in Egyptian Agriculture and Industry, 1882–1967*[31] argues that 'Egypt's dependence resulted from an essentially agricultural economy, geared almost unilaterally to the cultivation and export of cotton, and from the direct grip of foreign banks and corporations on the country's main centres of economic activity.'[32] Analytical consideration of Egypt's integration into the international division of labour as a dependent society is clearly an important advance on the earlier Leninist interpretations that followed 'Amir's approach. Nevertheless, Radwan, who relies upon André Gunder Frank and the dependency school, accounts for the changing class structure and the role of the state solely by reference to three phases of development:

> the export economy phase extending from the 1850s to the 1920s; the phase of import substitution industrialization which began in the 1920s and 1930s, gathered momentum during World War II and reached its peak in the 1950s; and finally the phase of 'planned development' covering the 1950s and the 1960s.[33]

Radwan's pioneering study is still unable to account for or interpret the changes in the forces and relations of production that dominated rural society during the period under consideration. His conceptualization of class relations is still based on 'Amir's particular use of the Leninist methodology, namely a reliance upon aggregate statistics for the presentation of a stratification of landownership, albeit in the context of a descriptive account of Egypt's location in the international division of labour.

The limitations inherent in Radwan's analytical framework are further exemplified in Mahmoud Abdel-Fadil's study, *Development, Income, Distribution and Social Change in Rural Egypt (1952–1970)*.[34] Abdel-Fadil too relies upon aggregate statistics, and presents a broad stratification of landownership and holdings rather than an attempt to examine forces and relations of production. Abdel-Fadil's suggestion that there emerged 'a new set of agrarian relations more conducive to growth and development'[35] and a tendency to transform poor and landless peasants into proletarians[36] is highly contentious. This is particularly so since his introductory chapter notes the creation of 'a vast class of small-holders'[37] which suggests that the state-initiated agrarian reform policies were 'more akin to the liberal ideal of a "regime of small peasant properties" rather than any *collectivist or socialist* ideals'.[38]

The attempt to re-examine agrarian relations initiated by Egyptian scholars also served as an impetus for a similar re-examination amongst some Western scholars concerned with rural Middle East society. Alan Richards, for example, in his study *Egypt's Agricultural Development, 1800–1980: technical and social change*[39] assumes the extension of capitalism and thereby implies the polarization of agrarian relations along capitalist lines. His central argument for the extension of capitalist relations in the rural sector derives from his suggestion that:

> the phenomenon of primitive accumulation in Egypt was inseparable from that country's integration into the capitalist world system. Capitalism came to Egypt with cotton; resulted in large numbers of peasants losing all decision-making power over their land. In short, they were dispossessed.[40]

The expanded development of capitalism in the agrarian sector constitutes a major theme in the writings of many other Middle East scholars who focus on rural aspects of these societies. Karen Pfeifer, for example, in her study, 'Algeria's agrarian transformation'[41] locates her analysis in the framework of Algeria's colonial heritage and dependent position in the present international division of labour in order to conclude that 'capitalism seems to be the main force transforming Algerian agriculture and paving the way for a new society by setting in place modern class relations'.[42] It is due to such forces, she points out, that the Algerian agrarian 'reforms have helped to eliminate vestigial precapitalist structures, fostered capitalist relations within the cooperative sector, and encouraged the movement of small agricultural producers into wage labor'.[43] Similarly Mahfoud Bennoune in his work 'Algerian peasants and national politics'[44] challenges Algeria's image as a socialist state by noting that capitalist relations constitute the major force polarizing politics in the rural sector. Similar arguments are used by several scholars writing on Sudan, Morocco, Syria, Iraq, etc.[45]

The tendency to locate the analysis of agrarian relations in the framework of an international division of labour has considerably advanced our understanding of rural society in the Middle East. Yet while we are in agreement that agrarian relations have been transformed as a result of colonial rule, integration into a world economy and the concomitant expansion of capitalism, the question still remains as to how far this has led to a process of proletarianization or to the emergence of new forms and relations of peasant production. Generally, Leninist scholars point out that the expansion of capitalism in agriculture generates increased economic differentiation within the rural population, creating a relatively small, landowning capitalist class and a growing agricultural proletariat. The nature of agrarian relations is then derived from such an analytical framework and, given its uniform application in most of the studies, it is not surprising that the conclusions also share a great degree of similarity. This is not to suggest that such studies deny diversification and specificity. It is simply to point out that in the studies which employ the Leninist model, diversification is subsumed by the logic of expanding capitalist relations and, therefore, the specific peasant responses to capitalism are denied any analytical significance.

At this point it is important to note that Lenin's thesis was far more sophisticated than what has been discussed above. As Tribe, in his 'Introduction to de Crisenoy'[46] argues, the process of proletarianization is not directly associated with dispossession by Lenin, but is connected

> to the organization of the peasant household, and the impact on this household of diverse forces that lead it to rent land out, hire labour or sell it, alter crop patterns and so on. The appearance of wage labour is associated by Lenin not with the loss by the peasant of his land, but rather with the inability of the household to fully support the family from the holding it possesses.[47]

Lenin indicates significant ways by which a peasant household can respond to being 'squeezed' by disadvantageous conditions other than selling or losing its land. Nevertheless, an examination of Lenin's 'Conclusions on the significance of capitalism in Russian agriculture'[48] leaves no doubt as to what he saw as being the dominant trend in agriculture. Lenin categorically concludes:

> that the peasantry have been splitting up at enormous speed into a numerically small but economically strong rural bourgeoisie and a rural proletariat. Inseparably connected with this 'depeasantising' process is the landowners' transition from the labour-service to the capitalist system of farming.[49]

Lenin's approach to the study of agrarian relations represents a particular tendency within the Marxist tradition. In fact it follows one of the two alternative interpretations found in Marx's own writings. According to Harold Wolpe, Marx discussed the effect of capitalist production on pre-capitalist modes of production but provided no clear and consistent answer as to what the effect was.

> [Marx's] first approach (what has been commonly accepted to be *the* approach adopted by Marx) is based on the assumption that the appearance of capitalism... signalled the more or less immediate and inevitable disintegration of PCMPs and the subsumption of the agents of these modes under capitalist relations of production.[50]

The second approach recognizes '... the differentiated relationships which may be set up between capitalist and other modes of production'.[51] These issues raised by Marx have long been of central concern to many revolutionary political movements, but have only recently been taken up by Marxist academics studying agrarian transition.[52]

William Roseberry in his article 'Peasants as proletarians'[53] which presents a historical analysis of small coffee producers in Venezuela, focuses upon the increasing domination of capital over the production process, but without the expropriation of the means of production from the producers. During the 19th century, as a result of the small farmers' dependency on credit from the usurer/merchant in order to grow coffee 'farmers were caught in a productive relation with capital which allowed for the *production of surplus value*' (our emphasis).[54] However, 'the exploitation was not as efficient as might have been',[55] given that the producers still maintained some control over the means of production.

In contemporary times, coffee producers in Venezuela continued to maintain their indeterminate class position. Usurer/merchant capital was displaced by industrial capital, with the state acting as a principal creditor and coffee buyer. Coffee producers continued to be 'neither fully peasant nor fully proletarian'.[56] Hence Roseberry argues against the notion that these peasants are 'proletarians in disguise' or are 'paid a "concealed wage" in their interaction with merchants'.[57] For, as his concrete analysis shows, peasants and proletarians in Venezuela 'occupy and perceive different structural positions'.[58] Concluding, Roseberry stresses the multifaceted nature of capitalist evolution and urges, 'we must at once be sensitive to variation and analyse processual regularities. This requires constant movement between abstract and concrete levels of analysis in the attempt to understand particular societies'.[59]

Henry Bernstein has also contributed to the theoretical reformulation of the changing class position of Third World peasant producers under the domination of capitalism. Taking as a case study the historical experience of African peasantries, and in particular Tanzanian peasants, Bernstein, in his article 'African peasantries: a theoretical framework',[60] focuses his analysis upon 'the destruction of natural economy by the spread of commodity relations'.[61] By this, Bernstein means the process by which 'the reproduction of households takes place increasingly on an individual basis through the relations of commodity production and exchange'.[62] As household production is increasingly subsumed in the circuit of capital in various forms and by various mechanisms, peasant producers are seen to become

> 'wage-labour equivalents', that is producers of surplus-value, but in less determinate conditions than the proletariat... thus peasants are 'wage-labour equivalents' in a relative sense that limits the subjugation and real subsumption of household labour by capital to the extent that the producers are not fully expropriated nor dependent wholly for their reproduction on the sale of labour-power through the wage-form.[63]

In many ways, Bernstein's analysis of the commoditization of African peasants is similar to that of Roseberry's analysis of the penetration of capital in the production process of Venezuelan coffee producers. Both stress the role of usurer/merchant and later industrial capital in transforming these peasant producers into producers of surplus value as opposed to being producers primarily of use values. Second, both also emphasize the importance of the incomplete expropriation of the producers from their means of production, which limits capital's efficiency in exploiting these producers.

However, differences arise in their conceptualization of the class position of these producers. Roseberry emphasizes the substantial difference between Venezuelan coffee producers and agricultural wage labourers in both economic and ideological terms, despite the incorporation of both in the circuit of capital. But in terms of conceptualizing coffee producers, Roseberry is only able to do this negatively: they are neither fully peasant nor fully proletarian. This is probably the most problematic aspect of his approach to the study of rural society. Roseberry fails to rise to the challenge of formulating a theoretical category which would help clarify the class position of this group of agricultural producers.

Bernstein formulates a new conceptual category of 'wage-labour equivalents' in his analysis of African peasants. However, this conceptualization is not particularly helpful in understanding the class position of African peasants, who are said to be like wage labourers, yet different. Underlying Bernstein's notion of 'wage-labour equivalents' is the commonly held assumption that all pre-capitalist forms of production are eventually disintegrated by capitalism. Based on this assumption (Marx's first approach), the only possible conceptual categories are those arising from the capitalist mode of production, given the clear domination of capitalism within the world economy. As a result, Bernstein is forced conceptually to formulate a theoretical category derived from political economy, namely 'wage-labour equivalents', in order to analyse the class position of African peasants *vis-à-vis* capital.[64]

Some recent contributions to the debate on the agrarian question, which have tended to focus on peasant commodity production, clearly show that despite a refinement of arguments the basic Leninist model is still adhered to. One of the most ambitious examples of this 'new' wave of intellectual production is the article by Peter Gibbon and Michael Neocosmos 'Some problems in the political economy of "African Socialism"'.[65] In the first part of their article the authors criticize in detail Bernstein's analysis of African peasantries, specifically his notion of variable commoditization amongst peasant producers. For Gibbon and Neocosmos 'the practical effect of rendering the commodity production element of petty commodity production residual (by dint of making its degree contingent) constitutes a slippage back toward not only a subjectivist form of analysis, but a *peasantist* form of subjectivism'.[66] They likewise criticize Bernstein's concept of 'wage-labour equivalents' as ambiguous in that the peasant or petty commodity producer is characterized neither as a form of wage labour nor as a particular type of capitalist enterprise, but 'by the distinctiveness of their "logic of production"'.[67] In the remaining part of their study Gibbon and Neocosmos attempt to present their own analysis of petty commodity production as a particular form of capitalist production. They argue that petty commodity production exists, historically and structurally, only under conditions of generalized commodity production, and hence is a capitalist form of production. It is not transitional, but is created by the contradictions of capitalism itself. It is clear from the above that Gibbon and Neocosmos's argument is a reaffirmation of the Leninist approach, albeit in a different form. Although differing from Lenin's analysis of petty commodity production as transitional, Gibbon and Neocosmos assume the generalization of capitalist relations throughout the globe, regardless of their different forms. In their view, the contradictory unity of wage labour and capital which characterizes petty commodity production enterprises is but one form of capitalist relations. No particular significance is given to the fact that those who labour control the means of production, in other words that there is no separation between the producers and their means of subsistence.

Despite Gibbon and Neocosmos's attempt to be theoretically 'rigorous', relying essentially upon classical Marxist texts (which they use selectively), their analysis is open to much criticism. They admit that they are unable to identify the precise mechanisms by which petty commodity production is brought into being, nor are they able to explain 'on what basis does it generally tend to be conserved in the areas where it seems to predominate such as agriculture'.[68] However, the major weakness of their analysis is their assumption 'that "capitalism" at the level of world economy implies general circulation of commodities in all its regions, leading them to conclude that all the conditions for simple commodity production exist everywhere, and that terms such as "peasant" which attempt to specify non-commodity relations (or dimensions of relations) are wrong'.[69] As Harriet Friedmann argues:

> There is irony in all this. Those of us who have criticized the underdevelopment literature must insist on bringing back its central insight, which has been lost in its evolution into a theory of the 'capitalist world-system'. Underdevelopment creates specific structures, *different from capitalism and from each other*.[70]

Less serious criticism is directed to the Gibbon and Neocosmos argument by Bernstein in his contribution, 'Capitalism and petty commodity production'.[71] He admits that the authors give more attention to the capital component of the contradictory unity of petty commodity producers.[72] Nevertheless, despite some reservations Bernstein accepts Gibbon and Neocosmos's theoretical understanding of capitalism.[73] He accepts that generalized commodity production exists, and he defends Gibbon and Neocosmos against the accusation that their argument converges with that of André Gunder Frank and the 'world system' school.[74] Furthermore, Bernstein defends the *method* used by Gibbon and Neocosmos which 'involves investigating phenomena and their characterization in relation to the essential relations and contradictions of capitalism.'[75]

However, what this method is at an operational level, and its superiority in providing the necessary analytical tools for the study of the complexity of agrarian relations, is not spelled out by either Bernstein or Gibbon and Neocosmos. On the contrary, what we are offered is the a priori assumption that generalized commodity production exists throughout the world and that the job of the researcher is to try to distinguish the various forms of capitalist economy, 'whether "backward" or "advanced", whether they have phenomenal similarities with pre-capitalist forms or not'.[76]

While Gibbon and Neocosmos as well as Bernstein have managed to salvage the category of petty commodity production, their particular conceptualization of capitalism in the contemporary world converges essentially with the underlying Leninist assumption that the fate of all pre-capitalist forms of production is their destruction, and that capitalist relations will replace them, despite their phenomenal appearances. Nevertheless, it should be pointed out that with regard to the study of Middle Eastern agrarian relations such developments in the Leninist approach have yet to appear in the literature.

Despite the predominance of the Leninist approach to the study of agrarian relations within Marxism and Marxist-inspired literature, which, as we have argued, is based on a particular reading of Marx, it does not represent the only path of analysis within the Marxist tradition. Kautsky, a contemporary of Lenin, produced his seminal work *The Agrarian Question* in 1899, in which he attempted to analyse the transformation of agriculture under the domination of capitalist production.[77] Like Lenin and his followers, Kautsky emphasized the progressive and historically inevitable role of capital 'in smashing the old forms of production and of poverty and establishing the new forms which *must* succeed' (our emphasis).[78] However, Kautsky's insistence from the start of his study that 'agriculture does not develop according to the same process of industry [sic], it follows laws of its own'[79] opened up new avenues of enquiry into the study of agrarian transformation.

Kautsky located the specificity of agriculture's development under the domination of capitalism in the particular and peculiar nature of land as the major means of production. Land, both fixed in quantity and varied in quality, cannot be multiplied as occurs with industrial means of production. Thus, it produces a differential and absolute ground rent which constitutes an increase in the cost of agricultural production as compared to industry. Second, economies of scale are not necessarily advantageous in agriculture: 'Diseconomies of distance grow at a faster rate than economies of size'[80] after a certain limit, whereas 'in industry large units of production are always superior to small ones.'[81] Kautsky notes that the above tendency is less applicable to forms of agriculture 'based on *intensive cultivation and heavy concentrated doses of capital investment*'.[82] Both the above factors are structural and accordingly are seen to be important in hindering capitalist development in agriculture.

Kautsky adds a third factor which he claims was the most basic cause for retarded capitalist development in agriculture, namely the shortage of manpower. The concentration of agriculture was seen to create its opposite, i.e. the dissolution of small holdings. This resulted in the simultaneous destruction of the main supply of agricultural labour on the capitalist farm. The seriousness of the growing labour shortage was stressed by Kautsky to the extent that he concluded that there was no remedy at that time under capitalism.[83] Due to the nature of his politics, his ideas were never adopted or developed by Marxists, and it was not until recently (1976) that a summary of selected parts of his work was translated for the first time into English. With regards to the literature related to Middle Eastern agrarian relations, Kautsky's ideas have yet to be considered and debated. Unlike Lenin's work, which is widely available in Arabic, Kautsky has yet to be translated.

## Elements of a new interpretation

During the last decade there has developed the start of a debate regarding the consequences of capitalist penetration in agriculture in the Middle East. Interest in this area was initially aroused by the apparent failure of Orientalism to grasp the dynamics and nature of the incorporation of Middle Eastern societies into an expanding European capitalist system, especially during the era of colonialism. The few scholars who were showing interest in this field were also highly critical of the mechanistic use of the Leninist model or for that matter the dependency framework in the analysis of agrarian relations during the colonial era. These social scientists began to re-examine the nature of the relationship between European (capitalist) and Middle Eastern (non-capitalist) socio-economic forces and their consequent articulation in Middle Eastern social formations.

### 1. Articulation of modes of production

Some of these scholars were inspired primarily by the emergence of a lively Marxist debate within economic anthropology.[84] For them capitalism's relation to other modes of production was *not* conceived:

> as a *succession or evolution* (as in the 'stages' model: primitive communal, ancient, slave, feudal, capitalist modes of production, with the 'Asiatic' awkwardly at a tangent); nor yet as some kind of dialectical *transcendence and dissolution*... nor even as a *transition* (unless prolonged to the point of analytical vacuity). On the contrary [for them] capitalism neither evolves mechanically from what precedes it, nor does it necessarily dissolve it; indeed so far from banishing pre-capitalist forms, it not only coexists with them but buttresses them, and even on occasions devilishly conjures them up *ex nihilo*.[85]

These scholars accepted the notion that pre-capitalist forms were 'being undermined and perpetuated at the same time' and pointed to 'complex forms of dissolution and conservation'[86] when capitalism expands in the Third World. Furthermore, and of greater significance for this argument, these scholars also responded to the fact that, although dependency might well suggest a macro-framework, it was unable to handle the shift from general statements to micro-fieldwork.

'Agenda for Ottoman history'[87] by Islamoghlou and Keyder is one such early contribution which attempts to 'provide the conceptual framework in which new research problems may be defined'.[88] Islamoghlou and Keyder start by presenting a critique of the conventional paradigm that 'by juxtaposing the assumptions of Oriental despotism and of the Orientalist paradigms [draws] a picture of society in "stasis" and "isolated" in its civilizational specificity'.[89] They then characterize the Ottoman social formation as 'a dominant Asiatic mode of production in which the control of the central authority over the production and appropriation of surplus constituted the crucial mechanism of reproduction'.[90] Within such an analytical framework independent peasant production is systematically theorized to constitute a component of the larger unit, but without the necessity to negate its autonomy. 'The peasant producer is integrated into the larger unit through the delivery of his surplus in the form of taxes to the state, and through the ideological-juridical apparatus that provides the matrix for the state's extraction of agricultural surplus. Thus, this integration ensures a political determination of the division of labour within the system.'[91]

This attempt by Islamoghlou and Keyder to locate the principal dynamic within the Ottoman Empire is important because it permits such societies to recapture their own history. This recapture is not simply at the level of making extensive use of indigenous archival material, as with many of the Egyptian scholars discussed above, but is a result of theorizing forms and relations of production. Islamoghlou and Keyder point out:

> The Asiatic mode of production does not create conflict or a confrontation between the producers and the appropriaters of surplus. The individual peasant comes into contact only with the tax-collector, who acts in the name of the central authority, only after the production process, which he carried out as a free peasant.[92]

Such a conceptualization allows for both the specificity of independent peasant production and the mechanisms by which surplus flows towards the world economy. It is, of course, the groups with a claim on the agricultural output through a determinate position in the social structure that constitute the mediating level between independent peasant production and the reproduction of a national and international economy. Independent peasant production therefore can adopt various forms and sustain such forms despite its incorporation into a capitalist world market.

Thus, independent peasant production becomes commodity production when it is incorporated into the capitalist world market, but such a change does not necessarily challenge the viability of peasant forms of production. Agricultural produce from peasant forms of production becomes a commodity only when it enters the circuit of industrial capital.[93] Of greater significance for this argument is the fact that it is not necessary to attempt to redefine the peasantry as 'proletarians', 'disguised proletarians' or 'semi-proletarians'. As Talal Asad, another early contributor to this part of the debate, points out in his study of Palestine during the British Mandate, 'in order to grasp the changing organisation of Arab villagers it is necessary to begin with a different set of concepts: the articulation of a capitalist with a non-capitalist mode of production mediated by the British colonial state'.[94] The preservation of peasant forms of production is once more accounted for by 'the intrinsic character of the European (British) colonial state [which] ensured the long-term economic growth of the capitalist mode of production at the expense of the non-capitalist mode, although it prevented the latter's complete elimination'.[95]

Asad elaborates some of the mechanisms through which surplus was transferred from the non-capitalist to the capitalist sector without causing any fundamental change in the nature of peasant forms and relations of production – that is, other than their increased marginalization and poverty. Rural property tax, for example, 'was levied as a fixed percentage on net productivity of the soil (i.e. minus cost of production) [therefore] capital-intensive Jewish agricultural enterprises paid proportionally less tax in relation to gross product'.[96] In such a scheme the low subsistence level of the Arab peasant producer – low wages or non-wage family labour – was the basis for the transfer of surplus from the non-capitalist to the capitalist sphere, mediated through the state (the British Mandate). Similarly indirect taxation, which was 'levied on necessities, was regressive and tended to fall most heavily on the poorer (i.e. rural Arab) population'.[97]

Asad's discussion of the causes for the deteriorating class position of Arab peasants during the British Mandate in Palestine is a particularly important contribution to the formulation of a new interpretation for the study of agrarian relations in the Middle East. Its importance is manifest when we attempt to explain the manner in which Arab labour was *not integrated* into the capitalist Jewish economy, but nevertheless contributed a substantial surplus for the reproduction of the latter. Such a relationship 'cannot be understood unless it is related to the process of surplus extraction from the peasantry that necessarily follows from the articulation of the capitalist with the non-capitalist modes of production within a single social formation'.[98] In other words, peasant forms of production can provide surplus to an expanding capitalist economy without being subsumed by the logic of capitalist accumulation. This is not to argue, of course, that peasant forms of production are never subsumed and dissolved in the advance of capitalism. We only intend to point out that it is not *necessary* for the expanded reproduction of capitalism that peasant forms of production be transformed into capitalist forms of production. To assume that the dominance of capitalism in a social formation implies the dissolution of peasant forms of production, as is argued in the Leninist model discussed above, is the result of a failure to examine in any detail forms and relations of production in the agrarian sector.

Talal Asad's and Islamoghlou and Keyder's contributions, both published in the mid-1970s, constituted pioneering attempts to reformulate the manner in which agrarian relations were being examined in the Middle East.[99] In a further contribution to this attempt to formulate a 'new interpretation', Caglar Keyder[100] attempts to investigate the response pattern of peasant producers facing the cyclical behaviour of the capitalist market in Turkish agriculture. His study shows that a particular form of peasant non-capitalist production (sharecropping) constitutes the most appropriate response on the part of peasants to their increasing indebtedness in the cyclical behaviour of the capitalist market. According to Keyder, sharecropping, which exemplified non-capitalist forms and relations of production, helped consolidate rather than dissolve small peasant ownership in Turkey.

The role of the state in contributing to the process of the consolidation of peasant forms of production is also examined by Keyder in the same study. Keyder points out that the combination of particular state policies and the preservation of peasant forms of production generated a dynamic *interval* to Turkish agrarian relations, which constituted the parameters guaranteeing the reproduction of the dichotomy between small peasant production and capitalist farming. He points out that Turkish migration to Europe was also one of the most important factors in consolidating peasant forms of production and family farm enterprises in rural Turkey. Thus Keyder is able to conclude that a *new, dynamic and radically transformed pattern of agrarian relations* constituted the basis for the flourishing of 'traditional' and non-capitalist social, economic and political forms in Turkish rural society.

This, of course, contrasts sharply with the interpretations of the functionalist–orientalist paradigm and the Leninist interpretations discussed above. It does not in any way imply that peasant forms of production are always consolidated by the exact same procedures outlined by Keyder or that they take the specific form present in the Turkish case. On the contrary, we are attempting to emphasize (through the selection of contributions to this volume) the great diversity both in forms that emerge and the nature of the forces that help bring them about or contribute to their reproduction. For the 'New Interpretations' are not static. The isolation of a particular form of non-capitalist production does not permit the automatic deduction of the nature of agrarian relations. Both the specificity of the particular form of peasant production and the role of the wider structures, such as the state and the international division of labour, constitute central elements in some of the 'new interpretations' in this volume. More empirically based research and theoretical debate is needed in order to develop the theoretical categories which will help us to understand the actual functioning of these forms of non-capitalist peasant production and their role within the wider capitalist economy.

**2. Articulation of forms (household) and modes of production**

Just as the Leninist-inspired contributions relied heavily on particular readings of Marx and Lenin, so some of the 'New Interpretations' in this volume derive from a critical application to Middle Eastern rural society of a number of recent theoretical debates from the wider field of rural sociology. In particular, a number of the 'new interpretations' consider two major areas of concern. First, the question of the specificity of agricultural production as distinct from industrial production,[101] and second, the nature of the internal dynamics of non-capitalist forms of production and the role that these forms of production play within contemporary capitalist economies.[102]

Of the many contributions[103] in this area of rural sociology, in our view the work of Harriet Friedmann has proved to be particularly innovative and thought-provoking. This is especially so when contrasted to the 'articulation of modes of production' contributions mentioned above. Friedmann resolves some of the limitations of the 'articulation of modes of production' approach, given the integrated nature of current world capitalist economy, through her main theoretical contribution of drawing a distinction between *mode* of production and *form* of production. Friedmann reserves

> ... the term mode of production for a broad historical period defined by characteristic laws of motion, existing at two distinct, but mutually dependent levels: the productive unit, and the totality of productive units.... the *form of production* consists of the relations and forces of production (machinery and techniques) at the level of the productive unit, or enterprise. The form of production is doubly defined by the internal relations, both social and technical, of the productive unit.... although the enterprise is the site of the labor process, its external relations (within the mode of production) enter into the determination of both the social and technical relations of production.[104]

Elaborating upon the theoretical category of form of production, Friedmann continues:

> Forms of production are more variable and transitory than the modes of production which provide their conditions of existence, but the variation is of two basic types. First is the form of production which constitutes the 'basic cell' of the historical epoch, and whose dynamic

> underlies the laws of motion of the economy as well as deriving from it. . . . the second type is a form of production dependent on the mode of production but not constitutive of it.[105]

According to Friedmann, simple commodity production, which typifies most farming in the industrial centres of the world, is of the second type of form of production.

Using the above theoretical distinction, Friedmann is not forced conceptually to analyse American family farmers at the level of enterprise via capitalist categories. On the contrary, she analyses these family farming enterprises in their own terms. Focusing on the internal logic of these enterprises, Friedmann characterizes the form of production as non-capitalist, given the lack of capitalist class relations within the enterprises. The labour process is governed generally by the principles of 'the gender division of labour, kinship obligations, and patriarchy'.[106] This kind of enterprise 'dispenses entirely with the category of profit as a condition of reproduction, and it replaces the inflexibility of the wage with a flexible cost of personal consumption'.[107]

As a result of the above, the simple commodity production enterprise is seen to have important advantages over capitalist enterprises within the same branch.[108] Hence, non-capitalist forms of production within the advanced capitalist countries have been able to persist.

In several ways, Friedmann's characterization of the internal dynamics of the unit of production within family farming is similar to that of Chayanov's. For Friedmann, however, this form of production – simple commodity production – is dependent upon a wider capitalist economy for its reproduction, namely the existence of markets in land, labour and credit. Here, Friedmann's position is antithetical to that of Chayanov, who argues for the independence and distinctiveness of a peasant mode of production *vis-à-vis* the capitalist mode of production. Friedmann's conceptual categories allow for the analysis of family farming at the level of enterprise and at the level of the wider economy without collapsing the one into the other. This is a theoretical step forward which has permitted some of the 'new interpretations' in this volume to go beyond the 'articulation of modes of production'.

Nevertheless, Friedmann's specific construction of simple commodity production's relation to the wider economy is perhaps the weakest part of her argument. Friedmann states:

> as a logical category, simple commodity production implies minimally that all external relations of the enterprise are commodity relations, that is, the enterprise sells all it produces, saving nothing for direct consumption, and buys all it consumes, both for means of production and for sustaining the life of laborers. . . . the continuous existence of any simple commodity production enterprise, therefore, implies generalised commodity production.[109]

On the contrary, at least some research has shown that the preference of family farmers is 'to maintain a pattern of diversified farming despite the potential higher efficiency of more specialized production'.[110] Farmers prefer such a pattern of farming as it ensures virtual self-sufficiency in domestic consumption and protects them 'against unpredictable price fluctuations and the vulnerability of a single commodity to the effects of natural hazards'.[111] In other words, the ideal pattern of family farming is the production of both use and exchange values, or commodities, although this pattern has become more difficult to maintain in the integrated world capitalist market.

Second, according to Friedmann another result of generalized commodity relations and thus the operation of the law of value within the wider economy is competition between enterprises. But again research has shown the centrality of co-operation between relatives and/or neighbours in family farming. This is clearly indicated in the volume edited by Professor Norman Long, *Family and Work in Rural Societies: Perspectives on Non-wage Labour*,[112] which draws on research from countries as diverse as Egypt, Poland, Israel, Finland, Argentina, etc. In Friedmann's analysis, however, there is no recognition of the importance of these particular non-commodity relations to family farmers within the capitalist centre. It is clear from the above that Friedmann's work, although a significant step forward, has yet to resolve the many issues involved in the debate relating to the 'persistence' of non-capitalist forms of production.

### 3. Gender and non-capitalist forms of production

Women's work in particular and gender issues in general still constitute a blind spot in most contributions in the field of political economy, as well as in the great majority of the literature in the social sciences. Recent feminist writings have been attempting to focus attention on these issues, whether with regard to societies in the Third World, in the West or in the socialist countries. These writings have contributed to a growing body of literature which has focused on such issues as the sexual division of labour, patriarchy, and the role of women in rural production.[113] This body of literature has highlighted the fact that society is differentiated not only along class lines, but also along gender lines and that this differentiation is first and foremost located in the most basic form of human social organisation, the family and the household. Thus, as Bernstein points out, materialist feminist scholarship 'has demolished hitherto residual, unproblematised notions of family and household ("the" family, "the" household').[114]

This process of deconstructing 'traditional' social categories has involved a systematic study of family and household structures in a variety of socio-economic settings. The major concern of these studies has revolved around the manner in which the internal structuring of the family and the household unit are affected by and affect (with the emphasis on the former) wider economic forces, specifically capitalism. In theoretical terms, the analysis of this process has taken two distinct paths, which are exemplified respectively in two recent contributions on the subject.

The first path of analysis reproduces a Leninist interpretation and sees non-wage labour (women's work) in the family or household as contributing to capital accumulation through the provision of labour power for capitalist production.[115] Veronika Bennholdt-Thomsen's contribution to this volume, 'Towards a theory of the sexual division of labour', is the clearest exemplification of this argument.

> We can finally sum up, then, that just as housewife production is not truly pre-capitalist, the sexual division of labor, which is based on the housewife, is not truly an historical remnant or even the dominant form throughout the history of mankind. *It genuinely belongs to our capitalist mode of production* [our emphasis].[116]

The second path of analysis is exemplified by Norman Long, who questions the possibility of explaining 'non-capitalist relations of production simply by reference to capitalist principles'.[117] Furthermore, Long notes that concentration on subsumption is likely to cause one 'to miss the important ways in which non-wage, non-capitalist forms ... resist the penetration of commodity relations to transform them in some way in accordance with existing non-capitalist principles'.[118] Instead, Long argues:

> ... if one wishes to achieve a deeper understanding of the social relations of production within specific economic units, then one should attempt to gauge the social estimation of the value of the labour in question as expressed by the individuals, groups, or classes involved.[119]

In other words, Long is suggesting that we should attribute equal validity to the social perceptions and symbolic meanings which actors attach to their social relationships.

With regard to the existing literature on agrarian relations in the Middle East, the attempt to deal with gender issues in the context of the persistence of non-capitalist relations has yet to appear. Much has been written during the last decade on the position of women in Arab/Islamic society; indeed it constitutes a favourite subject for many social scientists and publishers. The focus, however, has been directed towards placing women and gender on the research agenda rather than towards addressing specific issues concerning the manner in which gender can be conceptualized in different types of social formation. Thus, the two contributions in this volume constitute a pioneering attempt to deal with the issue of gender in the context of a particular type (household) of agrarian production relations.

What is clear from the above is that the debate on the 'persistence' of non-capitalist forms/modes of production has relocated peasant forms of production as a central concern of those social scientists who are concerned with agrarian relations. With regard to Middle Eastern agrarian relations, there is a real paucity of theoretically informed but empirically grounded studies which focus on the relevant issues, thereby helping us to understand better the complex relations between capitalism and other forms of production. It is hoped that the articles in this volume constitute an attempt at developing such a debate, albeit with particular reference to Middle Eastern agrarian relations. In general the articles address themselves to the three elements of the 'new interpretations' that have been discussed above: articulation of modes of production; articulation of forms (household) and modes of production; and gender and non-capitalist forms of production. All three elements constitute part of an attempt to develop a new interpretation of agrarian relations in the Middle East.

It should be noted that the contributions to this volume do not represent a coherent and developed alternative framework of analysis and no attempt has been made to impose any form of collective analytical framework. If the contributions do represent a new interpretation then this has to be decided *post factum*. The contributions attempt to explore a number of theoretical issues that have been discussed at some length in the fields of rural sociology and Marxist economic anthropology, and then relate them to the particular socio-historical realities of the Middle East. As such, this volume is more akin to an agenda for further research than to the presentation of definitive solutions or analytical frameworks. Furthermore, no attempt has been made to divide the contributions into 'theoretical' and 'substantive' sections. All the contributions, with the exception of this introduction which attempts to provide a general framework, attempt to integrate theory and substantive work and reject such a false dichotomy between equally central aspects of social analysis. Each contribution both stands on its own and is also part of an overall attempt to formulate a new interpretation of agrarian relations in the Middle East.

In editing this volume, the editors were guided by the manner in which particular contributors address themselves in a rigorous and analytical manner to the three particular elements from the recent debates in the field of rural sociology and Marxist economic anthropology outlined above. The sole concession to presenting the contributions within a unified and collective analytical framework is that they have been organized according to their particular theoretical orientation. As the central issue emanating from each of these three elements have already been discussed at some length, the presentation of the contributions has been kept to the minimum. It is left to the reader to compare and contrast the particular contributions with the general debates.

Chapters 1 to 4 address themselves to issues that emerge from the 'articulation of modes of production' debate, although each article takes up very different aspects of that debate. Nico Kielstra examines Iranian rural society and attempts to use the debate in order to formulate a theoretically inspired agenda for further research. Kielstra is primarily concerned with the macro level of analysis and the political implications of the new formulation of agrarian relations. In this sense, his work shares some aspects of Islamoghlou and Keyder's work discussed above. Sarah Graham-Brown's article addresses the role of the state in affecting transformations in the agrarian sector. Her study of Palestinian peasants under Israeli military occupation also operates at the macro level and raises a number of issues that have been referred to above in the discussion of Talal Asad's pioneeering work on Palestine. Salim Tamari and Alex Pollock focus on the micro level and examine the dynamics and persistence of a particular non-capitalist form of production (sharetenanch/ share-cropping) amongst Palestinian peasants under Israeli military occupation. In many respects their respective accounts share a common theme with the work of Caglar Keyder on sharecropping and the consolidation of small peasant ownership in Turkey.

Chapters 5 to 7 present a micro account of agrarian relations and attempt to theorize one particular form of non-capitalist production, the household. Stauth, Glavanis and Aydin examine different agrarian realities and attempt to analyse them in the context of the relationship between the household and national/state policies and structures. All three contributions add to the discussion initiated by Friedmann's work, though they are not necessarily derived directly from it (especially as each conceptualizes the role of the 'household' in a different manner). Chapters 8 and 9 take up the issue of gender and non-capitalist forms of production. Kandiyoti and Moors respectively theorize the role of gender along the two paths discussed above. As indicated above, both these contributions reflect a new and still restricted orientation in the study of agrarian relations in the Middle East and as such represent a challenge to other scholars.

## Notes

1. This discussion is partially derived from Kathy and Pandeli Glavanis 'The sociology of agrarian relations in the Middle East: the persistence of household production', *Current Sociology*, vol. 31, no. 2, 1983, pp. 5–9.
2. Henry Rosenfeld, 'An overview and critique of the literature on rural politics and social change', in Richard Antoun and Iliya Harik (eds.), *Rural Politics and Social Change in the Middle East*, Bloomington: Indiana University Press 1972, p. 46.
3. Ibid.
4. Ibid., p. 47.
5. Ibid., p. 53.
6. Ibid., p. 54.
7. Ibid., p. 48.
8. Also see his *Latin America: Underdevelopment and Revolution* (New York: Monthly Review Press, 1969) and his *Dependent Accumulation and Underdevelopment* (New York: Monthly Review Press, 1978).
9. Dale Eickelman, *The Middle East: an anthropological approach*, New Jersey: Prentice-Hall, 1981, p. 45.
10. Ibid.
11. Talal Asad (ed.), *Anthropology and the Colonial Encounter*, London: Ithaca Press, 1973.

12. Emrys Peters, 'Aspects of rank and status among Muslims in a Lebanese village', in Julian Pitt-Rivers (ed.), *Mediterranean Countrymen*, Paris: Mouton, 1963, pp. 159–202; and 'Shifts in power in a Lebanese village', in Richard Antoun and Iliya Harik (eds.), *Rural Politics and Social Change in the Middle East*, pp. 165–97.
13. Eickelman, *The Middle East*, p. 60.
14. Ibid., p. 56.
15. Talal Asad, 'Market model, class structure and consent: a reconsideration of Swat political organisation', *MAN*, vol. 7, no. 1, 1972, pp. 74–94.
16. Talal Asad, 'Two European images of non-European rule', in Talal Asad (ed.), *Anthropology and the Colonial Encounter*, London: Ithaca Press, 1973, p. 113.
17. Pandeli Glavanis, 'Historical interpretation or political apologia? P. J. Vatikiotis and modern Egypt', *Review of Middle East Studies*, no. 1, 1975, pp. 63–77.
18. Cited in Talal Asad and Roger Owen, 'Introduction', *Review of Middle East Studies*, no. 3, 1978, p. i.
19. Ibid.
20. Asad, *Anthropology and the Colonial Encounter*, pp. 14–15.
21. Samir Amin, *The Arab Nation*, London: Zed Press, 1978, p. 24.
22. This discussion is partially derived from Glavanis and Glavanis, 'The sociology of agrarian relations in the Middle East', pp. 9–20 and from Glavanis and Glavanis, 'Historical materialism or Marxist hagiography? A response to a positivist critique', *Current Sociology*, vol. 34, no. 2, 1986, pp. 173–198.
23. Amin, *The Arab Nation*, p. 50.
24. Mahmoud Abdel-Fadil, *Development, Income Distribution and Social Change in Rural Egypt (1952–1970). A Study in the Political Economy of Agrarian Transition*, Cambridge: Cambridge University Press, 1975, p. 103.
25. V. I. Lenin, *The Development of Capitalism in Russia*, Moscow: Progress Publishers, 1967.
26. Ibrahim 'Amir, *al-Ard wa'l-Fallah. al-Mas'ala al-zira'iyya fi Misr* ('Land and the Peasant. The Agrarian Question in Egypt'), Cairo: Matba'at al-Dar al-misriyya, 1958.
27. Ra'uf Abbas Hamid, *al-Nizam al-ijtima'i fi Misr fi Zill al-Milkiyyat al-zira'iyya al-kabira*, 1837—1914 ('The Social System in Egypt Under the Influence of the Large Landowners, 1837–1914'), Cairo: Dar al-Fikr al-hadith li'l-Taba'a wa'l-Nashr, 1973.
28. Peter Gran, 'Modern trends in Egyptian historiography: a review article', *International Journal of Middle East Studies*, vol. 9, no. 3, 1978, p. 370.
29. Pandeli Glavanis, 'Historical interpretation or political apologia?'
30. Salih Muhammad Salih, *al-Iqta' wa'l-Ra'smaliyya al-zira'iyya fi Misr min 'Ahd Muhammad 'Ali ila 'Ahd 'Abd al-Nasir* [Feudalism and Agricultural Capitalism from the Era of Muhammad Ali to the Era of Abd al-Nasir], Beirut: Dar Ibn Khaldun, 1979.
31. Samir Radwan, *Capital Formation in Egyptian Industry and Agriculture 1882*–1967, London: Ithaca Press, 1974.
32. Ibid., p. 233.
33. Ibid.
34. Mahmoud Abdel-Fadil, *Development, Income Distribution and Social Change in Rural Egypt (1952–1970)*.
35. Ibid., p. 116.
36. Ibid., p. 118.
37. Ibid., p. 23.
38. Ibid.
39. Alan Richards, *Egypt's Agricultural Development, 1800–1980: technical and social change*, Boulder, Col: Westview Press, 1982.
40. Ibid., p. 39.
41. Karen Pfeifer, 'Algeria's agrarian transformation', *MERIP Reports*, no. 99, 1981, pp. 6–14.
42. Ibid., p. 14.
43. Ibid.
44. Mahfoud Bennoune, 'Algerian peasants and national politics', *MERIP Reports*, no. 48,

1975, pp. 3–24.

45. For a further discussion of these contributions see Glavanis and Glavanis, 'The sociology of agrarian relations in the Middle East', pp. 17–18.

46. Keith Tribe, 'Introduction to de Crisenoy', *Economy and Society*, vol. 8, no. 1, 1979, pp. 1–8.

47. Ibid., pp. 6–7.

48. Lenin, *The Development of Capitalism in Russia*, pp. 315–23.

49. Ibid., p. 315.

50. Harold Wolpe, 'Introduction', in Harold Wolpe (ed.), *The Articulation of Modes of Production*, London: Routledge and Kegan Paul, 1980, pp. 1–2.

51. Ibid., p. 3.

52. Ibid., p. 5.

53. William Roseberry, 'Peasants as proletarians', *Critique of Anthropology*, vol. 3, no. 2, 1978, pp. 3–18.

54. Ibid., p. 12.

55. Ibid.

56. Ibid., p. 14.

57. Ibid., p. 15.

58. Ibid.

59. Ibid.

60. Henry Bernstein, 'African peasantries: a theoretical framework', *Journal of Peasant Studies*, vol. 6, no. 4, 1979, pp. 421–43.

61. Ibid., p. 432.

62. Ibid., p. 424.

63. Ibid., p. 436.

64. This discussion is elaborated on in Glavanis and Glavanis, 'Historical materialism or Marxist hagiography?', pp. 176–8.

65. Peter Gibbon and Michael Neocosmos, 'Some problems in the political economy of "African Socialism"', in H. Bernstein and B. K. Campbell (eds.), *Contradictions of Accumulation in Africa: Studies in Economy and State*, Beverly Hills: Sage, 1985, pp. 153–206.

66. Ibid., p. 162.

67. Ibid., p. 163.

68. Ibid., p. 178.

69. For a critique of this argument see: Harriet Friedmann, 'Postscript: small commodity production', *Labour, Capital and Society* special issue: *Rethinking Petty Commodity Production*, vol. 19, no. 1, 1986, p. 120; and Joel Kahn, 'Problems in the analysis of peasant ideology', *Labour, Capital and Society* special issue: *Rethinking Petty Commodity Production*, vol. 19, no. 1, 1986, pp. 36–69.

70. Friedmann, 'Postscript: small commodity production', p. 121.

71. Henry Bernstein, 'Capitalism and petty commodity production', *DPP Working Paper No. 3*, Milton Keynes: Open University, 1986.

72. Ibid., p. 28.

73. Ibid., p. 33.

74. Ibid., p. 34.

75. Ibid., p. 35.

76. Ibid., p. 34.

77. See 'Summary of selected parts of Kautsky's *The Agrarian Question*', translated and compiled by Jarius Banaji, *Economy and Society*, vol. 5, no. 1, 1976, pp. 1–49.

78. Ibid., p. 3.

79. Ibid., p. 2.

80. Ibid., p. 31.

81. Ibid.

82. Ibid.

83. Ibid., p. 40.

84. See John Clammer (ed.), *The New Economic Anthropology*, London: Macmillan Press, 1978; John G. Taylor, *From Modernization to Modes of Production: A Critique of the*

*Sociologies of Development and Underdevelopment*, London: Macmillan Press, 1979; and David Seddon (ed.), *Relations of Production: Marxist Approaches to Economic Anthropology*, London: Frank Cass, 1978.

85. Aidan Foster-Carter, 'Can we articulate articulation?', in John Clammer (ed.), *The New Economic Anthropology*, p. 213.

86. Ibid.

87. Huri Islamoghlou and Caglar Keyder, 'Agenda for Ottoman history', *Review*, vol. 1, no. 1, 1977, pp. 31–55.

88. Ibid., p. 31.

89. Ibid., p. 35.

90. Ibid., p. 37.

91. Ibid., pp. 37–8.

92. Ibid., p. 45.

93. Ibid., p. 35.

94. Talal Asad, 'Anthropological texts and ideological problems: an analysis of Cohen on Arab villages in Israel', *Economy and Society*, vol. 4, no. 3, 1975, p. 14.

95. Ibid.

96. Ibid., p. 15.

97. Ibid.

98. Ibid.

99. Not until 1981 did some of these scholars attend a workshop at the Sociology Department, Durham University, that attempted to develop this type of approach. Many of the contributors to this volume participated in this workshop and contributed to the central issue being debated, namely, how to theorize and account for the persistence and viability of peasant forms of production in the Middle East. The debates and discussions at that workshop constituted the impetus from which a number of projects were carried out in the following years. Our own work, *The Sociology of Agrarian Relations in the Middle East: the persistence of household production* was inspired by that workshop and constituted the basis for the organization of a second workshop in 1983, at the Sociology and Anthropology Department, Birzeit University.

100. Caglar Keyder, 'The cycle of sharecropping and the consolidation of small peasant ownership in Turkey', *Journal of Peasant Studies*, vol. 10, nos. 2 and 3, 1983, pp. 130–45. See also his study, 'Small peasant ownership in Turkey: historical formation and present structure', *Review*, vol. 7, no. 1, 1983, pp. 53–108.

101. Susan Mann and James Dickinson, 'Obstacles to the development of a capitalist agriculture', *Journal of Peasant Studies*, vol. 5, no. 4, 1978, pp. 466–81; and Patrick Mooney, 'Labor time, production time and capitalist development in agriculture: a critique of the Mann–Dickinson thesis', unpublished paper, undated.

102. Max Hedley, 'Independent commodity production and the dynamics of tradition', *Canadian Review of Sociology and Anthropology*, vol. 13, no. 4, 1976, pp. 413–21; Kostas Vergopoulos, 'Capitalism and peasant productivity', *Journal of Peasant Studies*, vol. 5, no. 4, 1978, pp. 446–81; and Harriet Friedmann, 'The family farm in advanced capitalism: outline of a theory of simple commodity production in agriculture', Toronto: University of Toronto, (unpublished ms.), 1981.

103. Joan Smith, Immanuel Wallerstein and Hans-Dieter Evers (eds.), *Households and the World Economy*, Beverly Hills: Sage, 1984; 'The household and the large-scale agricultural unit', *Review*, vol. 7, no. 2, 1983; and T. J. Byres (ed.): *Journal of Peasant Studies*, special issue: *Sharecropping and Sharecroppers*, vol. 10, nos. 2 and 3, 1983.

104. Friedmann, 'The family farm in advanced capitalism', pp. 7–8.

105. Ibid., p. 8.

106. Ibid., p. 12.

107. Ibid., p. 17.

108. Ibid., p. 13.

109. Ibid., p. 5.

110. Hedley, 'Independent commodity production and the dynamics of tradition', p. 417.

111. Ibid.

112. Norman Long (ed.), *Family and Work in Rural Societies: Perspectives on Non-wage Labour*, London: Tavistock Publications, 1984.

113. Maria Mies, *Patriarchy and Accumulation on a World Scale: Women in the International Division of Labour*, London: Zed Books, 1986; Maria Mies (ed.), *Women: The Last Colony*, London: Zed Books, 1988; Deniz Kandiyoti, *Women in Rural Production Systems: problems and policies*, Paris: UNESCO, 1985; and Nanneke Redclift and Enzo Mingione (eds.), *Beyond Employment: household, gender and subsistence*, Oxford: Basil Blackwell, 1985.

114. Bernstein, 'Capitalism and petty commodity production', pp. 28–9.

115. Veronika Bennholdt-Thomsen, 'Towards a theory of the sexual division of labour', in Smith, Wallerstein and Evers (eds.), *Households and the World Economy*, pp. 252–71.

116. Ibid., p. 266.

117. Long (ed.), *Family and Work in Rural Societies*, p. 11.

118. Ibid.

119. Ibid., p. 12.

# 1. Modes of Production and Class: Coalitions on the Iranian Plateau

*Nico Kielstra*

The present paper is intended more as a research programme, formulating some plausible hypotheses to guide further work, than as an accomplished piece of research. Its purpose is to place modern Iranian social history in a more explicit theoretical framework than has been done so far. At the same time I shall try to give a critical review and evaluation of the 'rent capitalism' interpretation of the traditional Iranian mode of production as presented by German (and Austrian) geographers (Bobek, 1959; 1961; 1974; Ehlers, 1978; 1980), and of the criticism of this view by Marxist authors (Leng, 1974; Massarat, 1977). In this context it will be necessary to give a more general review of the concepts and models (feudalism, Asiatic mode of production) used in the analysis of pre-capitalist modes of production. Geographically I shall concentrate my analysis on the Iranian plateau and the mountain ranges (Elburz, Zagros) that border it to the north and south-west. This includes most of the territory of modern Iran, but it does not include the humid south coast of the Caspian Sea and the plain of Khuzistan at the northern end of the Persian Gulf. Both areas have long been under Iranian sovereignty, and they have received the impact of national institutions, but ecological conditions are different here from the plateau and the mountain ranges. Both areas are important agricultural regions, but their populations have been too small and politically too marginal to exert much influence on the social structure of Iran as a whole.

Until the land reform of 1962, which did not in fact entirely abolish the system, Iranian agriculture was dominated by absentee landlords, who had their land cultivated by tenants on a sharecropping base. In 1960 only about 26% of the cultivated land was owned by the cultivators themselves (Ehlers, 1980: 229), and much of this was poor, marginal land. According to tradition five production factors were distinguished in agriculture: land, irrigation water, seed, plough animals and labour. The provision of each of these factors gave title to one fifth of the crop. Land and normally also water were provided by the landlord, labour by the tenant, seed and plough animals sometimes by the landlord, sometimes by the peasant and, in the case of plough animals, sometimes by separate entrepreneurs. Actual arrangements showed considerable regional variation, studied by Lambton (1953). The landlord's share in the crop varied accordingly between 30% and 80%. Since landlords usually lived in towns or cities, the system resulted in a large flow of agricultural surplus to urban centres. The bigger towns could therefore become much more prosperous and populous than would have been the case if they had simply functioned as market and administrative centres.

Historically the system had its origin in a system of land grants (*iqta'* or *tuyul*) granted by the central government to individuals on a non-transferable and sometimes temporary base. Holders were entitled to collect land rent in the area in exchange for various types of services rendered to the state. As in the case of the medieval European fief system the central government soon found itself unable to prevent the usurpation of *tuyul* rights or their transfer by inheritance, gift or sale. For all practical purposes *tuyul* holdings gradually became indistinguishable from private property, into which they were formally transformed after the constitutional revolution of 1906.

This system has often been called 'feudal' in a loose sense. Lambton (1953) had already pointed out, however, that one of the basic characteristics of early European feudalism as a political system, the close personal link between vassal and liege lord, was never present in Iran. Bobek (1959; 1961) elaborated upon these differences from European feudalism. He pointed out that the landowning class was not a closed and privileged aristocracy but a relatively open group, that titles to rent could be commercially transferred and that the motivating force in the system was more the accumulation of capital than control over men. He therefore qualified this system as 'rent capitalism', a mode of production which had in his opinion existed in the Middle East since the second millennium BC. In spite of this early origin and long persistence he still interpreted rent capitalism as a transitionary phase between feudalism and modern capitalism (Bobek, 1974). Characteristics of rent capitalism were:

1. a close link between political dominance and cities;
2. the exploitation of peasants and craftsmen by the expropriation of a large part of their produce as rent;
3. the commercialization of titles to rent;
4. very limited productive investment by capital owners;
5. the stagnation of the development of productive forces.

The capitalist element in this system lay in its dominant motivating force, the accumulation of wealth, though this was not yet embedded in 'rational economic behaviour' as in modern capitalism.

Leng (1974) has objected that Bobek defines capitalism not as a system of production but as a moral or ideological superstructure, just as he defines feudalism as a political and legal superstructure. Leng considers as an alternative the model of the Asiatic mode of production, characterized by:

1. communal landownership with an overriding claim to all land by the state;
2. a narrow link between agriculture and crafts in the villages without a well-developed division of labour;
3. the primacy of subsistence production over commodity production;
4. land rent as the main element of taxation;
5. economic stagnation;
6. the indifferent unity of town and country;
7. the importance of irrigation;
8. a despotic political and economic system.

Such an Asiatic mode of production could change into a feudal mode of production when land titles are no longer controlled by the ruler and his official but come into the hands of a large category of relatively independent landowners who do not cultivate the land themselves. Finally, however, Leng tends to the conclusion that there is only one pre-capitalist mode of production, characterized by the appropriation of agricultural surplus by a landowning ruling class that does not reinvest this surplus in new productive activities. Feudal, Asiatic or slaveholding systems only represent alternative types of legal and political superstructure within this simple pre-capitalist mode of production.

Such a discussion on terminology may seem futile, but it draws our attention to a basic weakness of both Marxist and non-Marxist studies of the Middle East, namely the weakness of the link between theory formation and empirical research. Bobek and his follower Ehlers have collected solid amounts of empirical information, but they stick to a simplistic theoretical model that cannot accommodate the complexity of their empirical information. A British author, A. K. S. Lambton (1953, 1969), has carried out even more comprehensive empirical research with hardly any explicit theoretical framework at all. As a result, her work remains a hoard of almost indigestible information for the reader, who can only draw isolated facts from it. On the other hand, rare Marxists like Leng and Massarat seem only to care about the correct application of given theoretical concepts. These concepts may enable them to ask relevant questions from the abundance of historical material, and the answers to these questions may lead to new theoretical models much more complex than the original ones. These authors seem to care little, however, about this potential wealth of historical information. Great works of theoretical synthesis based on as many available facts as possible are conspicuously absent from Middle Eastern studies (Hodgson, 1974, is an all too rare exception).

The first question to ask about any conceivable mode of production is, which institutional arrangements and balances of power enabled it to survive for any considerable amount of time in spite of its internal contradictions? These institutional arrangements and balances of power may take various forms, according to historical conditions, but they may also transform the original mode of production into something quite different. Capitalism could not have become dominant without the rise of the modern nation state, and it may demand the use of supranational forms of authority in its later stage. This development of the political superstructure has helped to propel the evolution of the capitalist mode of production all the way from associations of merchant adventurers to multinationals.

The state structures and ideological systems of Western feudal societies have been studied in so much detail that their economic basis has sometimes been neglected. We know, however, that feudalism has never been a self-sufficient economic system. All societies that we may want to qualify as feudal have had commercial systems based on capitalist principles. Feudal lords may have been important clients for the merchants, and feudal rulers ever since Charlemagne have attempted to regulate commerce; there is no feudal system of commerce. Commerce always constituted a capitalist enclave within feudal societies. It is not unusual to find various modes of production coexisting within a simple social formation, but the commercial sector within feudal systems was neither an atavistic survival nor a minor secondary arrangement, but an essential element of the whole system. It is therefore better not to speak of a feudal mode of production, but of a feudal social formation in which at least a landlord sector and a capitalist sector coexisted with sometimes also a sector of autonomous subsistence farmers, while political dominance was in the hands of the landlord class.

The type of Asiatic societies we think of when we speak of an Asiatic mode of production had a similar capitalist commercial sector. The difference is that in Western societies the capitalist sector became dominant gradually, whereas in Asiatic societies it remained in a subservient position. The question, then, is on what the despotic and therefore supposedly strong state is founded, under the Asiatic mode of production, if it is not on the support of a landowning or capitalist ruling class? Wittfogel (1963) has tried to answer this question by qualifying Asiatic societies as hydraulic societies whose existence was dependent on a centralized system of water control that could only be managed by a strong centralized state apparatus.

It would be outside the scope of this paper to discuss if any known historical society could really qualify as a hydraulic society. In many cases, including that of Iran, political units became far larger than would have been necessary for water control according to pre-modern techniques. In Iran, irrigation systems serve a single village or a small group of neighbouring villages. These irrigation units may be suitable for management by a big landlord, but the political unit of the state includes hundreds and thousands of such mutually independent irrigation units. The state has on occasion, from Achaemaenian times to the present, constructed large irrigation dams in periods of strong state structure, but even nowadays only 7.3% of the cultivated surface is irrigated by dams (Ehlers, 1980: 94, 231). The political unit, therefore, has always been much larger than would have been necessary simply for the management of water resources. It is true that ecological conditions on the Iranian plateau have played a fundamental role in the formation of both the social structure of Iranian society and the type of state structure uniting that society. I hope to show, however, that these influences have been much more complex than is usually assumed and that the socio-economic structures and political superstructures they have created are not adequately described by the models of either rent capitalism, feudalism or the Asiatic mode of production.

The historical heartland of Iran is made up of an elongated triangular high plateau bordered to the north by the Elburz mountains and their less impressive continuation in the Khorasan range. Toward the south-west the plateau is separated from the Euphrates–Tigris delta and the Persian Gulf by the Zagros range and its continuation in the mountain range of the Makran. In Azerbaijan in the northwest both mountain ranges meet. To the east, there is no clear natural border with Afghanistan and Pakistani Baluchistan, and the political borders have moved forwards and backwards in the course of history. It is only in the mountain ranges that we find sufficient rainfall to make unirrigated agriculture economically viable and a positive balance between precipitation and evaporation (Ehlers, 1980: 74–5). The climate on the plateau becomes gradually drier when we move inland and the central parts of the plateau are taken up by the uninhabitable Lut and Great Kavir deserts. The natural condition of most of the plateau, however, is not that of a sand or stone desert but of a steppe, where winter and spring vegetation provides pasture and maintains a high enough content of organic matter in the soil to make cultivation possible when irrigation water can be provided.

The most favoured agricultural areas and, since Achaemaenian times, the centres of the Iranian state are found along the foot of the mountain ranges, where relatively fertile plains can catch enough water. Along the coast of the Caspian Sea water comes from direct precipitation, but elsewhere it is provided by the run-off from impermeable rocky mountain areas. Some of this water may be caught on the surface from permanent or temporary streams or natural wells, but most must be caught underground in artificial wells or in the horizontal underground galleries, known as *qanats*, which are peculiar to the Iranian plateau. (In old texts and in some dialects the older term *kariz* is used.) *Qanats* are underground galleries which tap the aquifier on the lower mountain slopes. The water is then conducted through an underground tunnel, usually several kilometres long, to the lower surface level of the plain, where it can be used for irrigation. The original construction of *qanats* demands a large investment. An estimate from the early 1960s mentions a cost of $10,000 per kilometre (English, 1966: 140). Once constructed, however, a *qanat* demands only limited maintenance and gives a permanent stream of water. Vertical wells are much cheaper to construct, but until half a century ago traditional pump mechanisms could only draw a limited amount of water from them, at considerable cost. Wells were mainly used, therefore, for the intensive irrigation of small horticultural plots, while the extensive cultivation of wheat, cotton and other products on large surfaces depended on *qanat* irrigation. It is only since relatively cheap motor pumps have become available that well irrigation is gaining ground over *qanat* irrigation, a development that carries with it several risks. Limited groundwater supplies can easily get exhausted by an increasing number of wells. Moreover, the groundwater caught in wells has usually seeped through the soil over much longer distances than the groundwater caught in *qanats* and therefore often contains a higher amount of mineral salts. If insufficient care is taken of drainage, salt crusts may be found in the upper layers of the cultivated soil. Where centuries of *qanat* irrigation have left little or no salification of the soil, a few decades of well irrigation sometimes have.

In the late 1950s, when well irrigation was already winning ground, Goblot (1962) estimated that about half the irrigated land was still irrigated from *qanats*. In earlier periods the relative importance of *qanats* must have been even higher. I think that it is therefore justified to attach considerable importance to the peculiarities of *qanat* irrigation when we try to relate the Iranian rural social structure to ecological conditions. It was the permanent irrigation of large surfaces that made permanent settlement on a large scale possible. Once such settlement existed, the peasants might try to increase their production by the intensive cultivation of horticultural plots and by additional dry cultivation as a gamble that might provide a good crop once every few years.

With the exception of the Caspian Sea coast, the areas with highest rainfall, where vegetation can grow all year round, are found in the mountain ridges. The relief does not favour large-scale agriculture and the concentration of large populations, but good summer pastures can be found here, which can best be exploited by pastoral nomads. There is no complete agreement on the role of pastoral nomads in Iranian history. Pastoralism is at least as old as the Aryan invasion of the Iranian plateau in the middle of the second millenium BC, and may be much older. De Planhol (1968; 1969) has argued on the basis of classical sources that the older forms of pastoralism may have been a kind of transhumance in which limited numbers of herdsmen migrated over small distances with the flocks while the majority of their social group lived in permanent villages in the winter pasture areas in the plain. The pattern of nomads organized in large tribes migrating over long distances and without permanent settlements would only have been introduced, according to him, by medieval invaders of Turkish and Mongol origin from Central Asia. (Earlier Arab invaders in the 7th century had mainly settled in the cities, since the climate of the plateau with its relatively cold winters was not favourable for Arab nomads, whose flocks were adapted to a hot climate all the year round.) Because of their mobility, comprehensive but flexible tribal organization and the difficult accessibility of many of their pasture areas, these nomads gained a military superiority over the sedentary population that could only be broken by modern 20th-century armies.

They introduced a new power factor with a different social basis. From the 12th to the early 20th century an Iranian state could not simply be a hierarchy of landed magnates as European early feudal states were and as the Sassanian empire (3rd–7th century AD) had probably been. The usual political pattern was that a successful tribal leader united a sufficiently large force of tribesmen (paid by plunder) behind him to seize power over part or all of the plateau, and established a dynasty. If this dynasty managed to survive for a while, the ruler usually tried to make himself independent from his rather undisciplined and unsubmissive tribal followers. From taxes drawn from the sedentary (urban and rural) population he tried to pay officials and mercenary troops, the latter originally often recruited outside the Iranian plateau from the Caucasus, while the tribal confederacy that had brought him to power was allowed to fall apart into smaller, politically powerless tribal units. Only Reza Pahlavi after World War One no longer needed original tribal support, since the mercenary army corps that he commanded had by then become the strongest military force in the country.

Thus there developed a type of government that was not the representative of a class or a coalition of classes, but which constituted a 'political class' of its own: a group of people controlling a power apparatus that enabled them to collect taxes mainly for their own benefit. The rulers had renounced their original position of tribal aristocrats, while the sedentary landowners were merely taxable subjects, whose preference was for as weak a state as possible. Urban merchants and craftsmen were often taxed relatively mildly, since undisputed control over the cities was important, but were not given any say in political affairs. Within the state machinery, a relatively high degree of social mobility was sometimes possible. Rulers often preferred officials who depended on their sole favour and who had little or no political backing of their own. In the long run the weakness of such regimes lay in their lack of mass support. Internal political threats could only be met by reinforcing the state apparatus and this could only be done by raising taxes, which would increase social discontent. Moreover, a growth of the mercenary state apparatus usually led to a growth of corruption, so that the net effect on the efficiency of the state apparatus of higher expenditure remained very limited. Until the early 19th century the expenses of the Persian state were determined by the economic situation of the country itself. Then the need to keep up with foreign nations with a higher level of economic development and the introduction of foreign patterns of consumption to the upper classes led to an increasingly expensive state machinery to become financed from higher and higher taxes which could only be raised through increased repression. State revenues from oil production, which began around World War One and increased rapidly from the 1950s, lowered the burden of taxation. A basically corrupt state apparatus was unable, however, to use the rising oil revenues efficiently for the development of the country. It created a larger clientele by making new bureaucratic jobs, distributing orders to private entrepreneurs and maintaining a market for luxury goods and services, but at the same time it increasingly alienated all other groups of the population, a coalition of whom finally brought down the Pahlavi regime.

The rise to power of the Pahlavis had not been a social revolution but only a modernization of an old political pattern. They left no political institutions behind them which could have been transformed into a new political system, only a political vacuum. (Centuries of repression had created a religiously inspired popular protest culture, but this had always remained at the level of ideology and so far has provided an insufficient base to create new political institutions.) The Iranian political system, even before the land reform of 1962 was thus not based on the rule of a class of feudal landlords. That does not mean that landlords did not play an important role in Iranian society. The prominence and persistence of landlordism in Iranian history and the fact that, in contrast to European feudalism, it seems to have provoked very few peasant rebellions, remains to be analysed.

The origin of landlordism in Iran probably lies in the early importance of *qanat* irrigation. While this system did not demand a nationwide integration of the water control system, the construction of *qanats* demanded a much larger investment than small and poor peasant communities could provide on their own. A new settlement based on *qanat* irrigation could only be established by the initiative of a wealthy and powerful leader. Once a *qanat* has been constructed, however, its maintenance is relatively simple and can easily be carried out by a local community. A *qanat* is also relatively invulnerable. When maintenance is neglected, the water supply diminishes, but even such neglect can be repaired at relatively limited cost. *Qanats* may be destroyed by heavy earthquakes, which are not rare in Iran, but they only affect limited areas at one time. Moreover, the deliberate closure of *qanats* is a much too laborious job to be carried out by passing plunderers. Where *qanats* have been closed this seems usually to have been the work of new landlords who wanted to reorganize the cultivation and settlement pattern of the area. In a dry environment the abandonment of irrigation and cultivation may lead to the destruction of the organic components in the soil and thereby to a loss of agricultural potential that is difficult to repair. In the major agricultural areas of Iran, however, abandoned agricultural land reverts to a kind of steppe vegetation beneath which the fertility of the soil is neither permanently nor seriously damaged. The danger of exhaustion of the soil, salification, wind erosion etc. does not arise from abandonment of the land but from overcultivation, insufficient drainage or overgrazing of marginal lands. While for example in Iraq or nothern Libya the destruction of irrigation systems and the abandonment of cultivation because of nomadic invasions led to a loss of agricultural potential for many centuries, we see time and again that Iranian agriculture rapidly recovers after periods of warfare and insecurity. The long-term effects of the medieval 'Beduinization' of the country have not been so negative as they have sometimes been considered.

The involvement of at least 25%, and sometimes maybe as much as 50%, of the population in full-time nomadic pastoralism made possible the use of remote mountain pastures which could not easily have been used by sedentary or semi-sedentary populations. At least some of the nomadic tribesmen practised a certain amount of unirrigated cultivation in their summer pasture areas as a secondary source of income. Agricultural possibilities here were too limited and uncertain, however, to make permanent settlement possible. Only where relatively fertile valleys and mountain pastures could be found in fairly close proximity, as in the Elburz and parts of Kurdistan, did the old pattern of transhumance survive. If the same level of animal production had been maintained by fully sedentary populations, this would have led to overgrazing and permanent deterioration of the more easily accessible pasture lands. If a lower level of animal production had been compensated for by a higher production of cereals, this would – in the absence of modern productivity-raising agricultural techniques – probably have led to overcultivation and deterioration of marginal cultivable lands. Whatever damage the nomads may at times have done to agriculture and commerce, their activities probably prevented a worse long-term deterioration of ecological conditions.

We have seen how the military superiority of the nomadic tribes led to a special, parasitical type of government. It also led to permanent insecurity in the more remote rural areas. These two factors strengthened the position of landlords. We have seen that once an irrigation system had been constructed, the activities of a landlord were no longer necessary to run it. In the oral history of Iranian villages we often find the memory of periods when control by a landlord broke down and the village functioned as an autonomous community. After a while, it often happened that a new landlord took control and there is little evidence that this met with strong resistance from the peasants. Some such autonomous communities emerged as late as the late 19th century. A village without a landlord was not so much a free peasant community as a helpless prey to the depredations of government tax collectors and soldiers of roaming nomadic bands, who had much less interest in the continuation of a reasonable level of agricultural productivity and prosperity than did a permanent landlord. A landlord might also be a source of agricultural credit, even if not all of them were. Seeking credit on the free market – from urban moneylenders – often cost more than the rent to be paid to a landlord. Rates of interest on the open credit market were extremely high because of insecurity about repayment and probably also because of a general shortage of liquid capital. The recovery or resettlement of an area after natural disasters or periods of warfare was also something for which only a landlord might provide the necessary investments.

The combination of all these factors may help to explain the rarity of peasant rebellions. Landlords invested on average relatively little in agriculture, but they did invest in social contacts and political influence with both government officials and tribal leaders to ensure relative security for their tenants. A landlord was thus at least as much a political as an economic entrepreneur. Before the constitutional revolution of 1906, however, few landlords sought formal government office. The explanation for this is somewhat complex. It has often been noted that landlordism in Iran did not lead to the development of a stable landed aristocracy as in European countries. (The stability of Western landowning aristocracies should not be overestimated, of course.) This can be related to political insecurity, which could destroy the fortunes if not the physical existence of landed families. It has also been related to the Islamic system of inheritance, which prevents primogeniture and prescribes the distribution of estates between all heirs. This explanation nevertheless leaves open the question of why this system of inheritance persisted. The Koranic rules of inheritance have frequently been tampered with elsewhere, when local conditions made this desirable.

The Islamic system of inheritance is based on an economic system in which access to resources is relatively open, at least for those who can provide a modest initial investment. These conditions existed in the old Arabian Peninsula, where pastoralism on collective pasture lands, small-scale long-distance commerce, and raiding and plunder offered career prospects for every enterprising, energetic and moderately well-to-do man. They also existed in pre-industrial Iran, where land was not scarce but only became valuable when some initial investment could be spent on irrigation. Under such conditions it is less important to preserve an established estate intact than to provide each heir of a wealthy family with enough starting capital to develop his own estate. Only in relatively poor families might the division of an estate leave each heir with too little to start again on his own, and thus lead to downward social mobility. Descendants of wealthy families might remain wealthy over many generations, but since estates were split up in each generation the family never became associated with a particular estate, though it might well be dominant in a specific region.

This system did not lead to a flow of younger sons seeking lucrative (or at least honourable) government office, as was the case in European aristocratic families. A landowner might decide to seek government office, but that would have been a question of individual strategy. The possible gains in wealth and power had to be weighed against the risks of royal disfavour, expropriation and even execution inherent in government office under a despotic regime. Another well-known European phenomenon was even more completely absent: the flow of younger sons of the aristocracy into religious office. Though Islam has no priesthood, there is a category of religious professionals, the *ulama*, who serve as prayer leaders, preachers and teachers at religious schools, and in Iranian Shi'a Islam they have played an important and independent role. Religious office partly runs in families, who often but not necessarily claim descent from the Prophet, but the *ulama* constitute a free profession in which anybody who knows enough Arabic to read the Koran and is reasonably orthodox in his opinions can try to recruit a large enough following to earn a living. Religious higher education was and is relatively cheap, much cheaper than a modern university education. Institutions of religious education usually had their own revenues from property, and the poorer students were supported by public charity. Religious professionals did not usually come from wealthy aristocratic families but from more modest middle-class origins: from the families of urban merchants and craftsmen and some of the more prosperous peasants. As such, the *ulama* were not a group that would automatically support the political regime and the existing social system, though the government usually tried to remain on at least moderately good terms with them because of their influence on the urban population.

The more important tribal leaders were usually landowners also, but their political power was not based on their landed property but on the military force of their tribal clients. No single landowner would have been able to finance a force sufficiently large to overthrow the state apparatus, and landowners were always reluctant to arm their tenants. (Shah Abbas, a strong central ruler, once recruited a new musketeer corps from amongst the sedentary peasantry as a countervailing force against his own tribal levies.) Our information on the amount of taxes tribesmen paid to their leaders is rather poor, since detailed modern monographs were only written after tribal leaders lost much of their political power and autonomy. It seems to have been much lower, however, than the 30–80% of the gross produce that cultivators had to pay to their landlords, probably some 10–20% of their gross income. Moreover, this was not a tax on gross income but on capital, being based on the number of animals a nomadic family owned.

It is not surprising that nomadic tribesmen were taxed less than sedentary peasants since they were more difficult to control. They often also had some political alternatives when they considered themselves overtaxed: to join another tribal organization or support a political rival of the present tribal leader. They were clients, paying tribute to a political patron who was supposed to provide political co-ordination and protection in return, not tenants paying rent to a landlord. Only large tribal groups with some degree of central political organization could maintain grazing right over good pasture lands along long migration routes. There always were nomadic splinter groups which were not part of the large tribal organizations, but they had to content themselves with shorter migrations and poorer pasture lands.

Barth (1964) has described the double process of sedentarization of nomads at the top and the bottom of the tribal social hierarchy. The poorest nomads would no longer be able to live off their flocks and would be forced to seek employment as landless agricultural labourers. The wealthiest nomads might invest their surplus wealth in land and become small landowners. Nomadic tribes were far from egalitarian and dependent salaried herdsmen might be savagely exploited by their employers (Black, 1972). Tribal leaders usually recruited a professional personal bodyguard from amongst this tribal proletariat, but they had always to deal with a majority of economically self-sufficient tribesmen.

Leaders on the tribal level might own city houses, but usually shared the nomadic life at least part of the time. Branches of their families that did not inherit tribal political leadership might become urban citizens.

The large confederacies, the highest level of tribal organizations, had no economic but only political functions. Confederacies might be organized for national political purposes and would disintegrate when they lost these political functions. Their leaders were usually not nomads but sedentary urban aristocrats, and their position as political patrons of large tribal groups gave them a political power that other urban aristocrats had not.

A tribal leader founding a dynasty would normally already be a landowner and he would use his newly gained power to enlarge his own property, for example by expropriating political adversaries. Strong regimes would often prefer to administrate as much land as possible directly, collecting the same rents as private landlords and paying officials in cash instead of giving out *tuyuls* over which it might soon lose control. When regimes weakened they would give out state lands as *tuyuls* to gain political support or simply be unable to prevent regional magnates from usurping state lands. There was thus a direct conflict of interests between the state apparatus and the landlord class over the amount of land to be directly administrated by the state. Landlords who were usually able to protect their own interests often preferred as weak a government as possible.

As we have seen, one consequence of the land tenure system was that much more of the agricultural surplus was drawn toward urban centres than would have resulted from their marketing and administrative functions only. In consequence the percentage of the population living in urban centres was always relatively high considering the stage of economic development of the country. In the early 19th century, after a century of decline and insecurity, the urban population has been estimated at one seventh of the total population (Issawi, 1971: 26). At the end of the century, after a period of relative peace, the urban population had grown to about 25% (Ehlers, 1980: 183).

Before the second half of the 19th century this urban population seems to have been in a relatively favoured position compared to the peasantry. Strong independent municipal authorities never developed, but urban merchants and craftsmen were represented by well organized guilds. The *ulama* were at times willing to act as spokesmen for the urban middle classes with the authorities (Floor, 1975; Savory, 1980: 179–85). There was another category of urban workmen, directly employed in royal workshops, who were considered an especially privileged group amongst craftsmen (Savory, 1980: 188–9). Before the 19th century we hear little about the urban middle and working classes exercising an independent political role. During the 19th century the growing urban crowds did become a political factor, but they were just as likely to be brought out in favour of the government as in favour of any kind of opposition. The earliest known *petit bourgeois* reform movement, the Babis (1844–51) significantly failed to mobilize the urban crowds in its support (Floor, 1971a, 1971b).

From the second half of the 19th century onwards, the old balance of social forces in Iran gradually fell apart. An increase of population in the countryside led to the rise of a landless rural proletariat which began to seek work in the cities and even abroad (Abdullaev, in Issawi, 1971: 42–51). The growth of urban centres led to a growth of trade and in accumulation of merchant capital, but at the same time foreign competition in international trade and imports of foreign industrial products increased, upsetting both the position of craftsmen and the hitherto slightly positive balance of trade (Issawi, 1971: 130–51). On the whole we must assume a growing social inequality amongst the urban population and the rise of a growing part of the population no longer involved in or represented by the old guild organizations. The government became increasingly dependent on foreign credit to cover its rising expenses, and attempts to sell commercial concessions to foreign traders brought the government for the first time into decisive conflict with the urban merchant class supported by the *ulama*. When landlords, always opposed to strong despotic government, and the tribal leaders of the Bakhtiari confederacy, seeing their chance to grasp power from the hands of a weakening dynasty, joined this coalition, the stage was set for the constitutional revolution of 1906, which brought an end to the absolute monarchy. During the first few years of parliamentary government it seemed as if Iran was for the first time going to have a government representing a coalition of bourgeois interests. (In the position of the peasantry nothing changed.) The independent attitude of the new regime toward foreign interests in Iran led, however, to Russian military intervention in 1911, which broke up the ruling coalition.

The Bakhtiari leaders preferred to disband parliament and to try to concentrate power in their own hands rather than fight a desperate campaign against the Russians. The ruler who assumed power after the chaotic years of World War One, however, was Reza Pahlavi, a career officer of modest origins who commanded the Cossack brigades, the only effective regular army unit. He established his own dynasty in 1925. His regime constituted a return to the old traditions of rule by a parasitic group of military leaders, but these now based their support on the regular army instead of on tribal followers who were no longer able to resist a modern army. Such regimes had usually been founded by force, but had been obliged to maintain a careful balance between the other social forces in the country in order to maintain themselves in the long term. The Iranian class structure could no longer, however, be restored into an 18th or 19th century pattern.

The military power of the tribal leaders was definitely broken by the army, and in the economic field too tribesmen became more and more a marginal group. With this countervailing force gone, landowners could no longer play their role as mediators between the government, tribal leaders and their own tenants. The land tenure system lost such aspects of genuine patronage as it had had and became increasingly purely exploitative. In the growing and modernizing cities a merchant class continued to develop, which was denied political representation. Urban craftsmen were pushed from the market by industrial competition and joined the growing urban proletariat of rural migrants as a group without any links to the major social and political institutions. The *ulama* saw their purely religious position respected but lost their monopoly over learning and the access to important state positions that they and their students had had. The replacement of traditional intellectuals, trained in religious schools, by modern university graduates in the higher levels of the government bureaucracy meant a diminution of the traditional possibilities of rapid social mobility within the government apparatus. Traditional higher education had been cheaper and more easily accessible than modern universities. The new middle class of modern trained government employees also remained excluded from active political participation.

The nature of Reza Shah's regime itself prepared the ground for the coalition (merchants, *ulama* and traditional and modern intellectuals, with a badly organized urban proletariat as cannon fodder) which would finally overthrow the Pahlavi dynasty. Two events slowed down this development. The first was the overthrow of Reza Shah, suspected of pro-German sympathies, by the Allies in 1941. His son, Muhammad Reza, was maintained on the throne, but actual political power once more came into the hands of parliament in which bourgeois groups and big landlords were dominant. At this time there was a well-organized Communist Party with considerable support among some sections of the urban proletariat, but this party remained a minority against the landowners and big merchants who dominated the rural constituencies and the small towns. Like the constitutional revolution, this period of parliamentary rule was brought to an end when the regime clashed with foreign interests, this time mainly British oil interests. The oil concessions of what was to become the Anglo-Iranian Oil Company had first been established on the eve of World War One, when the Iranian state was at its weakest and unable to bargain for favourable conditions. Reza Shah seems to have respected British oil interests in exchange for British tolerance for his more verbose forms of nationalism. But no regime based, however imperfectly, on popular representation could in the long run ignore this foreign exploitation of the main source of national wealth. Attempts to nationalize the oilfields led between 1950 and 1953 to a diplomatic crisis between Iran and the Western powers, and to an economic crisis, since Iran was unable to sell a large part of its oil against the opposition of the international oil companies. The stalemate was broken by a CIA-supported coup in which the Shah supported by the army once more seized power. What remained of the period was a widespread sense of political frustration which the Shah was never able to overcome or suppress and a definitive split in the pro-democratic forces between Marxists and non-Marxists, between whom there has been very little co-operation since.

Another more structural intervening force was the influence of state oil revenues on the Iranian socio-economic system. These enabled Reza Shah to realize a modest modernization of the state apparatus and the national infrastructure, thereby stabilizing his regime. Since the mid-1950s, and especially during the 1970s, Iranian oil income increased rapidly because of rising oil prices, higher royalties and increasing production. Though the level of waste because of corruption and bureaucratic inefficiency remained high, the Shah realized that he had to provide rapid development for the country in order to maintain his throne. The rapid modernization of the country's infrastructure led to the rise of a new class of modern capitalist entrepreneurs: bankers, contractors of public works, property developers, import and export traders. These were recruited more from the old landowner class than from the traditional bazaar merchants, who were much less adapted to modern technology and business practices and resented the rise to power and affluence of these new rich. The major figures in the new bourgeoisie became part of the ruling élite together with the royal family and its sycophants and military and security leaders. Their influx decisively influenced the nature of the ruling élite, which became much more big-business orientated than it had been under former despotic regimes.

The old landowning class, liberal in so far as it was opposed to a strong state and royal despotism, was successfully eliminated by the land reform of 1962. The old land tenure system had now lost all the functions it had ever had and the national bourgeoisie lacked liquid capital. Fairly generous compensation was paid for the expropriated land, so that the landowners were transformed into an entrepreneurial bourgeoisie. The latter's members were much more dependent on government co-operation for their enterprises than had been the landlords, who thus had to pay for their new business opportunities with a loss of political independence. Business opportunities were such, however, that there was little opposition from landowners.

The land reform, coupled with some other measures for rural development, raised some popular enthusiasm in the beginning. A more reckless despotic regime less connected with big-business circles, like Peron's in Argentina for example, might have used the opportunity to raise a populist movement in support of the government against the established liberal bourgeoisie. The Iranian government carefully avoided any such populist agitation, however, and though the peasantry in general reacted favourably to the land reform, the latter failed to create for the government a popular reformist image.

In fact, the reform raised an anti-government populist movement from quite a different quarter. The major religious centres had enjoyed an independent income from the revenues of landed property. This property had been accumulated through the centuries from bequests and was administrated in so-called *waqf* foundations (foundations for religious or charitable purposes). According to Islamic law, *waqf* property could not be sold, expropriated or otherwise alienated. This independent income had long assured the religious leaders a large degree of economic and political independence from the government. Even the land reform did not propose the expropriation of *waqf* land, but it lowered the rent therefrom and placed the *waqf* foundations under closer government control. In spite of their traditional middle-class associations, not all religious leaders were opposed to social reform, but all of them feared a loss of autonomy especially as they had few illusions about the despotic nature and secularizing intentions of the government. A clash between religious leaders and the government took place in 1962–3, which led to the banishment abroad of Ayatollah Khomeini, the most outspoken and uncompromising of the religious leaders, and to a constant and gradually increasing religious agitation against the government.

The *ulama* had certainly not always been a progressive and dynamic element, and there was a considerable anti-clerical tradition both amongst the modern educated élite and in popular (both urban and rural) circles. Urban lower middle class groups were traditionally the most orthodox. The religious apparatus, however, was the only nationwide type of oppositional organization which the government did not dare to destroy, even though on occasion it persecuted individual *ulama*. Gradually, therefore, most of the Marxist opposition was drawn into a religious orbit. Such an Islamic populist opposition turned out to have a much larger appeal to the new urban proletariat that had arisen since the 1950s than did Western-style liberal or Marxist opposition groups.

The land reform had accentuated the already existing split between tenants, who now became small owners or landless labourers, for whom little had changed. The land reform triggered off the entrepreneurial activity of a new rural bourgeoisie of somewhat more well-to-do peasants. These started, for example, exploiting agricultural machinery which they rented to the smaller farmers, thereby diminishing the need for agricultural labour. Though the drainage of agricultural surplus to the cities had considerably diminished, the advantages of this for the peasantry were offset by a government policy of low agricultural prices. Iran with its large foreign exchange income could easily import food and thereby keep prices low. Government plans even went so far as to concentrate Iranian agriculture in a number of favourable areas and to sacrifice agricultural activity in the more marginal areas. Such plans were only realized to a small degree, but they kept Iranian agriculture in a constant state of depression. The result was a much larger migration of rural proletarians to the cities than had ever been seen before.

Urban employment was rapidly growing, though wages were low and hardly kept up with rapid inflation. Urban employment did not grow rapidly enough, however, to provide steady employment for the large number of unskilled rural migrants, and urban public services did not grow rapidly enough to serve the rapidly growing new urban slum quarters. The new semi-unemployed urban sub-proletariat responded easily to Islamic populist propaganda. Mullahs were not normally considered political leaders in village society, but their ideological terminology was more easily understood than that of the various Marxist groups or of Westernized secularist intellectuals. All alternative secular organizations that might have organized the urban poor were either successfully repressed or (like labour unions) monitored by the government. In these conditions the coalition of the whole non-Marxist opposition emerged, which overthrew the Pahlavi regime. To the surprise of the bourgeois intellectuals the *ulama* were able to communicate directly with the urban proletariat and sub-proletariat and lower middle classes and to recruit from amongst these their own corps of Revolutionary Guards, which became the decisive political power factor after the fall of the Shah, and prevented Marxist groups and non-Marxist secular intellectuals from assuming political control.

By its very nature the Shah's government was inherently unable to stem the rising tide of Islamic populism. Increased government spending, even on welfare projects, led more to an increase in corruption and bureaucratic inefficiency than to increased output. By the mid-1970s it had become clear that government development policies were unable to keep pace with the social and material problems of rapid urbanization. There was no 'silent majority' to oppose big-city radicalism. The government had alienated all classes and groups, and the religious professionals, as guardians of traditional values, were on the side of the opposition. The peasantry was probably still least opposed to the Shah and least influenced by religious agitation, but at the time of the land reform the government had failed to raise a peasant popular movement which might have supported it. Even government employees were not a reliable clientele, since their political and career ambitions had been frustrated.

Military spending had increased rapidly since the late 1960s when Britain first announced its intention of ending its military presence in the Persian Gulf area. This rise in military expenditure, however, did not result in the creation of a relatively small but highly privileged army that might have fought for the regime to defend its own interests, as some Latin American armies do. Instead, the Shah tried at enormous expense to create a military apparatus that would enable him to take over the British policing role in the Gulf area and the Indian Ocean. This policy may have gratified his own megalomania and the career ambitions of some senior officers, and it certainly served Western interests. It did not bring Iran any economic advantage, since the country was unable to take over the import and foreign investment markets in the Arab Gulf states against Western and Japanese competition. This policy, moreover, left Iran with excessively expensive and top-heavy armed forces that were nevertheless badly prepared to deal with large-scale urban demonstrations. Demonstrations had to be dealt with by an army of conscripts, who had little reason to consider themselves privileged and were led by junior officers who were somewhat better paid but, like most modern educated Iranians, frustrated in their social and political ambitions. As soon as the opposition was strong enough to organize a widespread and continuous series of demonstrations, it became clear that the army would not hold together if things continued. Even senior officers became inclined to drop the Shah in an attempt to preserve their grip on the army. It has now become known that they were encouraged in this attitude by the US Embassy, which at last realized that the monarchy had no future and hoped to be able to come to terms with a moderate new regime. Both the Iranian generals and the Americans failed to realize that the modern liberal bourgeois politicians had little effective support either.

Ayatollah Khomeini had well understood the nature of the Shah's regime, when he said about him in 1963: 'Poor man! Don't you know that not a single man of those who surround you shall stay at your side if there is the lightest sound or a single accident. They are not with you; they are either servants or brokers who have no religion; they have no loyalty and are the servants of the Pound....' (cited by Rizvi, 1980: 261). Khomeini seems, however, to have failed to see that even an Islamic regime needs a socio-economic base. For the moment the *ulama* maintain themselves by a kind of mob rule by the Revolutionary Guard and its hangers-on. They probably still enjoy considerable support amongst the urban proletariat and lower middle class, but they have done little to organize this support and have gradually alienated the modern intellectuals and technicians who were willing to co-operate with them. The *ayatollahs* are not simply reactionary fanatics who want to turn Iran back to the Middle Ages. They are in theory aware of the problems of the modern world, but their factual knowledge of the workings of that modern world is too limited to enable them to transform theory into praxis, while their cultural intransigence alienates modern educated people, even moderately religious ones, from them.

Intellectuals and the liberal middle bourgeoisie are powerless against the Revolutionary Guards and the urban mob. The armed forces are for the moment eliminated as an active political force. Many officers may not be happy about the regime, but for the moment no officer could hope to make his conscript soldier march against the *ayatollahs*' orders. The peasantry is probably the only group that has drawn some economic advantage from the situation. A sharp diminution of food imports has created a new demand for Iranian agricultural products and a revival of agricultural activity. The cultural changes brought about by the Islamic regime probably have little influence on the life of the peasantry, and they might well become supporters of the regime. So far, however, nothing seems to have been done to organize them.

The only active opposition so far comes from autonomist movements amongst the ethnic minorities, especially the Kurds, who control only limited and marginal areas, and from some Marxist groups who are too small to take over power even if the system should collapse. Its urban popular supporters may become disappointed with the Islamic regime if it fails to bring about social reforms and economic development, but such a process of disillusionment may take a long time. During that time there will probably be a stalemate in which the Islamic regime can neither be overthrown nor implement effective policies. Consequently, the development of the country as a whole will stagnate. What new class coalitions or ruling élites may constitute themselves in a more remote future can now only be a subject of speculation.

## References

Barth, F., 1964, *Nomads of South Persia: The Basseri Tribe of the Khamseh Confederacy*. Oslo.

Black, J., 1972, 'Tyranny as a strategy for survival in "egalitarian" society: Luri facts versus an anthropological mystique', *Man*, N.S. vol. 7, no. 4, pp. 614–34.

Bobek, H., 1959, 'Die Hauptstufen der Gesellschafts- und Wirtschaftsenfaltung in geographischer Sicht', *Die Erde*, no. 90, pp. 259–98.

——— 1961, 'Zur Problematik eines unterentwickelten Landes alter Kultur: Iran', *Orient* (Hamburg) no. 2, pp. 64–8, 115–24, 146.

——— 1974, 'Zum Konzept des Rentenkapitalismus', *Tijdschrift voor Economische en Sociale Geografie*, no. 65, pp. 73–8.

Ehlers, E., 1980, *Iran: Grundzüge eines geographischen Landeskunde*, Darmstadt.

English, P. W., 1966, *City and Village in Iran: settlement and economy in the Kirman basin*, Madison–Milwaukee–London.

Floor, W. M., 1971a, 'The Lutis, a social phenomenon in Qajar Persia', *Die Welt des Islams*, no. 13, pp. 103–20.

——— 1971b, 'Demonstraties als vorm van politieke mobilisering in Iran', *Sociologische Gids* vol. 18, no. 2, pp. 202–7.

——— 1975 'The guilds in Iran: an overview from the earliest beginnings till 1972', *Zeitschrift der deutschen morgenländischen Gesellschaft* vol 125, no. 1, pp. 99–116.

Goblot, H., 1962, 'Le problème de l'eau en Iran', *Orient*, no. 23, pp. 46–55.

Hodgson, M. G. S., 1974, *The Venture of Islam: Conscience and History in a World Civilization* (3 volumes), Chicago.

Issawi, C. (ed.), 1971, *The Economic History of Iran, 1800–1914*, Chicago.

Lambton, A. K. S., 1953, *Landlord and Peasant in Persia*, Oxford.

——— 1969, *The Persian Land Reform 1962–1966*, Oxford.

Leng, G., 1974, 'Rentenkapitalismus oder Feudalismus', *Geographische Zeitschrift* no. 62, pp. 119–37.

Massarat, M., 1977, 'Gesellschaftliche Stagnation und die asiatische Produktionsweise', *Geographische Hochschulmanuskripte. Göttingen*, vol. 4.
Planhol, X. de, 1968, *Les fondements géographiques de l'Islam*, Paris.
——— 1969 'L'évolution du nomadisme en Anatolie et en Iran', in L. Földes (ed.), *Viehwirtschaft und Hirtenkultur*, Budapest.
Rizvi, A. A., 1980 *Iran: Royalty, Religion and Revolution*, Canberra.
Savory, R., 1980, *Iran Under the Safavids*, Cambridge.
Wittfogel, K. A., 1963, *Oriental Despotism: a comparative study*, New Haven.

# 2. Agriculture and Labour Transformation in Palestine

*Sarah Graham-Brown*

The past two decades or more have witnessed significant changes in the importance of agriculture in the West Bank economy, not so much as a percentage of GDP but as a source of livelihood and employment. The value of land as a measure of social and political power has diminished, though as a non-agricultural commodity its value has generally been enhanced. The availability of waged employment in Israel has created a new 'commuting' workforce, many of whose members are still based in the villages of the West Bank but whose ties with the land and agriculture are weakening. These changes, which can be ascribed largely to the effects, direct and indirect, of the Israeli occupation, still have not brought a radical shift in relations of production among those who remain on the land. Despite the introduction of new technology these relations retain, for the moment, many of the characteristics of the pre-1967 era.

The process of rural migration to the cities is familiar to many other countries, but in the West Bank this process is complicated by a military occupation, and by a militant settler movement intent on taking over as much land as possible. Thus the rapidity of externally generated change is also a distinctive feature of this situation.

This chapter aims to explore some dimensions of the occupation's impact on agriculture, particularly its effects on patterns of labour. It should also be said at the outset that there are considerable geographical variations both in the state of agriculture and in the growth of migrant wage labour. Different parts of the West Bank are more or less climatically suitable for agriculture and historically their forces and relationships of production have developed in different ways.

## Developments in tenancy and labour during the Mandate

It is worth first returning to the agricultural history of the region when seeking explanations for some aspects of the present situation, particularly the apparent and surprising continuities that exist alongside the ruptures with the past. The changes in the West Bank since 1967 have been more dramatic than anything experienced since 1948. But both before and after this date the response in the countryside to externally imposed change has frequently been to adapt old relationships and methods rather than to espouse new ones, though this does not mean that the region can be regarded simply as an isolated and static periphery.

Palestine, it is often repeated, has never been a land with great feudal estates comparable, for instance, to those of Syria in Ottoman times. Nonetheless, until very recent times political and social power rested on ownership of land, predominantly rural land. This in turn enabled a class of *rentier* landlords to obtain land and merchant interests in the cities.

In the central hill region of Palestine, where even today dry farming is the norm (still only 5.8% of land under cultivation is irrigated), there were a number of fertile valleys, aside from the Marj ibn Amer, which were mostly in the hands of large landowners, though not necessarily in single estates. By the early 20th century these lands were generally farmed by tenants, more often than not under some form of sharecropping contract. In both what is now the West Bank and in the Galilee, however, there were also large numbers of small peasant farmers who grew field crops on small strips of land in the valleys (usually held in communal tenure – *mushaa*). These farmers also individually owned olive groves and fruit orchards on the hill slopes.

From the 1920s, and arguably from even earlier, many of these farmers were subject to some extent to market forces, both because of the growing monetarization of the economy as a whole and because they grew a range of crops beyond their subsistence needs. The world recession in 1929–33 and the accompanying drop in world commodity prices therefore filtered down to the peasantry. This caused considerable problems for small farmers and sharecroppers, who had been drawn into the market economy sufficiently to feel the effects of the drop in prices for the crops they produced. Reports written in the 1930s all stress the degree of indebtedness of most smallholders and tenants. This indebtedness increased their dependence on landowners and merchants, who were generally the only source of credit.

But at the same time, the existence of a market economy did open up new opportunities for agricultural production and this led to some adjustments and adaptations in the structure of agrarian relations as individuals tried to take advantage of the new conditions. One of those adaptations most relevant to discussion of present-day conditions was in the domain of sharecropping contracts. These developed into a spectrum of relationships between landlord and tenant.

These included what is usually thought of as the norm, in which the cropper contributes labour alone for an agreed share of the crop. But other, more complex compacts developed, with the cropper contributing some of the factors of production, for instance, a plough and ploughing stock. Yacov Firestone, who examined tenancy patterns in the 'Arabeh area in the

1930s, also found arrangements which he calls 'joint farming' under which the landowner, who also owns the stock, appoints a villager (who may himself own some stock) to operate the farm, making over a share of stock to him, debiting him its value and sharing out the crop according to their initial shares in the capital. The land itself was not included in the contract.[1] Such joint farmers could also take on croppers, which put them in an ambiguous position as both exploiter and exploited.

Such contracts, though not apparently very widespread, were to be found in various forms in olive growing and livestock rearing as well as in the cultivation of field crops. Although they still represented an uneven relationship between peasant and landlord, they offered opportunities for access to land on relatively advantageous terms at a time when land was scarce but market opportunities existed.

Another more common phenomenon, still to be found today, was that many farmers who did not hold enough land to make a living for their families sharecropped the land of a local landowner, a richer peasant or a relative while also working on their own plots.

During the Mandate period hill areas suffered from pressure on the land because of population growth but also because, failing the introduction of new, more intensive farming methods, there was a shortage of cultivable land. Although minor technical developments occurred, the only people with capital for investment, the landowners, generally retained their *rentier* mentality and were not prepared to put money into agriculture in this region.

This contrasts with the situation on the coastal plain and the Marj ibn Amer. While the hills were little touched by Jewish landbuying (except the Galilee in the 1940s), in the plains a good deal of land changed hands. It was in the plains that capitalist plantation agriculture developed, predominantly in the citrus groves owned by both Jews and Arabs. In these citrus groves and in public works schemes initiated by the British there was, by the 1930s, a substantial demand for wage labourers. Arab villagers were often employed because they could be paid at much lower rates than other workers, particularly unionized Jewish labour.

While most of these workers came from the villages on the coastal plain, Rachelle Taqqu in her study of Arab labour under the Mandate points out that in the early 1930s, with the slump in agriculture and in small workshop industries, workers were also being attracted into Haifa and its environs[2] from as far away as the Nablus area. Mostly wage labour would be done for a few months in the slack agricultural season. What we see here, then, was still a peasantry supplementing its main source of agricultural livelihood with off-farm work. There is little evidence that this had any impact on the deployment of labour on the farm. The family still remained the main unit of labour, whilst often the level of rural underemployment would allow a family member to go off and work in town for a couple of months without any need to seek a replacement from outside the family.

## 1948–1967: Jordanian rule

In the areas that came under Israeli rule after 1948, the Palestinian population was transformed within the space of a year from a settled, predominantly peasant society to a minority of village dwellers with drastically reduced access to land. By the 1960s, as the Israeli economy expanded, these village dwellers became a convenient pool of cheap labour on which to draw, since many were no longer able to make a living from the land. Today the majority of Palestinians who live in Israel form a kind of dormitory proletariat. They mostly live in what are still defined as villages (though in reality many are now towns) but land plays a limited role in their employment and in the definition of their social and economic status, whatever symbolic value it retains.

By contrast, Jordanian rule reinforced the West Bank's role as an agricultural hinterland. This was because the government, and British and American aid advisers, chose to invest money for industrial and service projects primarily in the East Bank. Such investment as there was in the West Bank was concentrated in the Jerusalem area.

The only exception was a major agricultural development project planned for the Jordan Valley. This was an area in which little agricultural development had taken place but which was seen to have vast potential if it could be irrigated. After 1948 a further incentive to develop it was the need to settle the large numbers of Palestinian refugees who lived in camps in the vicinity. For a number of reasons, however, primarily disputes over the division of the Jordan waters and the Israelis' unilateral decision to divert those waters in the north, the irrigation scheme was only in its early stages by 1967 and was subsequently developed only on the eastern side of the valley. The modest land reform programme launched in the 1960s had not been implemented in the western valley by 1967, so that many farmers were left without legal title to their land.

Despite the pool of cheap labour represented by the refugees in the valley, the introduction of new farming technology and the commercialization of agriculture, a pattern of capitalist farming employing exclusively wage labour only emerged on the fruit plantations, mainly centred around Jericho. In the cultivation of field crops and of vegetables, landowners employed landless refugees mainly as sharecroppers rather than as wage labourers, thus perpetuating the patterns of agrarian relations that had been common in the 1930s and 1940s.

In other parts of the West Bank, there was little fundamental change in either the structure or the technology of agriculture during this period. According to Hilal the trend in landownership was towards further fragmentation, mainly as a result of inheritance patterns (all the sons in a family inherit land), and an increase in landlessness. At the other end of the scale some of the largest landholders seem to have sold off some of their land, probably in favour of other business interests in Amman or elsewhere.

Land shortage appears to have increased the number of wage labourers in agriculture as well as sharecroppers. Hilal estimated that in the early 1960s, 3,226 large and medium landholders employed some 20,000 agricultural wage labourers. Opportunities for wage labour outside agriculture were available only on a modest scale.[3]

Outmigration was another solution for a peasant short of land or a refugee or wage worker with no land. Migration, especially to the Americas, had occurred in earlier times, particularly from the Jerusalem, Ramallah and Bethlehem areas, but in other regions it was a new phenomenon and was mainly focused on the Arab world rather than the West. In the 1950s and 1960s most of the migrants came from the refugee camps, especially those of Gaza, but a substantial number came from poorer agricultural districts such as Hebron.

The fact that the family remained the most common unit of production in agriculture meant that the agricultural sector carried a considerable burden of underemployment. A family's income would sustain its members, perhaps with the help of remittances, even when some of them were only partially employed.

## The impact of the Israeli occupation on agriculture

Up to 1967 agriculture was still the mainstay of the West Bank economy, providing the highest proportion of productive output and of employment. And it is in the sphere of agriculture and agricultural land that Israeli policies have had perhaps their most profound economic impact – on landholding, agricultural production and employment.

Some 70% of the population still lives outside the main towns, yet agriculture employs fewer and fewer people. At the same time access to land (whether by ownership or tenancy) has been decreased significantly by the closing off of large tracts of land either for settlement or for military purposes.

Estimates of the amount of land expropriated, confiscated or closed up vary. Benvenisti's 1984 study estimates that about 40% of the 5.8 million dunum land area of the West Bank is under Israeli control. Some 40,000 Jewish settlers are now thought to inhabit the settlements now completed or under construction in the West Bank (excluding East Jerusalem). According to Benvenisti, 1.1 million dunums, or 53% of the land under Israeli control consists of restricted military areas, though the Israeli defence force has also closed off further extensive areas which have subsequently been turned over to settlements or to other civilian purposes.[4]

Not all the land sealed off is cultivated, but from lists compiled by those who monitor settlements on a regular basis, it is clear that the amount of cultivated land that has taken over is substantially larger than the Israelis claim. Particularly affected have been fruit orchards and olive groves, as well as grazing land for animals. Certainly in some areas, the amount of cultivated land lost is extensive enough to be a factor in the decision of numbers of West Bank farmers either to give up agriculture altogether or at least seek a supplementary income elsewhere.

Israeli occupation and settlement policies have also had a serious impact on another crucial factor of production – water. At present farming is still largely dependent on relatively low and erratic rainfall. The village well provides water for domestic purposes and for vegetable and fruit growing, but only about 5.8% of the total area under cultivation is irrigated, compared with 4.8% in 1966. Irrigated lands are mostly found in the Jordan Valley, Wadi Far'a and in pockets in the Jenin and Tulkarem areas.

To expand irrigation would be one obvious way to raise productivity and improve agricultural income, but Israeli water policies have generally blocked large-scale development of this option. In the first place the Israelis have no interest in promoting a Palestinian agricultural sector on the West Bank that would compete with their own agriculture. Second, Israel has a very high rate of water use internally, with a large irrigated agricultural sector which takes up about 75% of the total volume of water consumed each year. The coastal water table is now in danger of salinity from heavy use and one third of Israel's present water resources are derived from groundwater in an aquifier lying under the western slopes of the West Bank.

Israel has therefore a clear stake in maintaining control over this source of water and has imposed strict limits on both agricultural and domestic water use in the West Bank. As a result the vast majority of villages, as well as some towns, suffer from water shortages in the dry summer months. Wells are metered and those who pump more than the stated limit are penalized. Agricultural water use is frozen at a level only 20% higher than it was in 1967. The authorities also forbid the drilling of new wells for agricultural purposes by Palestinians. In 1978, the military government's water department reported that Mekorot had drilled 17 wells for Israeli settlements in the Jordan Valley, which in the season 1977/8 discharged 14.1 million cubic metres (mcm) while the 314 Arab wells had only discharged 33.0 mcm.[5] Settlements in the occupied territories are not restricted in their use of water and are permitted to drill deep wells. According to Benvenisti, settlers form 2–3% of the population and consume 20% of total water used. Of this amount, 96% of settlers' water use is for irrigation.[6]

In the Jordan Valley where irrigation is vital for farming, the drilling of deep wells by the agricultural settlements there appears to have led in several cases to the drying up or reduction in flow to shallower neighbouring village wells and springs. Among the best documented cases are those of Auja at-Tahta in the central part of the valley, and Bardala in the north.[7]

These constraints form the basic context within which agriculture now functions. GDP from agriculture was 34.4% of the total in 1976 and 35% in 1980. Fluctuations in output on an annual basis depend largely on climatic factors and on the biennial cycle of olive production in which high yields generally occur only every second year. There has also been a noticeable change in the composition of the agricultural output with more emphasis on higher-value vegetables and fruit than on traditional field crops. While there have been no dramatic changes in production of field crops, citrus and olives, vegetable production went up from 149,400 tons in 1976/7 to 172,900 tons in 1982/3 and melons and pumpkins from a low of 8,900 tons to 74,900 in the same period. A substantial portion of this production is exported.[8] Meanwhile local agricultural employment is down from 42.1% in 1968 to 30% in 1980.

These figures do not indicate any fundamental change in the nature of either agricultural production or agrarian relations themselves but rather the shrinkage of the smallholding farming sector in the face of the constraints already described and the 'pull' factor of a better living to be gained outside agriculture. But in the agricultural economy that remains, the trends are more complex than mere decline.

From the British Mandate period onwards, agriculture has been shifting gradually from subsistence to market production, but the area has not experienced either land reform or a social revolution which would have matched relations of production on the farm with the changes that have taken place at the level of circulation.

Israeli policies have not encouraged change in these directions. Benvenisti comments:

> [their] strategy was termed 'improvement' as opposed to 'transformation'. The improvement strategy is characterised by the initiation of change within the existing resource base and infrastructure rather than by efforts to transform the rural infrastructure through heavy capital expenditure, land reform, a move to procession of produce, and improved structural support systems.

The existing infrastructure inherited from pre-1967 is 'a very low starting point', according to Benvenisti. He concludes, 'Implicit in the improvement strategy are a freeze on the agricultural resources available to the Arab population and complete Israeli control over growth potential.'[9]

Thus when the occupation began, there was neither secure access to land nor capital for much of the rural population. In these circumstances, the pressures of Israeli political and economic policies quite rapidly pushed, or enticed, many of those who were least secure away from reliance on agriculture for their family livelihood.

I will deal with labour migration from the territories at more length later, but it is relevant to point out here that in the West Bank the majority of those employed daily in Israel are classified as rural dwellers. Many of these were previously employed in agriculture, or not employed at all.

In the early days of the occupation, the demand for daily wage workers in Israel soaked up first those who had been underemployed or unemployed in agriculture. Then, because wage levels in Israel were higher than those offered in the West Bank, especially in the agricultural sector, former agricultural labourers (some of the 20,000 mentioned by Hilal began to seek work in Israel).

This in turn brought an increase in agricultural wage levels on the West Bank. One effect of this was to persuade farmers working marginal land that required them to hire in labour to cease cultivating it. More generally, higher labour costs combined with the disincentives to agriculture already mentioned to make many engaged in dry farming contemplate abandoning it wholly or partially rather than accept low returns that compared unfavourably with the income that could be gained from wage labour outside agriculture.

This story of decline is not, however, the whole picture. A certain amount of mechanization has taken place since 1967, initiated mostly by large landowners, or, to a lesser extent, by use of migrant remittances (mainly from the Gulf or the United States) by villagers to buy agricultural equipment which can be rented out. According to Hisham Awartani mechanization has developed in equipment ranging from small tools to heavy-duty tractors and combines. The number of tractors rose from 147 in 1967 to 1,534 in 1977, and 1,883 in 1979/80. There is also widespread use of Israeli seed stocks, which are certified and of higher quality than those available locally. Fertilizer use rose from 2.3 kg per dunum in 1968/9 to 9.5 kg per dunum in 1979/80.[10] All this technology is imported either from or through Israel, both increasing Israeli trade and importing Israeli inflation into agricultural costs in the West Bank.

The use of new agricultural technology has not been general throughout the West Bank. It has been concentrated in areas where conditions for certain reasons favour it. Tamari sums up this selective trend towards new technology as follows:

> [overall] agricultural productivity has not declined because large and middle landowners in the Jordan Valley and certain sections of the north, especially the Jenin, Tulkarem and Nablus areas, have introduced new agricultural technology – high yielding varieties of seeds, hot houses, mechanisation, labour-displacing machines. A number of wealthy peasants have substantially increased their income while a certain grouping of peasants have, without losing their land, lost agriculture as a main source of income and become workers in Israel.[11]

Thus it appears that in the dry farming sector, investment in new technology has mainly occurred among those with capital resources already at their disposal. Mechanization may have displaced some agricultural workers but its effects are probably limited compared with the impact of factors already mentioned: land loss, shortage of water, rising cost of agricultural labour, market constraints and the comparative attraction of non-agricultural wage labour.

In the small irrigated sector, the situation is different. The recent introduction of drip irrigation and plastic covers for vegetable growing in the Jordan Valley, Wadi Far'a and parts of the Jenin/Tulkarem region have created a minor technological revolution. Yields here, in contrast to most of the dry farming areas, have risen dramatically. The possibility of multiple cropping (three crops a year in the Jordan Valley) lessens the problem of land shortage, and drip irrigation with its economical use of water makes the constraints imposed by the Israelis less of a problem.

In these areas, agricultural employment has not dropped. In fact in the Jordan Valley there is a labour shortage in some places. Unlike the forms of mechanization employed in, for instance, cereal farming, drip irrigation of vegetable crops is quite labour-intensive. As a result, communities engaging in irrigated agriculture are less likely to have members working in Israel than those in the rain-fed sector.

Nonetheless Benvenisti points out that there is little prospect under present conditions of occupation for a significant expansion of the irrigated area in Palestinian farming because of the constraints on water use and well-boring. He adds: 'The shortage of land suitable for high-value crops under irrigation... is a major constraint. Such land is situated in the Jordan valley and is totally taken for Israeli agricultural production.'[12]

A further deterrent both to investment in new agricultural techniques and to the persistence of more traditional types of agriculture is the limitation on the markets available for agricultural produce from the West Bank. From the earliest days of the occupation, the Israelis have been determined not to allow agricultural goods from the territories to compete with or jeopardize markets for its own highly subsidized produce. Hence products that might compete with Israeli goods generally have to be consumed locally or exported via the Jordan bridges. When they are allowed into the Israeli market, they can be stopped if the interests of Israeli growers demand it. Military order 1039 of 1983 imposed quotas on production of grapes, plums, tomatoes and aubergines. Israeli producers are not prevented from selling in the territories and the 'import' of Israeli fruit and vegetables has contributed to the territories' large adverse balance of trade with Israel.

Much of the fruit and vegetables grown in the West Bank is shipped to the Arab world via Jordan. But even this export trade is wholly dependent on the maintenance by the Israelis of the 'open bridges' policy initiated soon after the occupation. Every now and then, for political reasons, a particular district or town will be 'punished' for a supposed misdemeanour or defiance by the closing of the bridges to its people and its produce. The result for farmers can be rotting fruit and vegetables and loss of income.

## Patterns of labour in agriculture since 1967

The deployment of the rural labour force inside and outside agriculture has changed considerably since 1967. But certain forms of tenancy, namely various types of sharecropping, have persisted, mainly it seems because they offer access to land and, in irrigated farming, to new technology not otherwise obtainable.

The West Bank is still a land of smallholders – 48% of holdings are 20 dunums or less and still employ family labour.[13] For a rain-fed farm, this amount of land may not be enough to provide a living for a large family. There are several alternative paths for its owners to follow: they can leave their land altogether; they can send one or two members of the family to work in Israel, leaving the others to farm the land as best they can with or without the help of croppers or wage labourers; if one member of the family is abroad, remittances may make up the income gap; or the family may choose to sharecrop someone else's land in addition to farming their own.

This last option is more likely in areas where there is less easy access to wage labour in Israel, in irrigated areas where the farmer has an uneconomically small plot, and where farmers have lost land through confiscations. For those who own no land at all sharecropping is still an option, a more attractive one if the land in question is irrigated.

The range of relationships which come under the heading of sharecropping has always been diverse and today there are still wide variations in the terms of sharecropping contracts, and in the shares allocated to each partner. 'Simple' crop-sharing arrangements are still used for olive groves and vegetable crops. It has, however, become less common, for a cropper to do the ploughing as part of his contract, particularly in olive groves. Tamari points out that this is mainly the result of the increased demand for labour elsewhere. Before 1970 a grove owner would give 50% of the yield to a cropper, who would be responsible for ploughing as well as harvesting. Today, for the same share, the cropper will only deal with the harvest. This, Tamari argues, has been a contributory factor in the neglect of olive groves which has been on the increase since the early 1970s.[14]

In the northern areas, traditionally the base for large and influential landowners, shares to the croppers remain much the same as they were in the 1930s, one third of the net yield. This share also applies to joint farming contracts, which are now used quite frequently in irrigated agriculture. In contrast, the share in the Jordan Valley in joint farming contracts is normally 50–50.

As in the 1930s, these joint farming contracts, in which the tenant participates in the capital investment (either by being designated a share in it by the landowner, or, more commonly today, by paying for all or part of the inputs, including fertilizer, extra labour and sometimes water), provide access to a type of agriculture which most peasants could not afford on their own. Furthermore they offer a means of circumventing the chronic shortage of agricultural credit prevailing in the West Bank today, and of spreading the risks inherent in a high-investment enterprise.

But another consequence of this type of sharefarming is a growing differentiation between the better-off tenants who can afford the extra outlay each season, and those who cannot and therefore remain 'simple' croppers. Also it is arguable that the more deeply the cropper is financially involved in this high technology farming, the more dependent he is on his landlord's wishes as far as choice of crops, marketing and so on, are concerned. Furthermore, the consequences of a sharp drop in prices (such as the one which occurred in the Jordanian market for tomatoes in recent seasons when there was a glut of production on both sides of the valley) can be severe indebtedness for croppers and share farmers.

Patterns of land tenure have not, therefore, changed dramatically, but have been adapted to fit new agricultural techniques. The evidence from the Jordan Valley - both west and east - suggests that sharecropping cannot be regarded as an inherently inefficient form of tenancy as far as productivity and net returns are concerned. More problematic is its perpetuation of inegalitarian relations between landowners and tenants which can only be solved by offering some alternative forms of access to land and to credit. In the West Bank these will clearly remain unavailable on a large scale while the Israeli occupation continues.

## The wage labour market's impact on villages of the West Bank

Two decades or more of Israeli occupation in the West Bank has created a marked trend away from agriculture as the sole source of rural family income. This process began on a small scale as far back as the 1930s, but today it has become a much more generalized phenomenon, affecting all but the most isolated communities, or those where agriculture is still profitable and demand for labour is high.

But this trend has not been accompanied, as it has in many Third World countries, by a large-scale drift of rural population to the cities. Nor has the region seen the development of full capitalist relations of production in the agricultural sector. The drift to the cities has not occurred because of the Israeli refusal to allow resident migrant labour inside the so-called Green Line. There are instead commuting migrants who return daily or weekly to the villages and towns of the West Bank.

The development of fully-fledged capitalist farming based on wage labour has been hampered by the controls imposed by the military authorities on access to factors of production and by competition from Israeli agriculture; and also by the lack of any kind of land reform by successive occupying powers: Ottomans, British, Jordanians and Israelis. Change has occurred on the land because of the progressive commercialization of agriculture but none of these governments have seen it as in their interests to initiate reforms that would disrupt the existing socio-economic power structure.

At the village level, there is no simple formula for the way in which this latest factor for change - the creation of a wage labour market - affects socio-economic relations in the community and its relations with the land. Among the mix of factors to be considered are the viability of agriculture in the village, access to land per capita, the number of people who have migrated abroad, and the proximity of village to main roads and of transport facilities to Israeli centres.

The wage labour force numbered, according to Benvenisti's estimates, some 49% of the total active labour force (131,000) in 1980.[15] Officially, the percentage is much lower, about 30%, but the first figure includes those who are not officially employed through labour exchanges (thought to number about 20,000 in addition to the 39,000 officially employed). It also adds in another 15,000 people employed in West Bank enterprises that serve as subcontractors to Israeli firms. Of those who work in Israel some 70% are from outside the main towns, either from villages or from refugee camps.

The employment they find varies from relatively secure, semi-skilled work in a factory, to washing up in a restaurant, to unskilled agricultural labour. Most common of all is work in the construction industry, which makes up almost half of West Bankers' employment in Israel. Some workers are hired individually through a labour exchange while others go every day to the so-called 'slave markets' (one is in Jerusalem, near the Damascus gate) where Israeli employers pick up casual day labourers, who are the worst-paid group of all (with the exception of the small proportion of women workers).[16]

But for villagers the most likely method of obtaining work is through a middleman, sometimes a relative or a member of the village who deals directly with the Israeli employer and who hires and employs a group of workers 'unofficially'. This is commonest in the building trade and in agriculture.

From the Israeli point of view the Territories' workers form a convenient and controllable force of unskilled and semi-skilled workers to do jobs which Israelis are less and less willing to do. The West Bank and Gaza Strip workers are largely unorganized. They cannot belong to the Histradrut (the Israeli trade union federation) and unions in the Territories are not recognized in Israel. Hence the employers can pay wages which would be unacceptably low for a unionized Israeli worker. A Histadrut survey in 1982 showed that hourly wage labour rates in construction for workers from the Territories were only 50–60% of those paid to Israeli workers. Until the mid-1970s, however, wages in Israel for workers from the Territories were higher in real terms than those paid in the West Bank. Since the advent of hyperinflation in the late 1970s, which has seriously affected the standard of living in the West Bank, these Israeli wages are no longer so attractive, but no better alternatives are available. The market for labour in the Gulf and other parts of the Arab world has now contracted and the stagnation in the local economy means there is little work available there either.

Not all of those who enter the wage labour market abandon their land completely. Some leave their land in the care of other members of the family, the women and older men, with children also helping. This means that the previously rigid divisions of labour in agriculture between men and women have been blurred; for instance, women can occasionally be seen ploughing or climbing olive trees to knock down the fruit, jobs previously reserved for men.

Another alternative for the wage-earning landholder has already been mentioned – to hire in a cropper or a labourer to tend the farm, though this often works out to be too expensive an option. Either way, wage earners who remain 'weekend' farmers are quite common in areas strongly affected by the pull of the Israeli labour market.

Land still represents a security, a fallback, even if most of the family's income does not now derive from it. Nonetheless, unless there is a major reversal in Israeli policy on workers from the Territories, it seems unlikely that even in the face of falling real wages migrants would return to full-time farming.

A study for 1980 quoted by Benvenisti (no source given) indicates that 33% of those heads of household working in Israel still cultivated land.[17] Of these about 50% had worked in Israel for 10 years or more and only 8.5% had worked for 2–4 years. But the larger proportion – two thirds of heads of households – had no land. Bearing in mind that some 70% of migrants are classified as rural dwellers, it appears that a substantial number of these workers are landless peasants. Some 45% of those without land had worked in Israel for more than 10 years. Some of these are undoubtedly those who had no land at the beginning of the occupation and were therefore attracted into the Israeli labour market. They have since been joined by others who have lost land or who have abandoned cultivation on marginal land, or, less frequently, have sold their land.

Among those who still cultivate land there seems to have been some stabilization of the spectrum of relationships to the land. Though there may still be a propensity for those who initially cultivated land when they went to work in Israel to cease doing so, a good many others have now worked in Israel for some years and remain part-time farmers.

The distribution of longer-term workers seems to suggest that those who still cultivate land are more likely to work in agriculture or construction, both of which allow for seasonal breaks to return to the farm for harvest time and other periods of the year when agricultural work is heaviest. For the rest of the year maintaining the farm will depend largely on how the head of household can deploy family and other labour. Tamari has described the situation in Ras et-Tin, a village where many of the men work on Israeli construction sites. Most families still own some land but few have it as a sole source of income, and most families have at least one member working in Israel. According to Tamari, maintaining agricultural production under these conditions depends very much on the individual peasant's 'proper utilisation of his household members' labour (including the labour of women and children throughout the year) so that he can derive optimum benefits from the opportunities for wage labour, without, at the same time, neglecting his farm totally.'[18]

In contrast to the choices for deployment of family labour in the 1930s, what has changed is the priority given to wage labour as the most important source of livelihood, the reverse of the previous situation. Success in the deployment of family labour depends very much on whose labour is available, and particularly on the abilityof the head of household to control his grown sons who are wage earners and who may not wish to work on the farm. Another variable in many rural households is the absence of one or more members working or studying abroad. If the migrants are sending remittances, this too will affect calculations on the balance between the needs of the farm and the attraction of the wage labour market.

Another potential agent of socio-economic change in the rural areas is education. The economic changes in the villages seem to have affected rural attitudes to schooling in various ways. However the net result of these pressures is not yet clear.

In general, education is viewed by most Palestinians as a way out of poverty and a counterbalance to the insecurity of their lives. But at the same time, it could be argued that in the context of the rural West Bank, where most of the work available is in Israel and is at best semi-skilled, time spent on, for instance, secondary and post-secondary education is time wasted because there are so few jobs available locally for the skilled and well educated. This attitude is noted by Mahshi and Rihan in their study of education in the West Bank (1980), though it is not clear whether this sentiment is very widespread.[19]

Enrolment of girls at primary schools has grown significantly in recent years, but in villages the fact that a large number of able-bodied men are employed outside the village can mean that the labour of women and children is important for agriculture and girls are pulled out of school to help in the fields or with domestic work.

Many men are reluctant to allow wives and daughters to work outside the village, though some go in groups under a supervisor to work in Israeli agriculture or in textile factories. But it is noticeable that more women from refugee camps work away from home than from the villages.

The money which comes into the villages, from those who work abroad or from wage labourers in Israel, does not by and large return to agriculture. A few people invest in agricultural machinery to hire out but generally any capital expenditure goes towards new houses, consumer durables, children's education or property speculation. Perhaps this more than anything else is a measure of how much the status of agriculture and agricultural land has changed in the rural areas. The exception is to be found only in areas where agriculture is still the primary source of livelihood. 'Land is no longer the criterion of wealth . . . indeed there does not seem to be a correlation in dry farming areas today between a peasant's wealth and the cultivable area he owns.'[20] Thus the nature of village society is also gradually changing, so that the hierarchy of power and influence resting primarily on ownership of land or access to it is being eroded, though not eliminated. This is a factor to take into account when considering not only the economic but also the political future of the area.

While some of the major landowners remain economically powerful, politically they have to contend with new forces in the village, as well as the urban middle class.

## A new proletariat?

Some would argue that by the creation of a migrant labour force the Israeli occupation is producing a new proletariat in the occupied territories. The empirical evidence on which this or any other opinion can be based is still patchy, so it is difficult to argue any case with complete conviction.

However, if proletarianization is taken to mean the divorce of the worker from his or her means of production, so that s/he depends entirely on the wages provided by an employer for subsistence, this has clearly not yet happened in the villages of the West Bank. In the Gaza Strip, where much of the population was declassed in 1948 by being made refugees, it is certainly possible to argue that people forcibly divorced from their means of production are now working in Israel as a wage-earning proletariat, though not a settled one. In the West Bank, however, the case of commuting workers from the villages is less clear than that of camp dwellers.

It can be argued that proletarianization in this 'pure' sense could not be said to have occurred in many Third World countries where migrant workers retain their roots – land and family ties – in the rural areas while working in the cities. This kind of halfway-house situation, it has been argued, is one which can continue for decades since it suits employers who, because of their workers' rural ties, do not have to pay what would otherwise be a full subsistence wage for a city dweller. Governments also point to the migrants' 'informal social security networks' as an excuse for not putting money into official social security programmes. Certainly these characteristics apply to the Israeli attitude to Territories workers.

But in the Territories there are further factors preventing 'full' proletarianization. Especially in the West Bank, the fact that the migrants commute from their villages means that family, social and economic ties are maintained. Also, if the example of Tamari's study of Ras et-Tin is anything to go by, the way in which much of this workforce is recruited serves to reinforce connections with the village. This is often done not through impersonal bureaucratic or market channels but through family and village connections. Tamari points out that particularly in the construction industry the 'hierarchical forms of organisation' keep Palestinian workers separated from their Israeli employers through the existence of Palestinian labour contractors and foremen. 'These hierarchies create not only a sense of "false consciousness" among rural workers, but an efficient system of labour management in the absence of workers' organisations and work tenure stability.'[21]

The overall insecurity of life in the West Bank and economic difficulties were factors in persuading villagers to work in Israel in the first place, but they are also factors in making people want to remain on the land, for political and emotional more than economic reasons. The land-grabbing of the settlers, especially over the last few years, has reinforced this feeling. There is a conflict between two sets of ideas. The first is that in the present circumstances the land cannot provide a proper living and therefore it is better to leave it, or treat it as marginal and look to different measures of affluence and status; the second, often held in parallel with the first, is that for Palestinians it has been a hard-learnt historical lesson that if you lose your land you lose your future.

The trend in the West Bank towards villages becoming workers' dormitories is certainly strong in some areas but it has not reached the same point as in the villages of Galilee and the Triangle where it would seem reasonable to describe the wage labour force as a proletariat living in villages. In the Territories, the permanence of the present pattern of labour deployment is a matter of debate. Some argue that the combination of wage labour in Israel and the settlement policies of the Likud government are creating a situation which, in the space of a couple more years, will be reversible only with very great difficulty. But the factors which have created this situation are fundamentally political rather than economic, which makes it harder to predict the future with any certainty.

While the Territories remain under Israeli rule, it seems likely that the Israelis will continue to use the pool of cheap labour, which is all the more crucial to many sectors of the Israeli economy – especially construction, agriculture, textiles – in the present climate of recession. Economically speaking, the only alternative would be to find another cheap labour supply from abroad to replace all or some of the Palestinian labour from the Occupied Territories.

What is clear is that even were Israeli rule to end in the near future, the question of how to employ those who now work in Israel would remain. Only a small proportion of the workforce now employed outside the Territories could be reabsorbed without major investment in industry, agriculture and infrastructure. Furthermore, in agriculture, a substantial change not just in agricultural methods but in the relation of production on the land would be required.

Land reform, of course, does not necessarily lead to a radical change in relations of production: in the eastern Jordan Valley, a limited land reform has slightly widened access to land but has left the basic system of ownership and control in many areas virtually intact. In the Palestinian case it would clearly depend very much on the political character of the government and on its base of support whether such a limited technocratic reform could be expected, or a more radical reordering of relations of power and production in the countryside.

## Notes:

1. Y. Firestone, 'Crop-sharing economics in Mandatory Palestine', *Middle East Studies*, pt. I: vol. 2, no. 1, pp. 3–23; pt II: vol. 2, no. 2, pp. 175–94.
2. R. L. Taqqu, *Arab Labour in Mandatory Palestine 1920–1948*. Unpublished PhD thesis, Columbia University, 1977, pp. 64–5.
3. J. Hilal, *Al-Daffa al-gharbiyya: Al-Tarkib al-ijtimai wa al-iqtisadi* ('West Bank: Economic and Social Structure') *1948–1974*, Beirut: PLO Research Centre, 1974, p. 164.
4. M. Benvenisti, *The West Bank Data Project: a survey of Israel's policies*, Washington and London: American Enterprise Institute for Public Policy Research 1984, pp. 19–23.
5. Ibid., p. 14, and H. Awartani, *West Bank Agriculture: a new outlook*, Nablus: Al-Najah University Research Bulletin 1, 1978, p. 7.
6. M. Benvenisti, *West Bank Data Project: pilot study report*, Jerusalem: 1982, p. 23.
7. For instance, see Tim Coone, 'Worries over West Bank water', *Financial Times*, 22 November 1979; S. Graham-Brown, 'Water: how Israeli plans hurt West Bank Arabs', *Arab Report* no. 9, 23 May 1979; Rami G. Khouri, 'Israel drains West Bank waters', *The Middle East*, September 1979, p. 38.
8. *Statistical Abstract of Israel*, Tel Aviv, 1980, 1984.
9. Benvenisti, 1984, p. 14.
10. Ibid., pp. 12–13 and Awartani, *West Bank Agriculture*, pp. 17–18.
11. Interview with Salim Tamari, *MERIP Report*, no. 100, Oct.–Dec. 1981, p. 31.
12. Benvenisti, 1984, p. 14.
13. Benvenisti, 1982, p. 11.
14. S. Tamari, 'From the fruits of their labour', in this volume.
15. Benvenisti, 1982, p. 6.
16. On the Jerusalem 'slave market', see Michael Meron, 'The Arab slave market: waiting on line for work', excerpted from *Yediot Ahronot* in *Al-Fajr*, 29 January 1982, and Colin Smith, 'Long wait in line for West Bank slave market', *Observer* (London), 21 February 1982.
17. Benvenisti, 1982, p. 7.
18. S. Tamari, 'Building other people's homes: the Palestinian peasant's household and work in Israel', *Journal of Palestine Studies*, Autumn 1981, vol. 10, no. 1, pp. 33ff.
19. C. Mahshi and R. Rihan, 'Education: elementary and secondary', in E. A. Nakhleh (ed.), *A Palestinian Agenda for the West Bank and Gaza*, Washington, 1980, p. 53.
20. Tamari, 'Building other people's homes'.
21. Ibid.

# 3. From the Fruits of their Labour: the Persistence of Sharetenancy in the Palestinian Agrarian Economy

*Salim Tamari*

When I first saw the share-rent levied – the fat smiling Lebanese landowner collecting his half of the heap of grain from the kneeling cultivator – I remembered that it was this very thing that the peasants of the Balkans had fought to abolish for over a century, from 1803 to 1918 . . . it seemed high time that this system should be abolished in the Middle East.

Doreen Warriner, *Economics of Peasant Farming*, 1964, p. xxxii.

The system of cultivation by *metayers* – contributes, more than anything else, to diffuse happiness among the lower classes, to raise land to a high state of culture, and accumulate a great quantity of wealth upon it. . . . Under this system, the peasant has an interest in the property, as if it were his own . . .

The accumulation of immense capital upon the soil, the invention of many judicious rotations, and industrious processes . . . the collection of a numerous population upon a space very limited and naturally barren, shows plainly enough that this mode of cultivation is as profitable to the land itself as to the peasant.

J. C. L. Sismonde de Sismondi, *Political Economy*, 1814

Sharecropping, the mode of agricultural tenancy by which the tiller is remunerated for his labour by a share of the yield, has been one of the most enigmatic features of agrarian studies. It has been variably characterized by its observers as semi-feudal (Bhaduri, 1973), feudal ('Ashour, 1948), peasant serfdom (Warriner, 1964), pre-capitalist (Wolf, 1966), and partnership in cultivation (Firestone, 1975b). This chapter aims at explaining the persistence of sharecropping arrangements in Palestinian agriculture over the last half century, through a number of agrarian regimes.

In order to place this discussion in its proper theoretical context, we will attempt to relate it to structural issues raised in the debate on the nature of sharetenancy in Asian agriculture. In particular, we will examine its relevance to three such problems: the nature of the relationship between the cropper and the landlord; obstacles posed by sharecropping arrangements to agricultural development; and the place of the sharecropper as a social category within peasant classes.

## Sharetenancy and 'semi-feudalism'

The controversy around the nature of sharecropping contracts was revived in the literature interpreting data collected from village studies in India. In his well-known study of 26 villages in West Bengal during the early 1970s, Bhaduri used the term 'semi-feudalism' to designate the condition of the Bengali *kishan* (landless sharecroppers), who constitute today 40–50% of the peasantry in the region (Bhaduri, 1973). According to the author, sharetenancy arrangements between the *kishan* and his Bengali landlord reduce the former to conditions of semi-serfdom. This subjugation is achieved through a combination of perpetual indebtedness of the *kishan* to the landlord, who supplies him with consumption loans at usurious rates, and through the *kishan*'s inaccessibility to the capital market. Although the *kishan* is 'free to move', his mobility is hampered by the lack of any creditworthiness among other landlords with whom no filial relations exist (Bhaduri, 1973: 122–3).

This model of semi-feudal sharetenancy rests on the operation of two modes of exploitation simultaneously, one based on the landlord's property rights to the land, and another on his monopoly of lending privileges to the *kishan* (ibid.: 135). Through the former mode, the landlord secures the sharecropper's continued landlessness or near landlessness, while through the latter, he maintains the *kishan*'s relative immobility on the land.

More recent empirical studies, however, raised serious questions as to the applicability of Bhaduri's model to sharecropping arrangements in general, or even to the contemporary conditions in northern India itself. One of the assumptions on which the above analysis rests is the double role played by the landlord as a supplier of both land *and* credit. Mabro and Griffin (1979) – and to a certain extent Bhaduri himself – point out that this is a feature of agrarian relations peculiar to West Bengal, but not to most Asian agriculture. Furthermore, due to state intervention and land reform in the last two decades, the credit market has become much more varied and accessible to the peasant (Mabro and Griffin, 1979: 90).

The same issue was investigated in a survey covering 334 villages in northern and eastern India (including West Bengal) whose authors find no evidence of usury, or even moneylending, being the main source of income for landlords (Bardhan and Rudra, 1980: 291). The authors reject also the equation of sharetenancy with 'semi-feudalism,' in both its European and Japanese varieties, on the basis of two crucial variables: one is the ability, in their contention, of the sharetenant freely to change his landlord from one agricultural season to another (the rate of 'lease-bondage', so to speak, did not exceed 8% of the cases in the most extreme example – that prevailing in Uttar Pradesh – ibid.: 290). The second condition of semi-feudalism rejected was the amount of 'unpaid and obligatory services (provided) by the tenant to the landlord'. Bardhan and Rudra found that in the majority of cases examined the tenants provided no labour services to their landlords whatsoever, while in those cases where such services were rendered, only a portion (between 2% in Orissa and 23% in the state of Uttar Pradesh) of unpaid or underpaid services to the landlord existed (ibid.: 291).

While these two writers seem to have uncovered a major flaw in Bhaduri's semi-feudalism thesis, their treatment of the sharecropper's market dependence is far from satisfactory. Bardhan and Rudra simply dispose of the issue by pointing to the evidence showing that only a minority of the tenants in their survey (less than 5%) sell their produce to the landlord. But, as we hope to show in the analysis below, there is much more to market dependence than the landlord's control of the peasant surplus. It is impossible, as Keith Griffin has pointed out (Griffin, 1979) to see market relations of sharecropping in isolation from the general agrarian system under analysis. Thus, when a landlord leases his land on a sharecropping basis, with credit advances, etc., 'wages, rental and interest rates, and even the price paid to the tenant for his marketed surplus, cannot be understood unless the entire relationship between the transactions is taken into account' (ibid.: xiv–xv).

## Sharetenancy and agricultural development

A more serious but related problem of sharecropping arrangements is their perceived role in blocking agricultural growth, in particular their function in discouraging landlords from introducing new technology in agriculture. This is how Bhaduri expresses the problem:

> ... technological improvements, which raise the productivity level of the *kishan*, become undesirable to the landowner to the extent that they increase the *kishan*'s available balance of paddy in relation to his consumption level so as to reduce his requirements for consumption loans. For it weakens the system of semi-feudalism, where economic and political power of the landowner is largely based on his being able to keep the *kishan* constantly indebted to him. (Bhaduri, 1973: 135)

Furthermore, the landlord

> ... will be discouraged from introducing any technological improvement so long as his gain in income from increased productivity brought about by technological change falls short of his loss in income from

> usury due to a reduction (or complete elimination) in the level of consumption-loan required by the *kishan*. (ibid.)

In Bhaduri's conception, the landlord who enters into sharecropping arrangements is predisposed against both short- *and* long-term improvement of the land. Against the former because it reduces his income (expressed in terms of a lower rent share), while maintaining the peasant's indebtedness to him; against the latter because it creates the conditions for the sharecropper's emancipation from dependence on the landlord – even though it may be economically advantageous to the landlord. Thus the sharecropping system fulfils a circular reinforcement of the conditions of agricultural backwardness. In a similar fashion, 'Ashour's survey of *muraba'a* (metayage) contracts in Syria, Palestine and Lebanon sees sharetenancy not only as *the* cornerstone of 'feudal relations in land' ('Ashour, 1948a: 47–8, 'Ashour, 1948c: 61–4), but also as a chief impediment to the rationalization and mechanization of agriculture ('Ashour, 1948b: 59) and even, surprisingly, to the production of cash crops (ibid.: 60).

Yet as in the question of 'feudalism', those positions have been seriously challenged in recent examination of the evidence. In the two cases of West Bengal and Syria/Palestine discussed above, we are fortunate to have studies which re-examined the data for the same period (1970s for northern India; 1940s for Palestine). In the case of Palestine, the work of Firestone (1975a, 1975b), which we will discuss later in greater detail, shows that cropsharing arrangements achieved an increased integration of the agrarian economy into market relations and a general expansion of cultivated land which would otherwise have remained idle. Similarly, in the case of northern India, Bardhan and Rudra (1980) found that there is no fixed pattern for cropsharing arrangements over time, or within the same region, a point confirmed by 'Ashour for Syria and Palestine ('Ashour, 1948a: 37–44). They also found a positive association between the landlord's share of the crop and his participation in production costs (Bardhan and Rudra, 1980: 289) and, conversely, between the introduction of high-yielding varieties of grains and increased tenants' share (ibid.). Both correlations indicate a significant flexibility for the development of agricultural technology within the sharecropping framework.

In the final analysis, however, the issue amounts to how much attribution must be made to the sharecropping component within traditional agrarian institutions as the decisive factor in agricultural backwardness. Perhaps the most far-reaching critique of Bhaduri's position in this regard has been made by Griffin (1979) who reviewed the impact of the green revolution in Indian agriculture on the relationship between landlord and tenant. The exceptional technological backwardness of the situation in West Bengal is seen by Griffin as due not to the landlord's fear of investment in his land that might incur his loss of political and economic control (as Bhaduri implies), but due to of the landlord's own surplus and the physical dispersal of tenants (Griffin, 1979: 91–2). On the other hand, under altered conditions, when a larger pool of tenants is available, and higher initial capital is invested, we find that 'large farmers have ejected their tenants and begun farming with wage labour. In other cases, the landowners have retained the sharecropping system and have simply reduced the share received by the tenant' (ibid.: 93).

In short, it is argued that the introduction of agricultural technology has not been hampered in most of Asia by sharecropping arrangements; on the contrary, sharetenancy is seen as having strengthened the political and economic hand of landlords in relation to their tenants as a class. Especially with the advent of the 'green revolution', sharetenancy is being absorbed into capitalist relations in agriculture and sharecroppers are being transformed into wage workers (cf. Bardhan and Rudra, 1980: 289).

## Sharecroppers as a category within the peasantry

A popular theme in the literature, but one not usually backed by evidence, is to treat sharecroppers as the lowest section of the peasantry, exchangeable with the rural proletariat. Perhaps one source of this assumption is the (mistaken) notion that sharecroppers in general offer only their labour power, while the landlord provides the land and all other factors of production. But this is the case only in one extreme form of cropping arrangements, namely the 'pure' *harrath* in the *muraba'a* system that prevailed in the Levant at the turn of the century (see Granott, 1952: 301). Yet even here the *harrath* (the ploughman-tiller) usually, though not in all cases, provided his own plough and work animals, access to which was not within the reach of most landless peasants, who had to sell their own and their family's labour on a daily basis.

The view of the sharecropper as the 'bottom of the heap' is rejected in a work by Bell and Zusman (also on India) who, in discussing land leasing arrangements, note that 'household operational holdings that are partly owned and partly leased greatly outnumber those which are wholly leased in . . . and the former [account] for the lion's share of all land leased in.' (Bell and Zusman, 1976: 579). They further note that sharecropping tenants are mainly drawn *'not from the mass of landless laborers, but from the ranks of the small peasantry possessing land of their own* as well as skills and capital (or access to capital), all of which are traded (if, indeed, they are tradable at all) in imperfect market' (ibid., emphasis added).

Clifford Geertz goes further in his study of Indonesian agriculture under Dutch colonial rule and treats sharecropping as a levelling mechanism (for both work and wealth) among the Javanese peasantry (Geertz, 1963). Although later criticized for not taking sufficient account of internal differentiation among cultivators (Stoler, 1977), and for what may be termed 'ecological functionalism' (see Kanõ, 1980: 11–13; also ibid.: 14–21 for an alternative interpretation) Geertz nevertheless seems to have illuminated an aspect of sharecropping that until then was ignored in the economic literature on the subject: namely the manner by which peasant traditional tenures devise methods of reducing the impact of peasant differentiation resulting from the uneven sizes of holdings. 'In share tenancy,' he wrote then, '... the ever-driven wet rice village found the means by which to divide its growing economic pie into a greater number of traditionally fixed pieces and so to hold an enormous population on the land at a comparatively very homogeneous, if grim, level of living' (Geertz, 1963: 100).

Geertz pointed out that the different statuses of 'sharetenant', 'wage worker', and 'landholding peasant' often portray different facets of labour allocation within the same peasant stratum. Moreover, the terms 'landlord' and 'sharetenant' may be misleading, at least in the Javanese context, since the sharecropper might often be the stronger party (ibid.: 99 and n. 24).

Similar patterns of overlapping categories can be observed historically in Palestine. There also the little differentiation that existed between cropper and hired worker during the Mandate period has been attributed to seasonal factors (such as the fluctuations of crop yield in dry farming), and to the relations of patronage which the peasant may have enjoyed. The fact that the rural worker received a fixed wage (whether in cash or in kind) and the tenant a share in the crop, was not significant (except in years of plenty) since, according to Firestone, '[the tenant's] actual take was geared to his subsistence and a *fluctuating debt accommodated the difference between that and his contractual share year after year*' (1975a: 10, emphasis added). Furthermore, the sharecropper enjoyed a higher measure of security in tenure which reflected itself in the landlord's delegation of higher status tasks to him, such as ploughing (ibid.: 11). In practice, however, such expressions of filial bonds meant very little in terms of differential monetary rewards.

Thus, a consequence of these perspectives (if we allow for some simplification) is that Granott saw a hierarchy of peasant strata in which tenants and sharecroppers constitute the middle segment (with hired tillers at the bottom); Carmi and Rosenfeld (1974), in contrast, portray a fluid 'bottom' composed of smallholders, tenants, sharecroppers, and even wage workers continuously exchanging positions. Despite their differences, both perspectives seem to collapse all gradations of sharecroppers within the generic category of 'tenant' and view them (at any point in time during the period considered) as secondary to the greater distinction between smallholder and landless peasant. Given the problematic nature of the notion of smallholder in Palestine at the period (since a substantial segment of the peasantry did not have title deeds to their land), and given the fact that, as we shall see, many peasant proprietors were *also* tenants and sharecroppers, such a view draws the 'class' line at the wrong edge. Basically, in our view, it underestimates crucial functional differentiation within the tenant peasantry – some of whom occupied positions superior to the peasant smallholder, and some of whom were simple croppers.

Reviewing the evidence for a number of cases in Asian sharetenancy (Cheung, 1969; Bell and Zusman, 1976; Bardhan and Rudra, 1980), one finds a disproportionate number of landless peasants among sharecroppers and also a substantial proportion of smallholders and even middle peasants who chose to supplement their income by leasing-in additional plots. What is common to all those categories is access to a minimal amount of capital stock (work animals, seeds, and ability to hire extra labour in peak periods) and – in most cases – a certain degree of patrimonial bonds to local landlords. It is these bonds, rather than nominal title deeds, that restrict *access* to profitable use of land to only a portion of the peasantry in Asia and Latin America today, as demographic pressures and poverty pushes masses of their kin and neighbours to search for employment outside the village economy. C. Keyder makes the important observation, in the context of modern Turkey, that only those sharecroppers who were embedded in semi-feudal relations become permanently proletarianized *in* agriculture; that is, within the village economy (Keyder, 1980: 26.)

We arrive at two tentative conclusions from the above. One is that sharecroppers as a group cannot be considered a *stratum* within the peasantry, but cut across several peasant fractions, depending on the cropping arrangement that they enter with the landlord.[1] The second is that sharetenancy as an institution is more properly understood as a highly adaptive mechanism of allocating rural labour in a variety of transitional agrarian forms, rather than as an agency of siphoning the surplus of landless peasants by landlords in traditional agriculture. That aspect of sharetenancy may be true, but it is a truth that is rendered superfluous by its application to tenancy in general and, in effect, characterizes relations of expropriation between landlords and peasants historically.

While Geertz may have misjudged the egalitarian character of the institution – 'the ancient weapon of the poor' – and even exaggerated the degree of exchangeability in the positions of the sharetenant and landholder, he nevertheless has properly guided us to seek the manner in which sharetenancy is embedded in the network of agrarian institutions through the particular historical linkages that wed the peasant to his village economy and beyond. What is needed, then, is a periodization and taxonomy of the various forms of sharecropping arrangements that prevailed in a particular region. With this in mind, we will now examine how and why the system continued to persist in Palestine as the agrarian regime moved from big landlordism to medium and small peasant holdings, from subsistence agriculture to capitalist relations.

## The forms of sharetenancy in Palestinian agriculture[2]

The generic name for sharecropping among Palestinian peasants is *muzara'a* (co-cultivation), or *muhasasa* (from *hissa* – 'share'), or *sharakah* (partnership), and is generally distinguished from *daman*[3] (cash tenancy).

The sharecropper himself is known as *qatruz* or *harrath er-rub'* (ploughman of the fourth) in simple cropping, a reference to the share of the yield that goes to the cultivator; or *shareek* (partner) and *muzari'* (co-cultivator) in the case of joint farming. (The term *muhasis* used by agronomists and social scientists is never used, to my knowledge, by the peasants themselves.)

The status of the cropper varies from the humblest *qatruz*, basically a rural proletarian, who used to crop during the harvest for one sixteenth of the yield (against three quarters to the farmer–landowner, and three sixteenths for the work of his family), to the full partnership exemplified in *sharikat mugharasa* (joint farming compact) in which a contract is drawn transferring part of the land to the cropper who rejuvenates it.

From the cultivator's point of view, there are three important determinants of the *form* of sharetenancy: 1) the nature of the crop, most particularly whether his work involves the cropping of trees, vegetables, or cereals; 2) whether the land is dry-farmed (*ba'liyya*) or irrigated (*marwiyya*) as these involve different contractual arrangements; and 3) the degree of investment in stock and labour provided by each party: landlord, cropper, and (today) the commission agent. The classic pattern of simple cropping, as distinguished from joint farming, until World War Two was the *muraba'a* system, in which the cropper was also the landless, or near landless, ploughman. Each village would have a number of specialized ploughmen whose land was hardly sufficient for their family's subsistence. Against the provision of land and the seed stock, the ploughman would provide the ploughing (usually using his own utensils and ploughing animals) and the work of his family and a hired tiller (*bahhash*) – the latter probably recruited from the absolutely destitute among the village population. The *harrath*'s duties included three ploughings (before the winter rains, turning the weeds over, and immediately before sowing, known respectively as *krab*, *thnayeh* and *tathleeth*).

In addition, the *harrath* was also expected to plough the landlord's orchards (for which he did not receive any share of the crop – Aranki, 1980), and the provision of his family's labour during the harvest season. His share for all this amounted to one quarter the yield allotted at the threshing floor after deductions for tithe etc. were made. Today, this practice has all but disappeared and ploughmen are paid in cash for the provision of their animals and labour. Croppers are hired directly and separately by the farmer.

Of the many forms of sharecropping contracts that prevailed in Palestine during the Mandatory period and subsequent Jordanian rule, two broad arrangements continue to operate today: 1) crop-leasing against a share of the yield; and 2) joint-farming partnerships. The first compact is known as *daman mahsul* (leasing the crop) and is referred to by most peasants as *'ala hissa* ('on a share basis') in the case of olives, and *'ala qism* ('on a part basis') for most fruits and vegetables (it rarely applies to grains).

In both cases, the sharetenant actually leases crops, but not the land, during harvest time, and only *after* the fruits are ripe. In case of vineyards and fruit trees, the leasee estimates the potential yield after the blossoming of the fruits and negotiates a cash deal with the peasant owner. The leasee (tenant) is bound by the terms of the contract and is responsible for all losses due to bad harvests *and* high yield estimates that he may have mistakenly made. In some areas, as in the Hebron mountains, the sharecropper is usually a rural-based merchant who hires his own croppers (or occasionally uses his family labour) and pays the peasant owners in advance (Jaradat, 1980).

In olive *'ala hissa* compacts, the sharetenant and his hired cropper (in case they are not members of his household) pick and press the harvest into oil *after* the orchard has been ploughed by the owner, the latter getting 50% of the net yield. Olive-cropping is unique in that it is the only crop where the share is still paid in kind, in terms of a portion of the fruit pressed into oil, although cash transactions are not rare. (This practice is probably due to the nature of olive oil, which lasts well and thus constitutes an excellent safeguard against high inflation of currency.)

The second compact, known as *sharikat muzar'a* (joint-farming partnership), usually consists of a shared investment by the landlord and tenant farmer in which the former acts, mainly, as a passive partner. The landlord receives half the net marketed yield against the provision of land and half of all inputs. In the case of irrigated farming, water is pumped from artesian wells at the expense of the landlord. Additional labour costs (for harvest, weeding, etc.) are usually born by the tenant. This is the system of sharetenancy predominant in the Jordan Valley today, especially in vegetable cultivation. Similar patterns prevail in the irrigated plains of Jenin and Tulkarem although (as we shall see below) demographic pressures and patronage alter the share division.

Since the mid-1960s, the export market in vegetable and citrus has generated an increased involvement of landlords and urban financiers (commission agents) in the introduction of capital-intensive agricultural technology (chemicals, plastic sheaths, etc., and – since the mid-1970s – drip irrigation; Dajani, 1979: 15–16; Sharab, 1975). Unlike the mechanization of agricultural production in cereal cultivation, such intensification brought about labour shortages rather than labour displacement. Extensive areas in the Jordan Valley, as a result, were brought under cultivation by sharetenants, especially during the period preceding Israeli occupation of the West Bank.

The trend seems to have accentuated the differentiation between tenants who had access to *some* capital, thereby enhancing their parnership status with the landlords in the tenancy compact, and those with no access to such capital. So far there is little empirical data in support of this interpretation for Palestinian agriculture (cf. Tamari, 1980: 47–8).

Of the sharecropping compacts that prevailed in Palestine over the last century, only a few survive today. These tend to retain the form of earlier compacts but in substance operate in the context of a transformed agrarian economy. It is necessary therefore to examine the history of these agrarian transactions as their function changed within each set of agrarian relations in which they were embedded.

## Three functions of sharecropping arrangements in Palestine

There seems to be a consensus that during the first half of this century, sharetenancy in Greater Syria involved primarily the cropping of the big estates of absentee landlords ('Ashour, 1948a: 32–3; Warriner, 1964: 77; Granott, 1952: 286). It seems also that the dismemberment of the big estates during the Mandatory period was accompanied by the decline of sharetenancy itself (Granott, 1952: 302). At its peak, Tannous estimated that 'not less than 50%' of all cultivated land in the Middle East, including Iraq, was worked by tenants or *metayers* (Tannous: cited by Granott, ibid.).

The increasing spread of sharetenancy during the first decades of the 20th century in Palestine (and perhaps even more so in Syria and Iraq) has been attributed to the peasants' perpetual indebtedness to landlords–financiers: a phenomenon that is rooted in turn in the uncertainty of grain yields in arid agriculture (Warriner, 1948: 22; Warriner, 1964: 77). This is a process in which peasants, compelled to borrow at cumulatively higher rates of interest, eventually become tenants on their alienated land (Carmi and Rosenfeld, 1974: 475).

Both French and British colonial land policies, despite their serious attempts at stabilizing the land tenure system and securing the peasants' title deeds, reinforced this pattern of indebtedness–borrowing–alienation–tenancy by their reliance on the landlords as their political base within the nationalist movement. Only the steep increases of food prices during World War Two seemed to have finally broken this cycle of indebtedness (Warriner, 1948: 62).

The complexity of sharecropping arrangements appears immediately, however, when one attempts to discover what *kinds* of land tenure patterns and ecological systems tend to favour the presence of sharetenancy as opposed to owner-operated farms and wage labour. A recent village study suggests that during the Mandate cash rentals prevailed in the coastal terrain where the monetarization of the economy had advanced rapidly, while sharecropping was dominant in the hilly region (Ammons, 1978: 116–17). Granott, however, cites the Valley of Esdraelon, the Maritime Plains, as well as the Coastal Plain as locations for *metayage* (sharetenancy) during the same period. (Granott, 1952: 294ff., 302). In fact, one of the earlier sources of clashes between Palestinians and Zionists involved the eviction of thousands of sharetenants from the Marj Ibn Amer (one of the major plains), after the sale of vast tracts by absentee Arab landlords to the Jewish National Fund (Ruedy, 1971: 131). Rather than attempting to establish a regional distribution of sharetenancies, it might be more useful to examine how land tenure systems accommodated different forms of labour arrangements in response to particular economic demands.

In order to establish a secure tenure on the land during both the late Ottoman period and the Mandate, it was not sufficient for the peasant to establish legal ownership on the land, or even *de facto* possession (in the case of communal – *musha'* – lands); he also needed access to credit. Since the peasant smallholder was almost invariably indebted to the landlord or urban financier for both his consumption needs *and* operating budget, with his land tied up as security for his debts, many of the peasants became, as we have noted above, sharecroppers on their own alienated land, or at least some of it, in this process. A countervailing trend was the *acquisition* of land by landless or smallholding peasants through the process known as *mugharasa*, primarily in groves and orchards. This involved the rejuvenation of the landlord's uncultivated land by the provision of labour and the sharing of stocks on the part of the peasant. In return, the landlord would transfer a part of the orchards to his active partner (i.e. the landless tiller) ('Ashour, 1948a: 42–3).

In the preceding decades, sharetenancy had the dual function of providing political protection from the authorities *tied into* the credit provided by the resident village potentates (*mashayekh*). These local landlords eventually became the peasants' last resort against the state's tax farmers (*multazimun*). In exchange for the potentate's mediation and supply of seeds, the peasants were obliged to supply a share of the harvest on the threshing floor (Granott, 1952: 296), and provide free labour for the ploughing (and sometimes harvesting) of the *sheik*'s land, in a system known as *awneh* ('Ashour, 1948b: 50). This practice, prevalent in central Palestine up to the 1940s, comes closest to the notion of corvée labour in Middle Eastern agriculture. However, the replacement of *wergo* and the tithe by the flat Rural Property Tax during the 1930s (cf. Doukhan, 1938: 99) helped, along with factors completely external to the village economy – such as the urban pull of wage labour – to reduce the peasant's dependence on the local potentates.

We can now conceptualize in three broad categories the central features performed by the institution of sharetenancy in mid-century agrarian Palestine:

1. It was the mechanism by which an undercapitalized peasantry acquired credit and stock from local landlords and urban financiers, often losing title deeds because of accumulated debts and low productivity.

2. Sharetenancy performed the reverse of this process also. It provided a mechanism for the acquisition of land by the land-hungry peasantry through the rejuvenation of 'dead' lands. The peasant here became a proprietor, or expanded his holding by becoming an active partner to the 'passive' landlord. (This process contributed no doubt to rectifying the impact of land fragmentation due to the prevalence of an egalitarian inheritance system, and acted in general as a safety valve for relieving the demographic pressure on the land.)

3. A 'feudal' function of sharetenancy involved the combined intercession

of local potentates on behalf of the peasants to reduce or alleviate the impact of state taxes (tithe, *wergo*, etc.), as well as to advance credit for stock and other items in return for a share of the crop and compulsory labour in the landlord's holdings (*awneh*). This third feature of sharetenancy lost its 'feudal' (i.e. both the intercessionary and corvée aspects) towards the end of British colonial rule, while retaining its patronage dimension.

## Firestone's conception of sharetenancy as a devolutionary mechanism

Ya'cov Firestone's two essays on the agrarian economy of Mandatory Palestine constitute a significant theoretical contribution on the regulatory nature of the sharecropping contract in the relationship between peasant and landlord (Firestone, 1975a; 1975b). Basically, Firestone constructs a schema to illustrate the progressive devolution of the landlord's control over his land in favour of the cropper, resulting from the intrusion of market forces into the peasant's subsistence economy. The form this devolution took was partnership and 'quasi-partnership' compacts in land, based on sharetenancy arrangements between peasant smallholders (and occasionally landless tillers) and landlords in the Jenin and Nablus districts.

The progression from full landlord's control over crop production to the ascendancy of the sharecroppers to the status of smallholders corresponded to the physical movement of rural potentates from their villages of residence to regional urban centres. Although this process did not quite constitute a linear progression over time – many absentee landlords retained direct control over the land through resident relatives – it did evolve historically in such a way that the big landlords gradually were divested of their estates in favour of local peasant 'partners'. This progression can be broken down into stages of cropping arrangements illustrated in Figure 3.1.

Within this schema, the cutting edge in agrarian evolution occurs when the share-rent is transformed into cash tenancy, indicating both the landlord's physical alienation from the land (usually associated by moving his residency to the district centres), and by the termination of his filial connection with the patronized cropper and his family. But in the transitional stages, the role of the cropper also undergoes an important qualitative transformation. Thus, while 'a share-rent farmer who sub-farmed out to others some of his land remitted to the landowners the whole of the rent share he had collected for it, making him the landowner's trustee rather than a middleman', by contrast, a peasant tenant under a lease is allowed to sublet for a profit (Firestone, 1975a: 183). When this happens, full market relations run their due course.

While economists have traditionally stressed the stagnating influence of sharecropping arrangements, Firestone treats share-rents of both the joint-

**Figure 3.1**
**Firestone's Conception of Sharetenancy as a 'Devolutionary' Mechanism**

| Cropping arrangement | Landlord's role | Peasant's role |
|---|---|---|
| 1. Direct cropping | Direct supervision of own (wage) workers on own land. | Hired tiller (*qatruz*) |
| 2. Joint farming | Delegation of supervision to an agent (*wakil*) who provides a share in the stock, and acquires a share in the yield. Landlord still a resident. | *Harrath* (ploughman-sharecropper) providing a minor share in the stock and all labour. |
| 3. Share-rent farming | Provision of land only; landlord becomes an absentee. | Supply of seed stock and capital; hiring of additional croppers. |
| 4. Tenancy | Absentee. Periodic leasing of land to croppers, directly or through an agent. | Tenant farmer; full provision of capital stock. |

Derived from Firestone, 1975a: 6–7, 175–182.

farming and the co-cultivation varieties as being fairer from the point of view of the peasant since they 'reflect the considerable fluctuations that take place in crop yields' (ibid.). This, in part, is the same position held by James Scott in discussing risks in tenancy systems in South-east Asian agriculture (Scott, 1976: 44–52). The crucial element in Palestine is not parity, however (or even 'claims to subsistence' as in the case of Filipino and Vietnamese peasants discussed by Scott), but the availability of surplus which the peasant can invest in cropping additional land. This is why the share-rent as a form of cropping was confined to very big landlords in Palestine who were able to make such provisions, while 'joint-farming' (that is, delegated sub-farming) spread among the middle and small farmers who took croppers on to compensate for the loss of family members who flocked to work in the main cities during the high employment seasons of the 1930s and 1940s.

Labour mobility and full employment also generated both labour shortages in the agrarian sector as well as a historic decline in joint (share) farming in favour of cash rents, a trend which was not reversed until World War Two, when prices of food began to soar (cf. Firestone, 1975b: 44). However, even today (1981), under conditions of intermediate and high technology in agriculture and with the availability of relatively easy credit arrangements, sharecropping compacts have not declined, and in some regions (such as Tulkarem and the Northern Valley) they continue to spread.

The picture that emerges from Firestone's analysis is thus one that attributes to the institution of sharetenancy and the intrusion of market relations in agriculture not polarization between wage labour and capital, and not the emergence of rural capitalism, but an actual ascendancy of the smallholding peasantry, and the demise of big landlordism by the middle of this century. Such a demise has led, at least as far as the Nablus district is concerned, to the increased homogeneity of the peasant strata, in a context in which the differentiation between rural wage workers (*harateen* and *ujara'*) became synonymous with the smallholding *fellahin*.

## Peasant ascendancy or subjugation?

How are we to reconcile this view with Granott's proposition that 'tenancy in *all its forms* brought with its spread the enslavement of the *fellah* in the countries of the East' (Granott, 1952: 291; emphasis added) and with his claim that, in Palestine, 'the position of the *fellahin* who owned holdings of their own was incomparably superior to that of tenants. Even in its outward appearance a village inhabited by landowning *fellahin* differed from those belonging to tenants' – the former being distinguished by the presence of gardens and orchards in its immediate vicinity (ibid.: 292).

At one level, the answer lies in Firestone's restriction of his analysis to one area of central Palestine, beyond which he hesitates to generalize except in a cursory fashion (cf. Firestone, 1975a: 184), while Granott establishes his position on the basis of cases derived from several regions. Nevertheless, Firestone discusses an area which includes hilly and plains terrain (the Nablus mountains and stretches from the Marj ibn Amer plateau bordering Jenin – the latter also examined by Granott). In our view, however, significant divergence between the two writers lies in the conceptual and ideological underpinnings which govern the perspective of each author.

Ideologically, Granott has established himself as a Zionist authority on land relations in Palestine and sought on a number of occasions to rebut criticisms of the political consequences of land transfers from Arab absentee landlords to the Jewish National Fund. Together with several Labour-Zionist historians, he saw this process as an act of deliverance of the *fellahin* from their feudal lords (Granott, 1956: 251–2; and Granott, 1952: 302–3; see also Sereni and Ashery, 1936: 17, 83–8).[4] Other writers, it must be added, who did not share Granott' s ideological predispositions, such as 'Ashour and Warriner, also saw in sharetenancy contracts instruments of oppression for the smallholding peasant.

Conceptually Firestone was confronted with the dilemma that, in its main thrust, his thesis ran counter to the empirical findings established by several authorities on Middle Eastern regimes. At one point, he himself refers to the work of Milliot, Pesle, Berque (in North Africa) and Lambton (in Persia) where

> instead of accession to capital ownership, or at least of contractual equality of some sort, there had been dire exploitation of labour; and instead of compatibility between religious law and actual practice, a

> clear dualism perpetuated by obscurantist jurists... [addressing] themselves primarily to the agricultural institutions dictated almost by definition by dependence and patronage. (Firestone, 1975b: 322)

The prevalence in Palestine of patterns of 'mutual benefit and solidarity' over patterns of direct exploitation is seen by Firestone as the product of a transitional peasant economy where market relations hastened a greater accession to capital ownership (including in land) by small landholders. It also reflected a coincidence of compatibility between normative principles of the Islamic *shari'a* and agrarian practices, rather than an expression of Palestinian exceptionalism (in the Middle Eastern context).

The zenith of this 'compatibility' is observed in the bond of association between peasants and landlord in the institution known as the *mugharasa* contract – a form of co-cultivation predominant in orchards and groves – in which the cropper acquires accession to ownership of part of the orchard after contributing his labour for a specified number of years. 'Ashour defined *mugharasa* as a

> ... long-term contract by which the landlord leases-out a designated portion of land to a tenant stipulating the planting of trees in it, with the provision of all expenses. At the termination of the contract period, the tenant peasant acquires title deed to a proportion of trees (only) or to both land and trees. ('Ashour, 1949a: 42)

The period of accession differs depending on the variety of tree: three to five years for mulberry trees (*tut*), four to six years for vineyards, seven to eight years for olives (but thirty years in Lebanon, indicating regional variations), ten years for orange groves, etc. ('Ashour, ibid.: 43).

Unlike Firestone, 'Ashour does not compare *mugharasa* favourably with other forms of sharecropping. The crucial variable he considers in this context is the density of the rural population. The latter is seen rather mechanically to be associated inversely with the size of the peasant's share of the yield ('Ashour, ibid.: 47). But even when rural density is low, the peasant is still enslaved by his dependency on long-term loans from the landlord; in the case of *mugharasa*, by the unfavourable conditions of the contract (ibid.: 48).

In contrast, Firestone sees *mugharasa* as a form of partnership or quasi-partnership in which the active partner (the peasant–worker) takes advantage of an expanding market by providing his and his family's labour to acquire land, while the passive partner (the landlord) makes available his capital stock as a form of investment.

Firestone's original insight lies in his reinterpretation of the nature of sharetenancy, under transformed economic conditions, in what most observers took to be the same immutable agrarian institution. In a classic case of old forms camouflaging new relationships, we obtain here a historical synchronism among the components of a triad: 1) the demands of new investment opportunities in land; 2) religious regulation of partnership contracts, which so far have been circumvented to legitimize a stagnant and exploitative relationship (i.e. Warriner's and 'Ashour's notion of share-tenancy); and 3) a 'socially approved' customary form of association – *muraba'a* and *mugharasa* – the 'primitive' and 'advanced' forms of sharecropping.

Firestone's insight becomes limited, however, in illuminating the nature of the Palestinian agrarian regime in a variety of ecological terrains, and in subsequent periods of change. Initially, he confines his interpretation to the Jenin area ('Arrabeh and Zar'een). Then he decides to expand it to incorporate the hilly regions of Nablus (Samaria), then to the mountainous regions of Palestine in general, and finally to 'the agrarian economy of the Levant in periods of transition' (Firestone, 1975a: 3–4, 179, 186; Firestone, 1975b: 311, 316, 322, 324).

But how do we explain the completely different agrarian development which occurred in the big estates of Gaza, Jaffa, Lyddah, Jericho and elsewhere in Palestine where – from the beginning of the century and up to the 1940s – wage labour and investment of surplus by resident and absentee landlords were wedded to create the opposite of a smallholder's regime, the form of capitalist citrus plantation known as the *bayyara*? All three components of the triad (sharetenancy, Islamic law and market expansion – in the form of exports) existed here; but two additional ingredients led to a radically different outcome. These were the substantial presence of indigenous and migrant workers (from Syria and Egypt) seeking work opportunities in the coastal areas, and the relative absence in these plantations of bonds of patronage.

Patronage goes a long way (when set in the context of stable and relatively immobile peasantry) on the other hand, to explain the peculiar role of sharetenancy (especially in its *mugharasa* form) in the central and plains region of Palestine. It will be recalled here that feudal relations had an exceptionally strong hold in the Nablus–Jenin–Tulkarem region throughout the 19th century and during most of the Mandatory period in Palestine. Unlike coastal Palestine or the Jerusalem area, we observe there a resident landlord class with strong patrimonial relations to its peasant base. Factional alignments divided central (and later on, most of the hilly regions) of Palestine along vertical coalitions in the course of 19th-century peasant wars, in which major landlords mobilized whole villages which were tied to them by bonds of reciprocity. Such bonds included, during various intervals: intercession on behalf of the village to alleviate the tax burden to the state; provision of corvée labour to the landlord (*awneh*); provision of stock, land and consumption loans by the landlord; extension of protection from Bedouin raids, etc., to the village holdings.

The objectives of these alignments differed with the transformation of agrarian Palestine through its increasing incorporation into the world market economy. Initially, the competition for tax farming posts gave way to the scramble over the more influential regional administrative offices, judgeships and other official posts, and then to the use of peasant factions for augmentation of the landlord's holdings. At a later stage, these alignments became crucial in the mobilization of peasant factions for and against the Palestine Revolt in its later years (1938–9) (cf. Hoexter, 1973; Porath, 1975; Tamari, 1981).

With the gradual institutionalization under British rule of private property in land (the Land Settlement), two aspects of the natural economy of Palestine became the plagues of peasant tenure in the hilly region. These were parcellization of land, resulting from the archaic system of plot rotation prevalent in the *musha'* (communal) mode, and fragmentation, resulting from the partible system of inheritance. Parcellization and fragmentation amounted to the same thing in posing obstacles to the effective use of limited land holdings by the peasant household. Population increase in rural areas created new pressures, and opportunities, for landlords to use their estates more effectively. Wage labour in the cities, when available, was the external outlet for these pressures. *Mugharasa* share-contracts were an 'internal' form of accommodation which used, profitably, the established procedures of an old traditional institution, based on patronage.

Firestone is cognizant of the centrality of patronage in the widespread attraction of crop-sharing contracts during a period of risk and uncertainty in farming investment. The problem is that his schema does not allow for the explanation of sharecropping arrangements outside of patronage. The emphasis in his analysis is on how, to many landlords, and from a purely financial perspective, the losses far outweigh the gains involved in share-farming ventures. They often lose by tying their capital to low-return investments in the form of consumption and loans to the cropper, or as capital loans to joint-farmers (Firestone, 1975a: 178), and even by collecting lower rent-shares than those called for by the prevalent market rates (ibid.: 193). Yet they continue in doing just that with the conscious aim of consolidating their political base. In tracing the fortunes of the Abdul Hadi clan, he further notes how the joint-farm, under sharetenancy arrangements, provided a 'perfect opportunity for a patron-client relationship (and) assumed pivotal importance and lever of influence in such circumstances (i.e. the rebellion of 1936). Its establishment was, indeed, a crucial stage in the evolution of a sheikly family into an absentee class exercising its economic and political control of the home villages in new ways' (Firestone, 1978: 182).

Firestone overvalues the exchange of political gains made by landlords in return for material less precisely because he was dealing with a period of political uncertainty. The situation had not and could not have existed over an extended period. But we still conclude that patronage (or feudal relations, if we use the term generously) under conditions similar to those prevalent in Mandatory Palestine, was an essential prerequisite for the mediation of sharetenancy in the consolidation of the landless and smallholding peasantry to a situation of ascendancy and relative security in their land tenure. Despite the paradoxical marginalization of peasant holdings and increased proletarianization, all the evidence we have seems to support this assumption. For in those regions with weak patronage relations, such as the coastal areas, the advance of market relations gave rise to rural capitalism or alternatively to widespread speculation in land and the emergence of a pure *rentier* class of absentee landlords. (The process towards agrarian capitalism was facilitated no doubt by the abundance of migrant labour supply – but that in our view is not the critical factor.)

Under those conditions, no political base existed for *rentiers* among the peasantry. Is it by chance that peasant displacement resulting from land transfers to Zionists during the Mandate occurred as it did, where landlords had weak or virtually no links with their peasants, and where absentee *rentier* landlords abounded? Where, by contrast, patrimonial bonds were strong and fulfilled functional needs, as was the case in the central mountains and the northern plains of the West Bank, a regime of smallholding peasantry prevailed and persists to this day. That Firestone does not come to this conclusion is related to the limitations of the historical period to which he confines his analysis, and to his preoccupation, in his essay on *sharika* contracts (1975b), with problems of correspondence between juridicial forms and economic practice.

We must now re-examine problems of sharetenancy when market relations prevailed over patrimonial bonds.

## Sharetenancy persists with the decline of patronage

The dissolution of Arab landed classes during the 1948 war led to the dispersal of hundreds of thousands of peasants who flocked to the West Bank, Gaza and Transjordan, and to the shattering of the system of patronage that existed until then. Nevertheless, the system of sharetenancy persisted. This phenomenon may be attributed to two main features of the new, dislocated agrarian regime. One was the acquisition of vast tracts of irrigated land in the Jordan Valley (on both sides of the river basin) during the early 1960s by resident and absentee landlords. In this endeavour, the landlords used refugee camps in the vicinity as recruiting ground for agricultural workers.

A second factor was the migration of young members of peasant households to the Gulf, and (during the 1970s) to Israeli construction sites. The two population trends thinned out the surplus rural population and induced new sharecropping arrangements devoid of the traditional relations of patronage.

In this context, we may speak of countervailing trends in sharetenancy. The commoditization of land and most other factors of agricultural production was facilitated by the availability of cheap and landless refugee labour, creating ideal conditions for plantation agriculture (in the Gaza district, Jericho and the lower part of the Jordan Valley). It also created tenuous conditions of sharetenancy highly unfavourable to the cropper (in the upper Jordan Valley, and the East Ghor basin).

On the other hand, the considerable migration of peasant-workers from the hilly regions seeking work opportunities in Israel or abroad did not result in any significant degree of land transfers or consolidations, aside from the areas referred to in the Jordan Valley (Sa'ati, 1980). Here we observe the migrant peasants, or rather the remaining members of their households, maintaining legal control over their lands and farming them out to sharecroppers under favourable terms to the latter.

The fact that these trends corresponded ecologically to the plains and mountainous terrains respectively was not, of course, an accident. The seasonal character of olive (and olive oil) production, and its biennual yield cycles, created a continual surplus labour force which was, and is, highly responsive to wage labour attraction external to the village, while the irrigated vegetable crops of the Jordan Valley provided for year-round intensive farming, with double- and sometimes triple-cropping seasons that required a stable agricultural force. In the Jenin–Tulkarem region, where the tail end of the fertile Marj ibn Amer plains intrude into the olive orchards of the Nablus hills, we witness a combination of several forms of sharetenancy (simple cropping, joint farming, partnership compacts, etc.). Only the *mugharasa* compacts seem to be on the decline, probably due to the depletion of surplus cultivable plots and the rise in the real estate value of land.

The increased demand for food items (especially in vegetables and fruits) in the Gulf States, and the improvement of marketing procedures, have enhanced the role of the landlord-financiers in sharetenancy contracts. Quite often the role of the financier has become separate from that of the landlord, who now provides the land itself and only occasionally the seed stock. The following description of sharetenancy contracts in the Southern Ghor of the Jordan Valley applies equally to the upper valley where thousands of refugee families sharecrop for absentee landlords who reside in mountain towns:

> A typical share-cropping family enters into an annual contract with the land-owner. The contract stipulates that the land-owner or his agent will provide the farmer with a subsistence loan or advance of between JD 200–500, which will be repaid with interest, at the end of the cropping season. The interest is usually in the order of 10% for a six to nine month period. The whole operation is either financed by the owner or by a separate investor. The farmer provides all the labor necessary, while the owner or his agent provides plowing machinery, seeds, fertilizers, insecticides, crates, transportation and marketing. For these services the owner or his agent sets the price, and the farmer cannot seek alternative services in the open market. All revenues and costs are split between the farmer and the owner on a 1:2 basis, i.e. the farmer gets one-

> third of the net revenues of the farm, after all expenses, as calculated by the owner or his agent. In cases where the owner is different from the financier-investor, the net revenues are split equally among the owner, financier and farmer. The contract is typically signed with two witnesses and a guarantor. It stipulates that if the subsistence advance is not repaid by the end of the season, the owner will confiscate any other property which the farmer has, unless the farmer renews the contract for another year. Should the farmer default on the provision of labor, the owner will farm the land at the farmer's expense. The farmer will also have to pay for any labor which he may have to hire at harvesting time. (Dajani, 1979: 16)

Dajani's claim (based on fieldwork in the Southern Ghor region) that most farmers 'will have no choice but to continue to work the land at subsistence levels, and to accept whatever terms are dictated upon them' (ibid.) cannot be extended to the prevailing conditions in the western Jordan Valley today. An examination of sharecropping arrangements conducted by this writer in the West Ghor found a much higher incidence of sharing in capital investment by the farmer than in the Eastern or Southern Valley regions. The division of net marketed yield on a 50–50 basis between peasant and landlord seems to be the prevailing ratio in the Western Valley. In the northern West Bank (the Jenin–Tulkarem region), the peasant sharecropper receives only one third of the net yield for irrigated plots (Tamari and Giacaman, 1980: 11).

The higher rate of return for sharecroppers in the Jordan Valley as opposed to those in the northern plains can be related to several factors: 1) the traditionally settled and stable agricultural communities in Jenin and Tulkarem, with an equally high number of owner-operated farms, has worked to the disadvantage of sharetenants, who had to compete over scarcer land resources; 2) the harsh climatic conditions in the Valley compelled absentee landlords to offer better conditions in order to attract a settled agricultural workforce; 3) the historical presence of tribal landlords (such as the Masa'eed) in the Jordan Valley, and their patronage of refugee tenants since the early 1950s, seems to have set the pace for subsequent contracts between the new urban-based landowners and their tenants in the Valley (ibid.: 11–13).

Thus, rural class relations in the Jordan Valley cannot be reduced, as suggested by 'Ashour above, to a formula of 'demographic pressures', i.e. the more pressing the ratio of potential tenants on scarce land resources, the more unfavourable tenancy contracts are obtained. The exceptionally high ratio of landless refugees to settled peasants in the Jordan Valley has worked in such a way as to create significant differentiation within the landless rural community, more favourable terms for sharetenants and lower wages for agricultural workers with no access to leaseholds. In this context, previous agricultural skills and personal bonds to absentee landlords and their agents (*wukala'*) (usually enhanced by proximity of living next to their holdings), have been major advantages to those landless peasants in acquiring tenancy contracts and raising their standards of living.

By contrast, no such visible differentiation is obtained in the mountain regions. The status of both small peasants and big landlords has been substantially transformed by large-scale internal migration from the villages to Israeli industries and construction sites. *Muhasasa* cropping is widely practised in the harvesting of olives (Nablus, Ramallah, Bethlehem districts) and grapes (Hebron district), but not in cereals and vegetables, which in those areas are predominantly cultivated for subsistence.

In the hilly areas, large-scale migration had a different impact on cropping arrangements. The landlord no longer leases the land to a ploughman-tiller (*harrath*), but has to hire one himself, at a substantial expense due to the rise in wages of agricultural workers. Those farmers whose family members are unable to help them with the harvest, farm-out the trees during the picking seasons, receiving only one half the yield. Until the early 1970s, i.e. before the major movement towards employment in Israel, the landlord used to receive the same half of the yield (in olive oil) by farming-out the orchard to the ploughman-tiller, or to another farmer, who undertook the whole operation himself, all expenses being borne by the leasee (Aranki, 1980). Because of the current scarcity of labour and the unprofitability of such arrangements, we witness today widespread neglect of olive orchards among small farmers (Farhat-Nasir, 1980: 13–17), who prefer to release the labour of the household members for wage work outside the village.

A final distinction should be made between the situation of sharetenants in the mountain villages and those in the Jordan Valley. Sharetenants in the latter, by virtue of their refugee (and therefore landless) status, work predominantly on leased land while highlands dry-farming, by contrast, has a preponderance of owner-cultivators leasing-in additional land to supplement their income. Since valley farming, both in the citrus plantations in the Southern Valley and in the Northern Ghor, is almost exclusively intensive farming based on irrigation, it is possible to speak of a *stratum* of sharecropping peasants. This is not the situation in the hills where sharecropping arrangements are embedded in the structure of seasonal labour allocation in a manner akin to that described by Geertz for Java. Here, social cleavages in the countryside are brought about by dynamics completely external to agriculture.

## Conclusions

I have taken the position in this chapter that sharetenancy is a highly adaptive mechanism for the allocation of rural labour in a variety of agricultural regimes, rather than viewing it primarily, or merely, as 'an agency for the siphoning of agrarian surplus' generated by landless peasants in traditional agriculture.

In the Middle East, in common with many Asian countries, sharetenancy has historically been associated with cropping arrangements in the large estates of absentee landlords. The stabilization of land titles in private hands, given the communal usufruct in villages and relations of patronage in land, led to the alienation of the peasant's access to his land and the flourishing of an intricate network of tenancy compacts throughout the first half of this century, mostly to the advantage of landlords.

But this aspect of sharecropping has camouflaged a more complex reality of agrarian relations. In Palestine particularly, absentee and big landlordism were a relatively minor phenomenon, and landlordship – as Doreen Warriner has noted – was a credit operation. In addition to providing a system for the cropping of big estates, sharetenancy performed several important functions. Those included the acquisition of consumption loans and stock by an undercapitalized peasantry; the rejuvenation of abandoned land and the consolidation of a middle stratum among the peasantry through *mugharasa* contracts and similar partnership arrangements; the alleviation of the impact of state-imposed taxes, etc., through patronage bonds which often worked to the economic disadvantage of landlords (Firestone); and the accession of landless refugees to a position of stable land tenure in a rural economy which, due to excessive outmigration and shortage of labour, began to favour the tenant.

Methodologically, the detailed study of sharetenancy arrangements helps us to dispel the misleading, and prevalent, use of the criterion of land possession as an empirical index for the examination of class differentiation among the peasantry. Since *access* to land, under conditions of scarce land resources, and the quality of land are frequently more important indicators of differentiation than the size of the holding or the legal title to the plot, the terms of tenancy become a crucial determinant of differentiation. The continued significance of the 'land factor' in the identification of sources of status and power among peasants suggest that the proper demarcation of cutting edges within peasant strata should use a combined index of 'land possession' and 'access to land' (sharecropped, rented, co-cultivated, etc.). The weight of the share-rent component of this index is dependent, obviously, on the nature of the share contract and on extra-economic factors, such as patronage relations and state intervention in the regulation of agricultural prices. Moreover, control of marketing outlets by landlords and of disposition of the yield by urban financiers today are decisive factors in defining the content of the share contract to the extent that agricultural production has become export-orientated.

The persistence of sharetenancy in Palestinian agriculture is explained here *negatively* by the failure of capitalist relations in agriculture to take hold in mountainous (dry-farming) areas, and, with few exceptions, in irrigated farming. It is explained *positively* by the continued injection of landless peasant refugees into the network of tenancy and sharecropping compacts with both big landlords and smallholders.

The magnitude of internal migration (peasant-workers seeking work in Israel) and emigration among rural households has sustained a strong demand for tenancy among all categories of farmers, including smallholders. The high risk factor involved in dry-farming continues to favour share-rent contracts as opposed to cash rents. In the midst of a stagnant urban economy today under Israeli rule, the adaptive flexibility of such sharecontracts are responsible, to a considerable extent, for the continued survival and resilience of the agricultural sector in Palestine.

## Notes

1. There are exceptions of course. Many of the sharetenants in the Jordan Valley, for example, are almost exclusively landless refugees (ex-) peasants who crop the lands of absentee landlords from the hilly areas. Their status is only an inch above those rural proletarians whom they hire in harvest periods as day labourers (Government of Jordan, 1961: 164ff.).

2. The material in this section has been collected from interviews the writer conducted between 1978 and 1980 from a number of farmers and residents of the West Bank. Special mention should be made here of Messrs Salemeh Abu Dabbus, Zbeidat (Jordan Valley); Ali Jaradat, Sa'ir (Hebron District); Hamdan Taha, Shuyukh (Hebron District); Rashid Aranki, Birzeit (Ramallah District).

3. In regions where cash rentals of land are almost absent, as in the Ramallah District today, the term *daman* is often used in sharecropping, especially in the leasing of the olive harvest to croppers on a share basis.

4. Granott sought also to minimize the number of tenants displaced. Thus 'according to a list made in 1931, the Jews had acquired from large landowners 261,388 dunums in 15 places; and of this area 140,650 dunums were worked by 688 tenants' (Granott, 1952: 303). The 'source' cited for this data is Granovsky's (i.e. Granott himself before he Hebraized his name) *Land and Jewish Reconstruction in Palestine*, p. 87. According to these figures each tenant subleased 204 dunums from landlords (!) yet 'plots of such a size never attained by tenants anywhere in the Middle East, including holdings cited in official figures for Palestine itself.

## References

Ammons, Linda L., *West Bank Arab Villagers: The influence of national and international politics on village peasant life*, Department of Anthropology, Harvard University (unpublished Ph.D. thesis), Cambridge, Mass., 1978.

Aranki, Rashid, personal interview by author with Rashid Aranki, former assistant director of the Department of Land Surveys (Government of Palestine), Birzeit, West Bank, 1980.

'Ashour, 'Issam, 'Nidham al-Muraba'a fi Surya wa-Lubnan wa-Filastin', *al-Abhath*, vol. 1, no. 3, 1948, pp. 32–48; vol. 1, no. 4, 1948, pp. 47–69; vol. 2, no. 1, 1949: pp. 61–72.

Bardham, P. & Rudra, Ashok, 'Terms and conditions of sharecropping contracts: An analysis of village survey data in India', *The Journal of Development Studies*, vol. 16, no. 3, 1980.

Bell, C. & Zusman, P., 'The Bargaining Theoretic Approach to Crop-sharing

Contracts', *American Review*, vol. 66, no. 4, 1976.
Bhaduri, A., 'Agricultural Backwardness under Semi-Feudalism', *The Economic Journal*, vol. 83, 1973.
Carmi, S. and Rosenfeld, H., 'The origins of the process of proletarianization and urbanization of Arab peasants in Palestine', *Annals of New York Academy of Science*, vol. 220, 1974.
Cheung, S. N. S., *The Theory of Share Tenancy*, University of Chicago Press, Chicago, Illinois, 1969.
Djani, Hani, *A Baseline Socio-economic Study of the Southern Thor and Wadi 'Araba*, Amman, 1979.
Doukhan, M., 1938, 'Land tenure', in Sa'id B. Himadeh (ed.), *The Economic Organization of Palestine*, Beirut.
Farhat-Nasir, S., 1980, *The Olive of Palestine and Its Problems* (in Arabic), Birzeit West Bank: Birzeit University Publications.
Firestone, Ya'cov, 1975a, 'Crop-sharing economics in Mandatory Palestine', in *Middle East Studies*, pt. 1, in vol. 11, no. 1, pp. 3–23 (Jan. 1975); pt. 2 in vol. 11, no. 2, pp. 175–94 (May 1975).
_______ 1975b, 'Production and trade in an Islamic context: *Sharika* contracts in the transitional economy of Northern Samaria 1853–1943 (II)', *International Journal of Middle East Studies*, pp. 308–25.
Geertz, C., 1963, *Agricultural Involution: the process of ecological change in Indonesia*, Berkeley.
Granott, A., 1952, *The Land System in Palestine*, London: Eyre and Spottiswoode.
_______ 1956, *Agrarian Reform and the Record of Israel.*
Griffin, Keith, 1979, *The Political Economy of Agrarian Change*, London.
Hoexter, M., 1973, *The Role of the Qais and Yasseri Factions in Local Political Divisions: Jabal Nablus Compared With the Judean Hills in the first Half of the Nineteenth Century*, Jerusalem: Jerusalem Academic Press.
Jaradat, Ali, 1980, Personal interview by author with Ali Jaradat (May 1980), Sa'ir (Hebron).
Jordan, Government of Jordan, 1961, *The East Jordan Valley: a social and economic survey*, Amman: Department of Statistics.
Kanõ, H., 1980, 'The economic history of Javanese rural society: a reinterpretation', *The Developing Economies*, vol. 18, no. 1.
Keyder, C., 1980, 'Paths of rural transformation'. ESA Working Papers, No. 11, Middle East Technical University, Ankara.
Porath, Y., 1975, 'The political organization of the Palestinian Arabs under the British Mandate', in M. Ma'oz (ed.), *Palestinian Arab Politics*, Jerusalem.
Ruedy, John, 1971, 'Dynamics of land alienation' in Ibrahim Abu-Lughod (ed.), *The Transformation of Palestine*, Evanston: Northwestern University Press.
Sa'ati, Hanna, 1980, Personal interview by author with Hanna Sa'ati, head of the Land Registry Office, Financial Section (August 1980), Ramallah.
Scott, James, 1976, *The Moral Economy of Peasants*, New Haven: Yale University Press.
Sereni, Enzo and Ashery, R. E., 1936, *Jews and Arabs in Palestine: Studies in a National and Colonial Problem*, New York: Hechalutz Press.
Sharab, H., 1975, *Agro-Economic Aspects of Tenancy in the East Ghor Jordan Valley*, Amman: Royal Scientific Society, Economic Research Department.
Stoler, A. L., 1977, 'Rice harvesting in Kalil Lozo: a study of class and labor relations in rural Java', *American Ethnologist*, vol. 4, no. 3.
Tamari, S., 1981, 'Factionalism and class formation in recent Palestinian history',

in R. Owen (ed.), *Studies in the Social and Economic History of Palestine in the Nineteenth and Twentieth Century*, London: Macmillan.

——— and Giacaman, R., 1980, *Zbeidat: The Social Impact of Drip Irrigation on a Palestinian Peasant Community in the Jordan Valley*, Birzeit: Birzeit University Publications.

Warriner, Doreen, 1948, *Land and Poverty in the Middle East*, London: Royal Institute of International Affairs.

——— 1964, *Economics of Peasant Farming*, London: Frank Cass.

Wolf, Eric, 1966, *Peasants*, Englewood Cliffs, NJ: Prentice Hall.

# 4. Sharecropping in the North Jordan Valley: Social Relations of Production and Reproduction

*Alex Pollock*

This chapter attempts to specify theoretically the key elements of sharecropping as a particular form of houschold-centred agrarian production unit.[1] The definition of sharecropping relations of production will be theorized within the paradigm established by the 'articulation of modes of production' debate. I will describe the setting of sharecropping in the northern sector of the Jordan Valley in the West Bank, and offer an explanation of why sharecropping has been conserved, consolidated and reproduced in this region of the West Bank agrarian sector.

## Modes of production and their articulation

For a long period in its historical development, much Marxist historiography and social theory has been marred by a contradictory teleological strand. This is grounded on the assumption, either implicit or explicit, that pre-capitalist forms of production would eventually be superseded by the capitalist mode of production. Among the purveyors of this view it was a taken-for-granted truth that the internal logic of capitalist expansion and accumulation carried within it the seeds of the dissolution of non-capitalist modes of production.[2] Indeed, there is much in Marx's own writing, particularly his polemical and journalistic works, which gives credence to this view.[3]

This conception does not fit very well with historical reality, particularly the historical reality of agrarian communities in the Third World. Numerous divergent theories, operating at both macro-level and micro-level analysis, have argued, for a variety of different reasons, that the Darwinian/stagist assumptions embodied in this conception are not only false, but dangerously so. The authors of the Latin American dependent development school, for example, have argued with some justification that far from laying the conditions for the dissolution of non-capitalist relations of production, the penetration of foreign-based capitalism has resulted, in the Latin American experience, in the integration of dependent capitalism and backward rural production.[4] This, they argue, has been largely achieved through the imperialist mechanism of unequal commercial exchange. In the heartland of the world capitalist system, the USA, Friedmann has shown that household forms of petty commodity production have been the normal mode of production in the great American wheat belt. She has demonstrated that the petty commodity production household has been by and large oblivious to the advances of capitalist agriculture.[5]

The failure of the Darwinian/stagist concept to cope with the contemporary reality of the Third World and the 'developed countries' has led to a series of debates around the notion of modes of production. These debates attempted to take account of the fact that different modes of production can coexist and be fully integrated into national and international economic contexts. We can usefully distinguish three sources of contemporary debate.

First, there is the Indian debate of the late 1970s, which centred around the contributions of Alavi, Banaji, Chattopadhyay, Patnaik and Rudra, on the question of whether Indian agriculture can be described as capitalist or not. The Indian debate was essentially substantive, though it did raise a number of theoretical questions which were never adequately resolved.[6]

Second, we have the Althusserian re-reading of Marx's *Capital* which culminated in the debate about the conditions of existence of social formations, modes of production and the combination of modes of production in different social formations. This debate was centred around the contributions of Althusser, Balibar, Bettelheim, Castells, Hindess, Hirst, Meillassoux, Poulantzas, Rey and Terray. A number of important substantive pieces of work came out of this debate, although the main line of the debate was to sustain a rigorous conceptual reading of Marx's mature work. Through this it was explained that it would be possible to introduce conceptual rigour into modes of Marxist theorizing which were seen to be increasingly marked by a sequence of epistemological errors, namely empiricism, economism, reductionism and humanism.[7] This attempt to proscribe empiricism introduced an equally useless list of epistemological errors, namely theoreticism, rationalism, formalism, logicism, structural–functionalism and non-substantialism. The main problem with the Althusserian approach is that it reduces substantive and theoretical issues to epistemological ones, yet fails to perceive that there is perhaps a third epistemological line of theory construction, namely a realist one. The realist approach is the one I would most clearly associate with Marx, who is neither an empiricist nor a rationalist.[8]

Third, there is the Laclau–Frank debate, a debate over André Gunder Frank's neo-Smithian definition of capitalism and the implications this had, both politically and economically, for understanding and explaining Latin American history. Frank defines capitalism as a world system of *exchange* characterized by links of monopoly and exploitation through which the developed countries dominate the countries of the Third World.

Laclau was, correctly, far from happy with this as a Marxist definition since it defined capitalism not in terms of class relations but, on the contrary, in terms of national (imperial) power defined at the level of exchange. Laclau argues:

> Of course, Frank is at liberty to abstract a mass of historical features and build a model on this basis. He can even, if he wishes, give the resulting entity the name capitalism.... But what is wholly unacceptable is the fact that Frank claims that his conception is the Marxist concept of capitalism. *Because for Marx – as is obvious to anyone who has even a superficial acquaintance with his works* – capitalism was a mode of production. The fundamental economic relationship of capitalism is constituted by the free labourer's sale of his labour power, whose necessary precondition is the loss by the direct producer of ownership of the means of production.[9]

All three of these positions have elements in common but they are also separated by major theoretical and meta-theoretical differences. For the purpose of my analysis of sharecropping I will veer most heavily towards a Laclauian position in debate, since Laclau offers some general definitions which are interpretable within a realist framework.

**Modes of production**

The contemporary debates on the theory of modes of production have their theoretical lineage in volume 1 of *Capital*, where Marx analysed in detail only one particular mode of production; the capitalist mode of production. Marx himself, and the classical Marxists who followed him, never thought it necessary to construct a general concept of mode of production. Marx, in the '*Formen*' section of the *Grundrisse*, did discuss pre-capitalist modes of production and outlined some general differences between the capitalist mode of production and pre-capitalist modes of production, but he at no time presented a rigorous concept of modes of production in general.

This has raised a number of problems for latterday analysts. A number of Marxists, particularly economists, have a tendency to conceive the capitalist mode of production as including both the *production* and *circulation* of commodities (labour, money and products). I think that a fundamental error is embodied in this position.[10] If this position were correct then we would expect divergent modes of production to have methods of circulation specific to these modes. This is clearly not the case. Let us consider the example of the capitalist mode of production. This *form* of production involves two analytically distinct processes: the first involves a particular organization of the *labour process* in which labour is purchased as a commodity; the second involves a particular mode of expropriating surplus labour in the form of surplus value in the *valorization process*.[11] These two processes are *internal* to the capitalist mode of production and distinct from the process of the circulation of commodities. Historically, commodity markets in produce and money pre-existed the capitalist mode of production. In fact, these commodity markets are a necessary antecedent condition for the capitalist mode of production to come into being, but there is no compelling reason why we should reduce the capitalist mode of production to its antecedent conditions or to view the antecedent conditions as part of this mode of production.

Marx clearly distinguishes the interrelatedness but structural independence of the capitalist mode of production (*Capital* vol. 1), the circuit of commercial capital (*Capital* vol. 2), the circuit of interest-bearing capital (*Capital* vol. 2) and the effects of the interaction of the three (*Capital* vol. 3).

The point I wish to extract from this is that the capitalist mode of production is both analytically and, by and large, organizationally distinct from the circuits of commercial and interest-bearing capital. However, the reproduction of the capitalist mode of production requires that these organizational forms be combined or articulated as a functional unity. Once this is grasped we can profitably differentiate between the capitalist mode of production (composed of the labour process and the valorization process) and the *capitalist economic system* (composed of the historical articulation of the capitalist mode of production, the circuit of commercial capital and the circuit of interest-bearing capital).[12]

The circuits of commercial capital and interest-bearing capital are just as often articulated, both historically and contemporaneously, with other modes of production; petty commodity, feudal, slave and lineage modes of production.[13] All that is required for this articulation to be possible is that a portion of the economic surplus generated in these alternative modes of production be produced as commodities for sale or market exchange.[14]

Now, in general terms a mode of production is a systemic combination of relations and forces of production that entails a determinate form of ownership of the means of production and a determinate form of appropriation of the product or surplus product produced in the mode concerned. The form of ownership is a critical aspect since it categorically determines the manner in which appropriation of the economic surplus occurs and the degree of control which the appropriator has over the productive activity of the producers.

For the purposes of conceptual specification of sharecropping as a mode of production I will adopt Laclau's definition of a mode of production as:

> ... the logically and mutually co-ordinated articulation of:
> 1 a determinate type of ownership of the means of production
> 2 a determinate form of appropriation of the economic surplus
> 3 a determinate degree of development of the division of labour
> 4 a determinate level of development of the 'productive forces'.
>
> This is not merely a descriptive enumeration of 'isolated' factors, but a totality defined by its mutual interconnections. With this totality, property in the means of production constitutes the dominant element.[15]

I contend that Laclau's definition encompasses, at this level of abstraction, the necessary conceptual elements for (re-)constituting the different modes of production in Marxist discourse; the feudal mode of production, the capitalist mode of production, the petty commodity mode of production, the slave mode of production etc. Moreover, it should enable us to construct the concept of modes of production *not* found in Marx's discourse, e.g. the lineage mode of production and the sharecropping mode of production. This will be clarified when I deal with sharecropping as a mode of production.

**Articulation**

By articulation we refer to the processes and mechanisms through which divergent modes of production become inserted into social formations at regional, national and international levels.[16] The main sites of articulation are the *economic*, the *political* and the *ideological*. In this chapter I am primarily concerned in bringing out the economic conditions necessary for the articulation of sharecropping with the social formation at the regional level.

At the economic level a mode of production, in which a fraction or all of the economic surplus takes the form of commodities, will be articulated to the home and/or the international markets through two complementary processes. These are: 1) the circuit of commercial capital; 2) the circuit of interest-bearing capital. At an institutional level these circuits take very heterogeneous organizational forms, which are not my concern in this paper.

The circuit of commercial capital is predicated on the logic of purchasing commodities in order to sell them at a price which is substantially greater than the purchasing price. The logic entailed in this circuit can be formally represented in the following form:

$$M - C - M'$$

where M is equal to the sum of money initially outlaid for commodity C and M′ is equal to the final income from the sale of C. The logic of commercial capital involves two transactions and one commodity. In this process the commodity undergoes no transformation of its elemental form. The merchant does nothing to the commodity in a productive sense except to bring it to the marketplace. The relationship of the merchant to the purchaser is not an exploitative relationship but one of *unequal exchange*. The relationship of the merchant to the producer from whom he initially purchases the commodity is also one of *unequal exchange* because he is buying the commodity at less than market price. Both these transactions take place in the sphere of *market relations* and they are charged with the function of consumption.

The circuit of commercial capital has mediated the relation between production and consumption in many historically distinct institutional forms; from the itinerant merchants who traversed Europe and the Orient through the Middle Ages to the multinational corporate organizations of advanced capitalism. The main institutional conduit in articulating the peasant commodity-producing sector of the north Jordan Valley to the home, Israeli and international markets is the merchant wholesaler of agricultural commodities, the owner of a *hisbeh*.

If we consider the circuit of interest-bearing capital, it becomes apparent that this circuit is a variation of the circuit of commercial capital. The main difference is that money is the commodity which is dealt in, but this commodity is not sold; rather it is *lent* to be returned at some future date in an augmented form. In the circuit of interest-bearing capital, loans can be used either as a means of consumption (indebtedness in order to consume) or as a means of production (indebtedness in order to capitalize). The logic of the circuit of interest-bearing capital can be formally represented in the following form:

$$M - M'$$

where a sum of money, M, is forwarded in return for the deferred payment of a greater sum of money, M′. The logic entailed is one of lending in order to increase the quantity.

Both of these circuits are processes that facilitate the articulation of different modes of production – slave, feudal, capitalist, petty commodity, etc. – with other modes of production in a social formation. However, as I said previously, these circuits only act to articulate the economic instances where the process of commoditization exists in either an extended or restricted way: they only articulate *market* societies.

There are, of course, non-economic instances of articulation which are conterminous with the economic instances of articulation. These are the political and ideological mechanisms and processes of articulation. The political instance is composed of relations of violence–legitimation and the ideological instance is composed of relations of consent–manipulation. These two instances always have a people–class specificity which is not simply reducible to class determination (e.g. bourgeois state or false consciousness). However, they always have a distinct class content if not a class form.[17] The constraints of space do not allow me to work through the ideological and political mechanisms in this chapter.

## The setting

The area which forms the contextualization of my specification of sharecropping is the northern sector of the Jordan Valley inside the West Bank. Located here are the villages of Bardala, 'Ain al-Beda, Marj Najeh, Zbeidat, Jiftlik, Frush Bet Dajan and 'Ain Shibli. The area in which the villages are located forms a triangle bounded on the east by the River Jordan, from Jiftlik in the south to Bardala in the north, and bounded on the north-west by Ghor al-Far'a, from Jiftlik in the south to 'Ain Shibli in the north-west.

The topography of the Jordan Valley is unique. At 200 metres below sea level, it is the lowest place on the earth's surface. It has an arid climate with, on average, less than 250 millimetres of rainfall per year. The winter climate is temperate and rarely falls below 10° C, while the summer temperature is, on average, a baking 38° C. Temperate winters have resulted in Jordan Valley farmers traditionally producing winter crops; these normally obtain higher market prices due to supply and demand factors.

A major problem facing Palestinian farmers in the Jordan Valley is the limited availability of water. This is not particularly a natural or even an economic problem but is essentially a political one. The Israeli military authorities have consistently refused to grant licences for the drilling of wells to Palestinian farmers. No new wells have been dug in the Palestinian sector since 1967. Existing Palestinian wells are no more than 100 metres deep, while wells in the Israeli sector range from 100 to 600 metres in depth. These deeper Israeli wells have lowered the groundwater table and affected the quality of water available to Palestinian farmers. These farmers now find a higher saline content in the water than in the past.

## Demographic characteristics

The total population of the seven villages I surveyed was 5,451 persons.[18] This was equivalent to 0.7% of the total population of the West Bank in 1983. The villages varied widely in their population distributions, as Table 4.1 shows. The village of Jiftlik is by far the largest in the area and its population constitutes 45.0% of the regional adult population.

**Table 4.1**
**Village Adult Population by Sex**[19]

| Village | Male | Female | Total |
|---|---|---|---|
| Bardala | 171 | 176 | 347 |
| 'Ain al-Beda | 186 | 201 | 387 |
| Marj Najeh | 65 | 73 | 138 |
| Zbeidat | 108 | 118 | 226 |
| Jiftlik | 599 | 601 | 1,200 |
| Frush Bet Dajan | 136 | 144 | 280 |
| Other | 12 | 0 | 12 |
| 'Ain Shibli | 35 | 40 | 75 |
| **Total** | **1,312** | **1,353** | **2,665** |

The north Jordan Valley is an almost exclusive agricultural economy. In 1983 74.2% of the adult population worked in the agricultural sector. Only 1.6% of the resident adult population was engaged in the commercial or industrial sector, both of which are regionally underdeveloped.[20] Commuter proletarianization of the local workforce was marginal: only 6.6% of the adult population were wage labourers.[21]

The general adult (15 years and over) illiteracy rate was 47.7%, while the gender-specific illiteracy rates were 64.4% for adult females and 30.4% for adult males.[22] Only 56.1% of the adult population had attended school for some period in their life.[23] Of those who attended school only 10.3% had stayed on after 15 years of age and 52.2% never managed to remain beyond elementary level.[24] Only 4.0% of the adult population had qualified in the *tawjihi* (final leaving examination). Of the adult female population only 0.7% qualified in the *tawjihi*.[25] Furthermore, there were only 28 university graduates and students living in the region, six of whom were female.[26]

Housing conditions in all but one village (Zbeidat) were squalid and cramped. The majority of houses consisted of mud brick constructions and one-room shacks. Overcrowding was a serious problem with an average housing density of five persons per room. 67.0% of houses had no latrine facility and 79.5% had no electricity.[27] Most cooking was carried out on primus stoves. These households have continually been refused licences to upgrade the standard of their housing by the Israeli military authorities.

**Agricultural and agrarian characteristics**

The unique topographical and climatic conditions of the Jordan Valley have enabled the region to be placed at the forefront of a veritable 'green revolution' in agriculture. During the early 1970s a number of foreign non-governmental organizations (NGOs) became interested in what they perceived as backward rural production conditions and underdeveloped social conditions. They proceeded to make development interventions into the local community modelled along classical diffusionist lines. That is, they perceived the problem of agrarian poverty and underdevelopment, the constraining factors posed by Israeli rule notwithstanding, as essentially a technological problem stemming, in the main, from technological backwardness *vis-à-vis* local, national and international market competitors. The main policy to emerge was one geared to sending an agricultural extension agent into the region to diffuse the backlog of technical and technological knowledge about new equipment, plant species, seedlings, fertilizers and insecticides. This equipment was then made available through international aid transfers provided by foreign NGOs. The efforts of the NGOs resulted in a radical change in the pattern of agriculture in the region. Peasant farming locally became biochemically based and augmented by plastic water irrigation systems. The major changes involved:

1. a crossover from traditional earth-furrow irrigation systems to plastic pipe drip irrigation systems;
2. a change from local seed strains to high-yield hybrid strains with saline resistant properties; and
3. a move from organic to inorganic fertilizers.

This 'green revolution' had important consequences for the pattern and extent of crop production. Subsistence production has become marginalized; almost 70% of all farmers reported that they did not produce any crops purely for household consumption. Concomitant with marginalization of subsistence production has been a move to the specialization in

**Table 4.2**
**Dunumage of Crop Production by Crop and Agrarian Class**[28]

| Crop | Share-cropper | Shepherd | Cash tenant | Smallholder | Landlord | Total |
|---|---|---|---|---|---|---|
| Vegetables | 10,182.5 | 326.5 | 1,284.0 | 1,989.5 | 281.0 | 14,063.5 |
| Fruit | 342.0 | 33.5 | 67.5 | 377.5 | 159.5 | 980.0 |
| Field crops | 2,896.5 | 257.5 | 165.5 | 1,087.5 | 169.5 | 4,576.5 |
| **Total** | **13,421.0** | **617.5** | **1,517.0** | **3,454.5** | **610.0** | **19,620.0** |

a few crops and the development of what was potentially a regional export enclave economy (this trend would be expected to continue if stable export outlets can be established). Table 4.2 shows that of the 19,620 dunums under cultivation 71.7% were producing vegetables, 5.0% fruit and 23.3% field crops. Of the 14,063.5 dunums under vegetable production 40.1% of these were producing tomatoes. Tomatoes, aubergines, courgettes and cucumber accounted for 77.8% of all vegetable production.[29] Tomatoes were also the major export crop with over half of all tomatoes produced being directly exported from the farm to Jordan via landlords and commission agents.

**Table 4.3**
**Forms of Landholding by Agrarian Class**[30] **(dunums)**

| Landholding form | Sharecropper | Shepherd | Cash tenant | Smallholder | Total |
|---|---|---|---|---|---|
| Owned | 753 | 159 | 198 | 1,912 | 3,022 |
| Cash rented | 1,226 | 260 | 1,478 | 416 | 3,380 |
| Share rented | 9,899 | 198 | 284 | 727 | 11,108 |
| **Total** | **11,878** | **617** | **1,960** | **3,055** | **17,510** |

If we consider the basic agrarian characteristics we find a total of 17,510 dunums were held in three landholding forms (personal ownership, cash rental and sharetenancy) by four class categories (see Table 4.3). This table shows that sharetenancy was the most extensive form of landholding with 63.4% of all tenured land held by sharecroppers, while personal ownership and cash rental were almost at parity in terms of land tenured as 17.3% and 19.3% of all tenured land was held in these forms respectively. The arithmetic mean for holdings in each of these forms was varied. The mean for personal ownership was 32.2 dunums, the mean for shareholding was 24.7 dunums and the mean for cash holding was 39.9 dunums. The arithmetic mean is not, however, a very good measure of distribution because one or two large holdings increase the average significantly. A better measure is the mode. The modes for the different forms of holding were: personal ownership 10–14 dunums; cash rent 5–9 dunums, and share rent 20–24 dunums.[31]

An important feature to bear in mind, which Table 4.3 highlights, is that individual farmers can and often do occupy more than one class of location simultaneously. It is possible for a peasant household to be engaged in sharecropping and/or shepherding and/or cash tenancy and/or smallholding.

**Table 4.4**
**Numerical Analysis of Landholdings, by Village and Agrarian Class[32]**

| Village | Sharecropper | Shepherd | Cash tenant | Smallholder | Total |
|---|---|---|---|---|---|
| Bardala | 52 | 3 | 3 | 18 | 76 |
| 'Ain al-Beda | 74 | 0 | 6 | 22 | 102 |
| Marj Najeh | 9 | 0 | 2 | 15 | 26 |
| Zbeidat | 31 | 3 | 20 | 1 | 55 |
| Jiftlik | 208 | 6 | 7 | 12 | 233 |
| Frush Bet Dajan | 26 | 5 | 4 | 24 | 59 |
| Other | 3 | 0 | 2 | 3 | 8 |
| 'Ain Shibli | 6 | 0 | 1 | 0 | 7 |
| **Total** | **409** | **17** | **45** | **95** | **566** |

While Table 4.3 shows that sharecropping was the most extensive form of landholding, Table 4.4 gives a numerical breakdown of landholdings according to class and village location. These figures show that sharecroppers held 72.3% of all land tenures, smallholders 16.7%, cash tenants 8.0%, and shepherd-farmers 3.0%. Quite clearly sharecropping was the dominant form of land tenure and agrarian class relationship. There were, however, village variations to the general pattern. For example, in Jiftlik, 'Ain Shibli, Bardala and 'Ain al-Beda sharecropping was the dominant tenure form, constituting 89.3%, 85.7%, 68.4% and 72.5% of the tenure of these respective villages. Sharecropping was marginally predominant in Zbeidat also but here cash tenancy was more important than in any other village, constituting 36.4% of the village tenures. In Marj Najeh smallholding was the dominant form of tenure (57.7%). In Frush Bet Dajan sharecropping and smallholding were almost coequal, constituting 44.1% and 40.7% of their village tenures respectively.

## The sharecropping mode of production

In this section I will argue that sharecropping is a specific agricultural mode of production and that we can construct a rational concept of this mode of production. In stating this I know I will transgress certain clericist assumptions. It is only, however, by attempting to explain and conceptualize forms of social production relationship that do not fit neatly into the conceptual legacy of modes of production, which Marx looked at in his own work, that we extend the bounds of Marxism as a science. Marx himself perceived sharecropping as a transitional arrangement between feudalism and capitalism.[33] Historically Marx is mistaken since sharecropping existed in social formations where neither capitalism nor feudalism existed.[34] A way out of this teleological dilemma is to specify sharecropping at the same level of conceptual analysis as other modes of production.

In order to do this we will operationalize the four elements entailed in Laclau's definition of a mode of production, that is:

1. type of ownership of the means of production;
2. form of appropriation of the economic surplus;
3. degree of development of the division of labour;
4. level of development of the productive forces.

**Type of ownership of the means of production**

By the term 'means of production' we refer to those elements which are combined in the actual process of production to produce specific use values (e.g. tomatoes and aubergines). In agricultural production such means of production would include land, water, drip irrigation, farm machinery and equipment, labour, seeds, fertilizers and insecticides.

The term 'ownership of the means of production' entails two interrelated concepts: 1) a relation of *property*, and 2) a relation of *economic possession*. These two elements have to be brought out analytically so that we can begin to give a class-relational dimension to ownership.

The *property relation* specifies what we commonly refer to as *juridical* or *legal* ownership. For the purposes of this chapter I shall follow the practice of bourgeois-liberal jurists by referring to legal ownership in the form of private property. In the context of the West Bank the concept of private property in land is problematic because property is largely defined by the Ottoman Land Law of 1858 which enumerates four categories of juridical ownership. These are:

1. '*Mulk* land', which gives full rights of ownership as private property in the modern bourgeois sense;
2. '*Miri* land', in which right of full possession remains symbolically in the in the hands of the state (sovereign), but where usufruct is in the hands of a private owner;
3. '*Waqf* land', which is owned by Islamic institutions;
4. '*Mushaa* land', land which is collectively owned.[35]

In sharecropping it is invariably the case that juridical ownership resides not in the hands of the direct producer but in the hands of the non-labourer. This is invariant. The cropper never has legal ownership of land. Further, it is juridical ownership which legitimates the landlord's *power* over his sharetenant. This power has its base in the political–juridical structure of the state, which sustains this power through property and contract law. The generation of state-legitimated power relations – at this specific level – becomes intensified with the generalization of forms of social interaction where property–contract relations obtain, i.e. market societies. In this way the state underpins all social relationships through the institutionalization of property and contract law.[36]

When we consider ownership of the means of production other than land, we discover that this is open to a wide degree of variation, from the landlord providing all inputs except labour, to the labourer providing all the means of production except land.

In the Jordan Valley the ownership of water rights varies considerably depending upon the source of the water. For example in the villages of Bardala and 'Ain al-Beda, the village domestic water supplies now come from the Israeli water grid, although for the purposes of farming farmers still use artesian wells and springs which are owned by landlords and private individuals. The villagers in Zbeidat and Marj Najeh get their water supplies from artesian wells for farming purposes and from a village tap for household consumption. The artesian wells are independently owned by landlords and other individuals. The villages of Jiftlik, 'Ain Shibli and Frush Bet Dajan get their water from a canal which flows down from the Nablus mountains and which is canalized through an aqueduct as it reaches Jiftlik. The water is used collectively by the villagers in 'Ain Shibli and Frush Bet Dajan, but property rights apply to the aqueduct in Jiftlik. As well as using this water, Jiftlik farmers also use artesian wells which are the property of landlords and private individuals from whom they rent water rights. Nevertheless, 79% of all sharecroppers had their farm water supply procured through their landlords.[37]

The ownership of agricultural machinery, such as tractors, ploughs and other accessories, is not widespread among sharecropping households. 74% of all sharecropping households did not own any mechanical equipment.[38] All sharecroppers use tractors and accessories, but they generally hire this equipment from other farmers (mostly smallholders who are petty commodity producers) and from individuals who act as commercial operators; 87% of all sharecroppers rented some if not all of the mechanical equipment they used on their farms.[39]

The purchase of seeds, fertilizers, insecticides and drip irrigation equipment is usually shared by the landlord and tenant on a 50–50 basis, thus ownership is shared. Labour is, of course, the property of the

**Table 4.5**
**Juridical Ownership of Means of Production**

| Means of production | Landlord | Tenant | Shared | Rented |
|---|---|---|---|---|
| Land | X | | | |
| Water | X | | | X |
| Machinery | | | | X |
| Seedlings | | | X | |
| Insecticide and pesticide | | | X | |
| Drip irrigation | | | X | |
| Labour | | X | | |

sharecropper and his family. This labour is bound to the landlord in the form of a contract with reciprocal obligations.

The juridical ownership of the means of production is represented in Table 4.5. From the table we can see that juridical ownership of the means of production is subject to *diffuse* ownership between landlords, sharecroppers and *rentiers*. One important fact stands out here: there is no generalized capitalization of the most costly equipment.

The second component of ownership, economic possession, refers to the control of the means of production as they are combined in the labour process. The labour process involves the combination of three elements:

1. labour activity (work);
2. the object of labour, e.g. the raw materials, seeds, fertilizers etc.;
3. the means by which labour acts on the objects of labour, i.e. tools and equipment.

Marx defines the labour process as:

> ... the activity whose aim is the production of use values, the appropriation of external substance for needs, is the general condition for exchanges between man and nature, a physical necessity for human life, and therefore independent of all human forms, or rather common to all.[40]

Thus the labour process and its three constituent elements are components of all forms of production. In the capitalist mode of production, for example, economic possession or *real economic ownership* of the means of production are unified by the capitalist and his agents, where they economically control and direct (manage) all the inputs into the labour process: labour, objects of labour and means of labour. Capitalist control attempts to control in minute detail the work of the labourer, the quality of the object of labour and the pace of the means of labour. The aim of this control is to produce commodities as quickly as possible and to use labour to its maximum degree. This is necessary since labour is the source of surplus value. The capitalist mode of production in its earliest stages of development seeks the real subsumption of the labour process so that capitalists can control and direct all the elements in the labour process in a scientific synthesis, in which commodities can be produced as quickly and as cheaply as possible so that the rate of surplus value can be maximized.

If we consider economic control of the labour process under sharecropping, we find that real subsumption of the labour process to landlord's control has not occurred. That is, the fundamental ability of the landlord to control and direct the labour process in all its aspects is not operative in sharecropping.

This becomes clear if we break the labour process down into its constituent elements and analyse them in terms of economic possession or real economic control. Thus the following emerges. First, economic possession of the sharecropping household's family *labour* resides directly in the hands of the tenant household. The sharecropping household allots specific quantities of labour time to the different jobs in the production process. This allotment is, of course, subject to ecological–agronomic constraints on labour activity, but this in no way diminishes the fact that the tenant exercises managerial authority over labour. The landlord does not spend enough time on the farm, either himself or through an agent, to control labour activity. Second, the case of the objects of labour, i.e. land, water, seeds, fertilizers and insecticides, is slightly more complicated for a number of reasons. First, let us consider water; when water comes from artesian wells and from the Israeli water grid it is subject to partial control by the military authorities, inasmuch as the amount of water permitted for agricultural purposes is tightly controlled. However, this control is not economic possession and, leaving aside problems associated with water shortages, the tenant has real economic control over the use of water in production. The tenant supervises and controls its utility function. Second, the landlord has partial power to determine *what* will be produced, what seeds, fertilizers and insecticides will be used, what section of land will be used for production. These are important powers, but they do not essentially constitute real economic control over the objects of labour. They may give the landlord partial control, when, as in the case of the 'green revolution' technology used in the region, they surreptitiously introduce quality and quantity control into the labour process. In the Jordan Valley the introduction of biochemically based improvements in seeds, fertilizers and insecticides has stabilized productivity. These improvements also underplay the role of labour in controlling the quality of production: they act for the landlord as a sort of 'technological management' in absence. These improvements, it may further be said, initiate the process of de-skilling the agricultural producer by separating traditional farm skills from scientific development. For example, seed stock selection and breeding has been taken out of the hands of the farmer and placed in the hands of biochemical–agronomic specialists and companies. Now, this process does not lessen the fact that the tenant still has economic control over seed productivity, but it does mitigate this control and opens up the possibility of the landlord contracting with less skilled tenant–labourers. It potentially widens the landlord's tenant pool. Third, when we consider the *means* of labour – drip irrigation, farm machinery – we find economic possession and control invested in the hands of the labourer. The tenant exercises management and planning control over their use.

Thus we can draw up a table of economic possession, as in Table 4.6. While the sharecropper has juridical control *only* over his own labour power, he has real economic and managerial control over all the elements in the labour process. This means that the sharecropper controls work rhythms, job schedules, labour time, intensity of effort, crop cycle (within ecological constraints) and crop fertility. The landlord has very little

**Table 4.6**
**Real Economic Possession of Means of Production**

| Means of production | Landlord | Sharecropper |
|---|---|---|
| Land | | X |
| Water | | X |
| Seedlings | partial | X |
| Insecticide and fertilizer | partial | X |
| Drip irrigation | | X |
| Machinery | | X |
| Labour | | X |

economic and managerial control of the means of production in this particular system of production.

This particular method of producing commodities bears a remarkable structural homology to the 'putting-out system' that was common among artisanal labour in Europe during the transition from feudalism to capitalism.[41] Under the 'putting-out system' the artisan provided labour and means of labour (machinery, tools and equipment) and the merchant provided the objects of labour (raw materials or unfinished products).

The resemblance between sharecropping and the putting-out system concerns only juridical ownership and economic possession. They differ significantly in the form of the appropriation of the economic surplus from the direct producer: in the putting-out system the artisan was paid a piece rate for the job, in the sharecropping system the sharecropping household is given a portion of the crop.

**Form of appropriation of the economic surplus**

The form of appropriation of the economic surplus is normally the most visible aspect of class relations in modes of production. The manner in which the economic surplus is appropriated from the direct producer by the non-labourer is the precise criterion for outlining the specific class natures of different modes of production. Different modes of production are differentiated by their differential modes of exploitation.

I shall attempt to bring out what is specific about the form of exploitation internal to social relations of production in sharecropping. The first thing to note is that sharecropping is based upon a *legal contract*, whether verbal or written, which stipulates the provision in designated proportions of certain inputs into the labour process by both the landlord and sharecropper. The contract further designates the proportion of the final crop yield, or sale of crop yield, which each party will receive. In 1983, 80% of share contracts were verbal and 97% were contracted on a yearly basis.[42] The actual specification of the contract itself is open to numerous variations. There are three common ones.

First, and most widespread, is the contract where:
(a) the cropper provides his own and his family's labour, and also wage

labour if required, e.g. at harvest;
(b) the landlord provides land, water, water pump (if required) and fuel for the pump;
(c) all the other costs of inputs – seeds, fertilizers, insecticides and drip-irrigation equipment – are equally shared.

On the basis of this contract the final crop yield is shared between the landlord and tenant on a 50–50 basis, normally of market price.
Second is the contract where:
(a) the cropper provides his own and his family's labour, and wage labour if required;
(b) the landlord provides land, water, water pump, fuel for pump, seeds, fertilizers, insecticides and drip-irrigation equipment.
On the basis of this contract the sharecropper receives one third, and the landlord two thirds, of the final crop yield.

Third is the contract where:
(a) the landlord provides only land;
(b) the sharecropper provides all other inputs.
On the basis of the contract the landlord receives 15%, and the tenant 85%, of the net yield. This contract is almost a form of cash tenancy.

The *formal legal contract* is the important characteristic in specifying the particular method of surplus appropriation of the agricultural product, i.e. of specifying the form of exploitation. This legal contract has two aspects which need to be brought out. First, persons undertaking a sharecropping compact do so *freely*. The sharecropper is formally free to undertake, or not to undertake, cropping as a form of employment. There is no legal or political power *forcing* the sharecropper to contract; his is not forced labour. Second, in order for sharecropping to exist it is a necessary but not sufficient condition that there be commodity markets. The contract requires the development of extended or restricted commoditization within the social formation.

The process through which exploitation or the appropriation of the economic surplus occurs is variable with the degree of commoditization. The economic surplus is appropriated at the end of the circuit of production when the landlord acts to receive his legally sanctioned share of the total product. The actual quantity of produce that the landlord can appropriate depends, apart from technical, climatic and market pricing factors, on the sharecropping household's ability and predisposition to produce, e.g. the psychological desire for self-improvement and betterment of the household's economic condition. This is important to the supplementation of the landlord's income, and is subject to market constraints; higher productivity does not necessarily mean higher income, because of supply and demand factors at sale.

We might of course expect a tendency on the part of the sharecropper to procure as much as possible for himself by concealing quantities of produce from the landlord. This was found to be the case by Keegan in his study of sharecropping in the South African Highveld.[43] In the Jordan Valley, absentee landlords appear to be aware of this probability, since at harvest time they visit the farm on a daily basis checking and overseeing the product quantity. The potential quantity by which the tenant can augment his legally designated share in this way is severely restricted; the landlord will have assessed a very accurate approximation of crop productivity per dunum, since one of the results of the introduction of new varieties of seeds, fertilizers, etc., is to produce stable production rates.

From the foregoing discussion, I would suggest that the following elements are necessary to conceptualize sharecropping as a mode of production:

1. the antecedent existence of product markets in which the process of commoditization may be either extended or restricted;
2. the diffusion of juridical ownership of the constituent elements of the means and objects of production, but with landlords invariantly holding juridical ownership of land;
3. the concentration of economic possession of the constituent elements of the labour process in the charge of the sharecropper;
4. the appropriation of the economic surplus is legitimated on the basis of a private contract between consenting parties which is sanctioned in law and tradition;
5. the class relation between landlord and sharecropper is based on formal economic freedom.

These elements allow us to construct the concept of sharecropping as a mode of production.

Commentators such as Fatimah Halim are mistaken when they consider that the appropriation of the economic surplus is based on a form of 'forced labour'. Halim argues:

> Lacking access to the means of production, labour is forced to sell its power in a system of low remuneration. The price of labour within the sharecropping system has no determinate level. It is the outcome of relations of servitude existing within the village.[44]

This passage reveals a gross misunderstanding of Marx's notion of free and unfree labour. For Marx, labour (in the capitalist mode of production) is free in a dual sense. First, the labourer is 'freed' from ownership of the means of production, i.e. he is legally alienated from the means of production. Second, the only force making the labourer return to his workplace each day is the economic need to feed and clothe himself and his family. In general, the proletarian enters the factory because he has no means of economic existence other than the sale of his labour power. Unfree labour, on the other hand, is labour which is forced by extra-economic compulsion to work, that is, labour which is *forced* to work on threat of violence (normally military and most commonly, sanctified by law and social convention). Two notable examples of unfree labour are slavery and serfdom. The slave is the property of another person and is legally forced to do that person's bidding, normally within certain moral parameters. The serf is normally forced to contribute a certain portion of his labour for work on the lord's demesne. Both these forms are marked by the threat of violence. The same cannot be said for sharecropping; no person or power forces the tenant to sign the contract. We should also be clear on Halim's first point. 'Low remuneration' is not a sign of unfree labour. It may be an index of lack of economic power but not of unfree labour.

**Degree of development of the division of labour**

The social division of labour of enterprise in the sharecropping system is normally based on simple forms of co-operation compatible with household-type production. Job designations tend to be broken down on sexual lines, and there is very little job fragmentation. Men normally do the skilled work such as ploughing, harrowing and irrigating, and most of the other work is shared between males and females, e.g. sowing, transplanting, harvesting and packing. Women and children tend to do the weeding.[45]

In recent years, with the introduction of drip irrigation, there have been seasonal changes in the division of labour. Increasingly, wage labour is being employed at harvest time, due to the increase in productivity brought about by 'green revolution' technology. This has resulted in a 500–800% increase in crop yield.[46] This crop abundance is often greater than the harvesting capacity of the peasant household and thus the household division of labour, for some households, is complemented at harvest time with the addition of day labourers through the main harvest period: 48% of sharecroppers employed day labourers for some period during harvest time.[47] These day labourers are predominantly female and their introduction does not fundamentally alter the family division of labour on the farm.

In recent years, however, we can begin to trace a number of important changes in the sexual division of labour on the sharecropping household farm. These changes are determined by both internal and external factors. The internal factors are linked to the introduction of intermediate technology, which has reduced the labour time required for irrigation. For example, under the furrow system earth furrows had to be constructed manually – by fathers and sons – and these had to be checked and repaired on a daily basis. The introduction of drip irrigation ended this menial cycle since this irrigation system, once in position, needs very little labour time spent on repair and maintenance. Drip irrigation has further labour-saving features that greatly reduce the time spent in the fields, e.g. fertilizers and insecticides can be introduced into the fields by mixing these in at the pressure pump, so fertilization and insecticidation can be carried out without the farmer having to go into the fields to spray or spread fertilizers by hand.

From fieldwork experience we can begin to detect a new pattern in the division of labour on a number of farms, particularly in the village of Jiftlik. This pattern shows that the work of the female family members is becoming much more important and that female family workers are almost numerically equivalent to male family workers at a ratio of 49:51.[48] The new pattern shows the sharecropper working with his wife and daughters as opposed to with his wife and sons. The pattern is not as yet generalized but it is clearly emergent. I would hypothesize two reasons for the emergence of this pattern, one economic, one cultural.

First, the opportunities for economic employment outside the indigenous sector have greatly increased with the expansion of an urban settlement policy under the Likud version of colonization. This has increased the number of jobs available for Palestinian workers in construction. There is now also the additional possibility of work in agriculture on kibbutzim and moshavim. This increased opportunity for employment is contiguous with a decrease in the amount of labour time required on the farm for traditional types of male labour. While the numbers are not substantial, more males have shown a willingness to partake of these opportunities, which have certain real economic benefits, not least a regular source of income on a weekly or monthly basis. This is particularly true of the village of Jiftlik, where 60% of peasant households have their permanent residence in other towns and villages.[49] The older sons of the Jiftlik peasant household tend not to follow their parents and work on the family farm. Rather it is the unmarried daughters who accompany their parents to the family farm while their brothers remain in the permanent residence (most commonly Tubas or Tamun) where it is easier to commute to the Israeli economy on a daily basis.

Second, as opportunities for work outside the farm increase for males, daughters and wives extend their activities in production. Cultural barriers still largely stand in the way of daughters working outside the home, but the family farm is still within a symbolically pure environment where the family honour can be safeguarded.

Thus any increasing proletarianization of male members of the family farm is concomitantly offset, to some degree, by the peasantization of family daughters. The division of labour in sharecropping is still centrally constructed around the household as the unit of labour supply and with the reduction of manual tasks and the increase in work opportunities outside the farm for male offspring, increasingly women are constituting the more important source of labour supply in sharecropping.

Finally, the division of labour remains based on relatively simple levels of co-operation in the labour process. The introduction of intermediate technology has not radically altered this position. The reasons for this stasis are not difficult to adduce: the production process is constrained by the natural processes of crop germination, climatic and ecological conditions. The difficulty of speeding up these natural processes imposes constraints on labour specialization and job fragmentation.

**Development of the productive forces**

By productive forces Marx refers to the development of technological and scientific innovations which increase the productivity of labour. The term also refers to developments in methods of organization and planning of labour activity which augments the productivity of labour.

In the north Jordan Valley, as we have seen, there has occurred a virtual revolution in the development of the productive forces, which since the early 1970s has increasingly extended its impact over the whole agricultural sector in the region. The important point is that these 'green revolution' improvements all belong in the category of *intermediate technology*, and they have been introduced without high levels of capitalization costs. All these improvements are within the potential financial horizons of most farmers in the region. The important effects of these innovations are fivefold. First, they considerably cut down the amount of labour time required for irrigation. Second, because the drip irrigation system is water-conserving, and because the water restrictions imposed by the military authorities refer to volume of water and not land under irrigation, farmers are able to bring most, if not all, their fields under irrigated production. Third, problems of ground and water salinity in the area (in artesian wells due to depth restrictions) has led to specialization mainly in tomato and aubergine production. These two vegetables have been developed in high-salinity resistant strains. Other vegetables are grown, such as peppers, courgettes and cucumbers, but not to the same degree as tomatoes and aubergines since they don't have the same saline-resistance qualities. This has almost, but not quite, led to duo-crop agriculture in sharecropping. Fourth, the introduction of this technology has increased crop tonnage five- to eight-fold per dunum, making agricultural production in the region much more desirable to farmers and other groups. Farming has become both more productive, and was initially more profitable to sharecroppers and landlords alike. Fifth, the 'green revolution' has made farmers more dependent upon market relations. The number and extent of market relations have multiplied as all farm inputs (e.g. seeds, fertilizers, drip irrigation equipment and pumps) have now to be purchased rather than being produced on the farm.

In the region as a whole, the forces of production are uniform throughout the different modes of production functioning in the region (sharecropping, cash tenancy and petty commodity production). What differentiates them is the degree of capitalization. Sharecroppers are the most advanced in capitalization of intermediate technology but the least advanced in the capitalization of machinery and equipment.

## Articulation and reproduction of sharecropping

In the previous section I attempted to identify sharecropping as a mode of production specified by determinate relations which are *internal* to its cohesion as a distinct form of agrarian institution. However, this internal structure of relations does not exist in isolation from the wider social formation of which it is a part. In fact, it is not inconceivable that the most important parameters of social determination lie not in the internal form of sharecropping but the external processes of articulation which determine its reproduction. In the following section I consider the problem of reproduction and articulation from three interrelated aspects. These are, first, the process of commoditization, second, the function of merchant capital and, third, the blockage of the capitalist mode of production and capital accumulation.

**Commoditization**

By commoditization, I refer to a process with dual aspects.[50] These consist of on the one hand relations of commodity *production* and on the other hand relations of commodity *consumption*.

Commodity production refers to the process of the production of goods as commodities for sale on the market. The majority of peasant societies produce at least a portion of their crop for market exchange and retain a portion of their crop for self-subsistence. It is of course possible that an agrarian producer may not be engaged in any form of market exchange but be producing solely for purposes of self-subsistence; this is normally referred to by the concept, *natural economy*. In the context of the West Bank and historical Palestine the phase of natural economy belongs to prehistory. In the contemporary situation of sharecropping in the Jordan Valley, crop production is wholly dominated by commodity production. Sharecroppers in the region meet very little of their consumption requirements from their own production activity. This phenomenon is not generalized to other modes of production that exist alongside sharecropping in the region; it is a phenomenon unique to sharecropping. For example, petty commodity producers and cash tenants, while being mainly geared to commodity production, produce significant quantities of crops – e.g. lentils, corn, wheat, onions, garlic and spices – for family subsistence requirements. Subsistence production is absent from sharecropping because the landlord contractually specifies the use of available land, and it is not in his economic interests to have a proportion of his land used for family subsistence production. In this situation the tenant can siphon off for subsistence requirements only a small portion of the crop he is contractually bonded to produce. Moreover, this ability to siphon off is severely restricted by the process of agricultural specialization. Specialization in the production of particular commodities is almost inevitable once production comes under the sway of market forces, since it is only by specialization, particularly on smaller farms, that farmers can achieve limited economies of scale. Specialization in sharecropping is, as we have described, limited to vegetable crop production.

Specialization in commodity production is the obverse side of another phenomenon: the intensification of relations of commodity consumption. Commodity consumption refers to the process of meeting subsistence and production needs through purchases on the market. With specialization in commodity production the sharecropper's relations of commodity consumption become intensified at two levels; first as a consumer and second as a producer. We have seen that sharecropping households are not engaged in subsistence production in any significant degree. They therefore have to use the market in order to meet their most basic nutritional requirements. Here we have the paradox of producers of food having to buy all their foodstuffs on the market place. The more important side of commodity consumption, however, is the intensification of commodity relations at the level of production. This intensification increased significantly from the early 1970s with the introduction of new production techniques. These new techniques accentuated the process of market consumption and made the farm economy more dependent on pricing factors outside the direct control of the direct producers, such as rising costs of seeds, fertilizers and drip irrigation equipment.

The sharecropper in the Jordan Valley is under the sway of complete commoditization and this process is becoming more intensive the more the sharecroppers' productive needs are met through agricultural technology produced for the world market. Sharecropping is now dependent on a pricing system which is largely determined at the international level.

**Merchant capital**

The harbinger of international market relations – of commoditization – is merchant capital. In the first section of this chapter I presented a formal outline of the circuits of commercial and interest-bearing capital. I suggested that these circuits act as articulating instances through combining divergent modes of production in the social formation through the principle of market relations. I want to consider how this model is useful for understanding the articulation of sharecropping.

The sharecropper, at the end of the cycle of crop production, encounters commercial capital in the form of the commission agent, who operates as a wholesaler in the *hisbeh*. This function is generally centred in Nablus, but it is to be found to a lesser degree in Jenin and Tulkarem. The commission agent sells the crops at auction, either in the West Bank or Jordan, and takes 5–12% of the market price of the crop for the function of sale. Moreover, the commission agent provides further services which tie the sharecropper and landlord (if he is not himself a commission agent) to him. Thus, all tomatoes have to be packed in regulation boxes for transportation. The commission agent sells these boxes to the farmers for 40 shekels each – in a season the farmer will use hundreds, if not thousands, of these boxes – and when the sharecropper returns the box he receives a refund of 35 shekels. This is lucrative since in the course of a season the commission agent will deal in hundreds of thousands of boxes. The commission agent is often the main transporter of produce for which service the sharecropper has to pay him. Commission agents are further engaged in the sale of the means of production: seeds, fertilizers, insecticides, plastic and drip irrigation equipment.

There is a visible trend towards *vertical integration* of market functions in a number of powerful merchant families (but particularly with the al-Masri family who acts as commission agent for almost one third of the sharecroppers in the north Jordan Valley).[51] Vertical integration encompasses the auctioning of crops, transport, packaging and provision of agricultural inputs. Vertical integration allows the merchant to extensify and intensify the process of unequal exchange. But although the process of vertical integration is well established, monopoly pricing is not a relevant outcome since landlords and sharecroppers remain independent from the commisssion agent. Landlords and tenants can still obtain the best possible price for their produce by marketing in some *hisbeh*s rather than others.

There is another process at work which offsets the relative freedom of sharecroppers from commission agents. This is the process of the *horizontal integration* of commercial capital and the sharecropping mode of production. Under these conditions the commission agent is also the sharecropper's landlord. In this situation the dual exploitative processes of surplus appropriation and unequal exchange are unified in the figure of the merchant–landlord. The result of this process is not just the juxtaposition of two processes of exploitation but the concentration and intensification of both processes. The sharecropper is increasingly faced with problems associated with monopoly pricing in which he has to purchase seeds, fertilizers, insecticides and drip irrigation equipment at prices set higher than those on the free market. A not insubstantial 14.3% of sharecroppers have landlords who are also their commission agents.[52] The actual process of concentration of landlord and merchant functions is inhibited due to the fact that a property market in land has not emerged. The failure of a property market to develop is a direct result of Israeli colonial practices.

In the Jordan Valley we can discern a trend, associated with the extension of commoditization, for commercial capital to dominate the sharecropping mode of production through the processes of vertical and horizontal integration. Articulation in this instance is also associated with integration.

**Capital accumulation and the blockage of the capitalist mode of production**

There are a number of possible reasons for the non-dissolution of sharecropping and for the failure of capitalist relations of production proper to replace sharecropping.

Most commentators have a tendency to view sharecropping as either a backward or transitional form of agrarian social system. The majority of Marshallian economists, for example, focus on the 'technical inefficiency' of sharecropping. Marx viewed sharecropping as a transitional form of capitalist ground rent, which was destined to be superseded by capitalist ground rent proper. Timothy Keegan is notable for contradicting current opinion and analysing sharecropping as an exceptionally rational mechanism (under determinate conditions) of capital accumulation.[53]

In the context of the Judaization and colonization of land, as it was outlined in the Allon Plan, and its effects on the Jordan Rift Valley, the revitalization and consolidation of sharecropping was an eminently rational response on the part of landlords and landlord–merchants to the problems of capital accumulation. This is the case for a number of reasons.

Sharecropping was revitalized in the region through the introduction of intermediate technology. This outcome was largely brought about without any concomitant capitalization in expensive machinery and equipment, since sharecroppers typically rent mechanical equipment such as tractors and their accessories. Capitalization in intermediate technology involves, by and large, an annual expenditure on the purchase of seeds, fertilizers and insectitides. The exception to this is drip irrigation equipment, which has a maximum life expectancy of no more than a few years provided that it is properly maintained. The main item of depreciation on account is drip irrigation, but compared to the purchase of tractors, harrows, carts, buildings, etc., this is a relatively negligible item of expenditure.

The phenomenon of annual capitalization contains the clue to the causes of the consolidation of sharecropping during the early 1970s and in particular of landlord–merchant integration with the sharecropping mode of production. In the context of the ongoing Zionist colonization of the region, it would require an unfounded optimism on the part of any investor to proceed on the path of capitalization of the means of production along capitalist lines. This would involve a substantial investment in mechanical equipment (tractors, accessories, etc.), storage facilities, farm buildings and intermediate technology. With some of these items the capitalist farmer would be presenting a budget for capitalization and depreciation that would cover expenditures over periods from 10 to 30 years.

Given the ever-present and very immediate danger of land expropriation, water restriction, crop control and market control by the military authorities, such a long-term investment plan becomes an unwarranted financial risk. If a landlord has his land expropriated, or his water supply restricted to such a degree that farming becomes unprofitable, or the authorities impose crop restrictions, or if the authorities impose market restrictions, the farmer will lose a great sum of money. If the above scenario emerges in the sharetenancy situation, however, the landlord or landlord–merchant in general stands to lose only half of one year's capitalization and drip irrigation costs. This may be quite considerable but is not nearly as much as the sum involved for the capitalist farmer.

The appeal of sharetenancy over agrarian capitalism under the present constraints is that it offers an extremely lucrative interim solution to the drive for capital accumulation in the money form. The result of the policies of the Israeli state is thus indirectly to discharge conservation effects on the sharecropping mode of production.

One would expect once these conservation effects were discontinued, for example if the *de facto* annexation of the West Bank becomes *de jure*, or if a non-socialist Palestinian state was established in the West Bank and Gaza, that sharecropping would be superseded. But this is not a foregone conclusion and cannot be argued for on the basis of a teleological explanation. This supersession could occur either through sharecropping's subsumption in the form of capitalist ground rent or in the transformation to capitalist forms of agrarian production. Whatever the short-term outcome, the long-term future of sharetenants is sure to be one of social mobility, whether upward mobility to the ranks of petty commodity producers or capitalist producers (the least likely outcome) or downward mobility to the rural proletariat (the most likely outcome for the majority).

## Conclusions

If we work with a *restricted* concept of modes of production, to use Wolpe's terminology, this allows us to develop a pluralization of different modes of production. The main conceptual innovation I have introduced is to present a theoretical concept of the sharecropping mode of production and to argue that sharecropping can be specified at the same level of analysis as other modes of production in Marxist discourse, e.g. slavery, feudalism, capitalism, etc. If we accept the legitimacy of this, the concrete analysis of sharecropping can usefully supplement ongoing debates on the articulation of modes of production.

## Notes

1. The work on which this chapter is based was carried out as part of a socio-economic development study for the Arab Thought Forum in Jerusalem.
2. For a trenchant restatement of this classical position see Warren, 1980.
3. See Marx and Engels, 1962: pp. 37–8.
4. See Frank, 1978: pp. 140–72.
5. See Friedmann, 1980.
6. For a summary of the debate see McEachern, 1976.
7. See Althusser and Balibar, 1970.
8. For a summary of the realist position see Bhaskar, 1978.
9. Laclau, 1977: p. 23.
10. Wolpe points out a similar distinction to the one I am making. Wolpe defines 'restricted' and 'extended' concepts of a mode of production. The restricted concept defines a mode of production in terms of production relations, whereas the extended concept includes the process of circulation in the definition. See Wolpe, 1980: pp. 34–42.
11. See Marx, 1976: pp. 283–307.
12. Compare Laclau, 1977: pp. 15–50.
13. Compare Dupré and Rey, 1980: pp. 138–60.
14. See Kay, 1975: pp. 84–124.
15. Laclau, 1977: p. 34.
16. For an excellent account of the concept of articulation see Foster-Carter, 1978: pp. 210–43.
17. This points to the neo-Gramscian approaches to politics in Marxist discourse which are most ably developed by Poulantzas, Laclau and Mouffe, and Jessop.
18. All figures in this section come from *The Jordan Valley Development Survey* which I carried out for the Arab Thought Forum, Jerusalem, during 1982–3. The table sources will be given in the following format: ATF: table 1.1.1, etc.

19. ATF: table 4.1.1.
20. ATF: table 1.6.5.
21. ATF: table 1.6.7.
22. ATF: table 1.3.2.
23. ATF: table 1.3.3.
24. ATF: table 1.3.4.
25. ATF: table 1.4.10.
26. ATF: table 1.5.2.
27. ATF: table 3.1.9 and 3.3.1.
28. ATF: table 6.1.1.
29. ATF: table 6.1.2.
30. ATF: table 4.1.1a.
31. ATF: table 4.1.2.
32. ATF: table 4.1.1.
33. See Marx, 1981: pp. 938–50.
34. For a relevant historical account of sharecropping in Palestine see S. Tamari, 1983.
35. See Bonne, 1948: pp. 116–7.
36. See MacPherson, 1968.
37. ATF: table 4.3.13.
38. ATF: table 6.3.1.
39. ATF: table 6.3.3.
40. Marx, 1976: p. 283.
41. This important thesis is largely absent from the contributions to the *Journal of Peasant Studies* special issue on sharecropping, vols. 2 and 3 (1983).
42. ATF: tables 4.3.12 and 4.3.3.
43. See Keegan, 1983: pp. 201–25.
44. Halim, 1983: p. 262.
45. See Tamari in Tamari and Giacaman, 1980: pp. 26–30.
46. Ibid.
47. ATF: tables 4.4.10 and 4.4.12.
48. ATF: table 4.4.20.
49. ATF: table 3.1.1.
50. For a very important study and conceptualization of commoditization, see Bernstein, 1979.
51. ATF: table 6.6.3.
52. ATF: table 6.6.5.
53. See Keegan, 1983.

## References

Althusser, L., and Balibar, E., 1970, *Reading Capital*, London: New Left Books.

Banaji, J., 1975, 'The peasantry in the feudal mode of production: towards an economic model', *Journal of Peasant Studies*, vol. 3.

Benvenisti, M., 1982, *The West Bank and Gaza Base Project Interim Report* no. 1, Jerusalem.

Bernstein, H., 1979, 'African peasantries: a theoretical framework', *Journal of Peasant Studies*, vol. 6.

Bettleheim, C., 1972, 'Theoretical comments', in A. Emmanuel, *Unequal Exchange*, London: New Left Books.

Bhaskar, R., 1978, *A Realist Theory of Science*, Sussex: Harvester Press.

Bonne, A., 1948, *State and Economics in the Middle East*, London: Kegan Paul.

Carmi, S. and Rosenfeld, H., 1974, 'The origins of the process of proletarianization and urbanization of Arab peasants in Palestine', in Krausz, E. (ed.), *Studies of*

*Israeli Society: migration, ethnicity and community.*
Dupré, G. and Rey, P., 1980, 'Reflections on the pertinence of a theory of the history of exchange', in H. Wolpe (ed.), *The Articulation of Modes of Production*, London: Routledge and Kegan Paul.
Foster-Carter, A., 1978, 'Can we articulate "articulation"?', in J. Clammer (ed.), *The New Anthroplogy*, London: Macmillan.
——— 1974, 'The modes of production controversy', *New Left Review.*
Frank, A. G., 1978, *Dependent Accumulation and Underdevelopment*, London: Macmillan.
Friedmann, H., 1980, 'Household production and the national economy: concepts for the analysis of agrarian formations', *Journal of Peasant Studies*, vol. 7.
Halim, F., 1983, 'The major mode of surplus labour appropriation in the West Malaysian countryside: the sharecropping system', *Journal of Peasant Studies*, vol. 10.
Harris, W. W., 1980, *Taking Root: Israeli settlement in the West Bank, the Golan and Gaza-Sinai, 1967–1980*, Chichester: Research Studies Press.
Kay, G., 1975, *Development and Underdevelopment: a Marxist analysis*, London: Macmillan.
Keegan, T., 1983, 'The sharecropping economy of the South African Highveld in the early twentieth century', *Journal of Peasant Studies*, vol. 10.
Laclau, E., 1977, *Politics and Ideology in Marxist Theory*, London: New Left Books.
MacPherson, J. B., 1968, *Possessive Individualism*, London: Oxford University Press.
Mann, S. A. and Dickinson, J. M., 1978, 'Obstacles to the development of a capitalist agriculture', *Journal of Peasant Studies*, vol. 5.
Marx, K., 1976, *Capital* vol. 1, London: New Left Books.
——— 1981, *Capital* vol. 3, London: New Left Books.
——— and Engels, F., 1962, 'The Manifesto of the Communist Party', *Selected Works* vol. 1, Moscow: Foreign Languages Publishing House.
McEachern, D., 'The mode of production in India', *Journal of Contemporary Asia*, vol. 6.
Meillassoux, C., 1972, 'From reproduction to production', *Economy and Society*, vol. 1.
Nakhleh, K. and Zureik, E., 1980, *The Sociology of the Palestinians*, London: Croom Helm.
Pearce, R., 1983, 'Sharecropping: towards a Marxist view', *Journal of Peasant Studies*, vol. 10.
Poulantzas, N., 1975, *Political Power and Social Classes*, London: New Left Books.
——— 1975, *Classes in Contemporary Capitalism*, London: New Left Books.
Rodinson, M., 1973, *Israel: A Colonial Settler State?*, New York: Monad Press.
Roseberry, W., 1978, 'Peasants and Proletarians', *Critique of Anthropology*, no. 11.
Tamari, S., 1983, *The Dislocation and Re-constitution of a Peasant Society: the social economy of agrarian Palestine in the West Bank Highlands and Jordan Valley.* Draft PhD thesis.
——— and Giacaman, R., 1980, *Zbeidat: the social impact of drip irrigation on a Palestinian peasant community in the Jordan Valley*, Birzeit: Birzeit University.
Warren, B., 1980, *Imperialism Pioneer of Capitalism*, London: New Left Books.
Wolpe, H. (ed.), 1980, *The Articulation of Modes of Production*, London: Routledge and Kegan Paul.

# 5. Capitalist Farming and Small Peasant Households in Egypt

*Georg Stauth*

The submission of households to the needs of capitalist development has been discussed on various levels.[1] In recent economic discussions on the 'household' and 'home economics', much attention has been given to the 'value of domestic work' and to the methods of an evaluation of 'unpaid work in the household' (Goldschmidt-Clermont, 1982).

In this chapter, I would like to show how the organization of the production process in a market-oriented agricultural production system determines the structure of income of a subsistence-oriented, small peasant household in rural Egypt. Household studies in the main are interested in bridging the borderlines between production and consumption, and between monetary and non-monetary transactions in coventional economics. The problem posed here is not the problem of separation or measurement of transfers between 'different' spheres of the economy; the problem followed here is rather one of the distinction of various types of transactions. A better understanding of the relations between the 'household sector' and the 'market sector' would have to deal not only with the 'quantitative' mechanisms of their interactions, but would also have to look to the underlying structures, which in the last instance define the quality of life and work relations in the different sectors. Thus, all my attention in this article goes to the problem of how specific types of transfers between a given production system and a number of households determine the type of social and political interaction between the various households themselves, and between a network of households and the system.

The households observed here are those of the *fellahin* in a village in Egypt, and the production system in question is the *'izba* system as applied in Egyptian capitalist farming.

## The agrarian farm versus the small peasant household

Egyptian capitalist farming was and still is to a large extent the cultivation of cotton, although in recent years the so-called new crops – fruit and vegetables – have gained major importance. The unit of production for cash crops, the *'izba*, was in its classical form based on peasant wage labour. The *'izba*[2] – the corporative property of the families of local state representatives or of families with a strong village background competing for their integration into the 'state class' – is a creation of the 19th century, a creation of Egypt's agrarian capitalism as it developed in the framework of the rising world market. It is thus comparable with the hacienda and other big farming units being created under relatively similar conditions in other regions of the world. Today, the *'izba*, as the classical unit of cash-crop production, has lost its former importance in Egyptian agriculture; in the areas of my own research, the big estate as a production unit separated from the village economy has in fact almost completely vanished.

This is due mainly to the fact that Nasser's land reform of the late 1950s and early 1960s, and the mechanisms of state agricultural policies established at district and village levels, led to a division of the land of the old *'izbas* and to a political and social reintegration of the landowning class into the framework of village life. As a result, the landlord became part of village society. Apart from the partial social and political deprivation of the old landowning class, the *'izba* system of organization of the working process in cash-crop production occurred without discontinuity in the remaining big agricultural units.

It was then put under local control and became embedded in local communal structures as it, on the other hand, inverted the old networks of securing and distributing subsistence. The maintenance of subsistence farming within the *'izba* system served to reduce the overhead cost of reproduction. In addition, a state apparatus whose revenue remained basically tied to agricultural surpluses was fully engaged in the development of various types of agencies for securing the system's reproduction – that is, the reproduction of the given relations of production (and also, of course, for observing and securing the reproduction of the individuals subsumed under the system). While in other parts of the world new changes in agriculture arose, the state mechanisms intervening in Egyptian agriculture prevented basic changes. All over the world, agribusiness implemented changes resulting in the speedy displacement of small, so-called inefficient producers (see, for example, Feder, 1977). New forms of control of agricultural output and its distribution were introduced through the production contract system as a 'rational' way of integrating small producers to the system in cases where the type of product or social constraints seemed to require the prevalence of small producers. In Egypt, only some of these changes implemented by the 'new' subsumption of agriculture in the world economy were experienced as effects of state intervention in agriculture rather than as effects of direct-system operations in the form of agribusiness.

The maintenance of the *'izba* system meant the opening of the option of keeping agriculture as the 'excellent' business of the state bourgeoisie in securing both its private and its public revenues. Thus, the *'izba* system remained the form of keeping the small peasantry alive by incorporating their labour force into a system of internationally articulated commodity production and by externalizing the networks for securing and distributing the necessary means of subsistence. But then externalization of the local communal structures of reproduction on the 'economic' level only meant their exclusion from levels of integration that were set up by the system itself. That is, the systematic integration of the spheres of production and the life situations of the people were left to realms that took the characteristics of very old forms of integration and regulation: coercion and political power, but also passion and sentiment.

The development of the *'izba* system marked the patterns of social differentiation within Egyptian rural society: the rise of a state military and/or local patriarchal landowning class on the one hand, and a process of proletarianization of the small peasantry on the other.[3] These processes can best be studied on the level of organizational and economic structures of households.

Households that are relatively self-contained and self-sustained units have become rare, while households whose incomes are based entirely upon remuneration through the wage mechanism have never been fully developed or remain entirely exceptional cases. On the big farm, the household more or less becomes an income-pooling unit that recruits its members through kinship: a monetary system. Here, the non-monetarized subsistence processes and transfers remain necessary to this system only in a non-economic sense: they are used to maintain loyalty and to keep the heads of households in power. In other words, the integration of Egyptian agriculture into the world economic system has created a putting-out system which then subordinates all *necessary* relations as work *useful* for accumulation.

The proletarianized peasant households, on the other hand, remain basically units of consumption and production for the reproduction of their members. The self-sustained processes of production for direct consumption are kept within a rigid system of division of labour between sexes, topographically separated between field and household: these processes remain the necessary basis of reproduction of the working peasants, while through the selling of their labour force to the given putting-out system, the *'izba* system provides for income for the purchase of commodities that are now considered necessary.

Wage relations occur in various forms – daily wage labour, seasonal migratory labour, and all-year-round migratory labour – and they play an important part in the consumption funds of the small peasant as well as in sharecropping arrangements and occasional reciprocal work relations.

All these relations entail different levels of social relations and experience: the production of subsistence means and small commodity production entail a specific network of social relations tied to reproduction and to the defence of the known modes of securing survival and making a living. This network is shared among individual households. Within the construction of the moral economy, the opportunities offered 'on the market' are a well-calculated part of interaction and dealing within the neighbourhood and among the village fellows.[4]

These spheres of normative *and* rational action are basically separated from the functional mechanisms operating through the *'izba* system. The striking discrepancies of social interaction are thus based on the contradictions between the moral traditions of everyday practice and the functioning necessities of the system. On the local level, then, the coercive political structure compensates for the weakness of the economic apparatus of the *'izba* in regulating and smoothing these contradictions. Coercion tied to the distribution of the subsistence base, on the one hand, and political dominance of the tradition, on the other hand, are the means of compensation for the system's lack of functioning for and within the local contexts.

## The internal *'izba* processes and their variations

The internal processes within the *'izba* system are grouped around three major areas of concern:[5]

1. distribution and allocation of property;
2. division and allocation of crops; and
3. division and disposition of labour.

The *'izba* system entails a distinct logic – of an apparatus that did and still does function so as to tie the specific local tradition of an intended autonomous reproduction of self-producing and personally interrelated individuals to the world economic system. I want now to show how this function has developed a specific and, in its own logic, dynamically operating set of interconnections between property, produce and labour. I illustrate my argument with reference to 12 units to which the *'izba* system was found to be applied. All these cases differ very strongly in their size and property, in their selection of specific crops, and in the extent to which they employ labour; they are all similar, however, as far as the channels of interconnecting and combining these basic elements of the production system are concerned.

### Property relations

For all the holdings to which the *'izba* system applies, proprietorship is a trust, consisting of an incorporated family (*'aila*) that regroups its members through the various channels of kinship relations. The members of these trusts belong to a class of landholders that has separated itself strongly from the rest of the rural population, basically since the times of the Muhammad Ali regime. The employment of the *'izba* system depends on kinship descent of the trust proprietors and not primarily on the size of the holding. There exists an obvious division between various forms of distributing and allocating landed property, and because of this the organizational structure of the holding is strongly differentiated.

Depending on either form of descent – whether rural (local, patriarchal) or urban (state military and exceptionally mercantile) – the immediate commitment of the trustee family of proprietors in local affairs takes various forms; two generalizations could be made. First, big holdings, with proprietors of no or little kinship base in the village, tend to be managed as production systems strongly oriented toward pure commercialization. Second, holdings with strong kinship ties in the village tend to maintain strong subsistence-based cash production systems.[6] Thus, in all the cases studied, a general pattern of farm management can be observed.

The family trust nominates one of its members to exert the effective possession of its land in a form of usufructuary relations. He, the cultivator (*muzari'*), or the owner (*ha'iz*), is sometimes the only member of the trust to remain in the village. Often, but not always, the *muzari'* is the most dominating figure within the trust and, if he is not the village headman (*'umda*), he has close relations to him. All the trust members together combine a variety of functions and potentials of access to various resources that, only by means of their interconnection, can provide for the securing of property, the appropriate market channels, and the use of the labour force. The interdependencies between the members of the corporative family could be best described as follows: no property without access to high-ranking state functions; no symbolic presentation of power without access to land.

The trustees benefit not only from formal transfers made on a regular basis in return for leasing their land and other facilities to the farmer, but also from irregular, informal, and reciprocal transfers taken from the *'izba* household and from the field.

**Allocation of crops**

The land of the big farm unit is cultivated in four separate parts, each part fulfilling specific functions within the reproduction process of the apparatus of the *'izba* itself:

1. One part of the cultivated land is entirely devoted to production for the consumption of members of the household unit (and also, though not in a strictly regulated way, for the consumption of the households of the trust members). Other factors determine the size of the land devoted to this part: basically state regulations on crop rotations or the needs of the livestock. The subsistence crops maintained in this part are wheat, clover and maize.
2. Another part of the land is cultivated to sustain (*ma'ash*) the permanently employed labourers of the household and the farm, so this part too is entirely reserved for subsistence crops.
3. In most, but not all cases, a small part of the *'izba* land is let under leasing terms, tying the farm closer to the villages' small peasants. The rationale here is social rather than economic: the land is leased either to tenants who are poor members of the *'aila* or to confident small peasant labourers who care for maintaining loyalty to the *'aila* among the poor villagers. Again, in most cases this land is cultivated with subsistence crops for direct consumption in the tenant's household.

4. In a strict sense, there remains only a part of the productive land for the cultivation of essentially marketable produce, such as cotton, vegetables and fruits (i.e. cash crops).

The subsistence crops devoted to the household (category 1) are, in fact, not distributed entirely inside the unit itself: feeding the livestock ultimately leads – at least for the greater part – to a marketable produce. Grains and poultry are also used for the frequent subsistence transfers to the households – urban or village-based – of trustees of the farmland. In 1977–8 a part of the grain produce was to be transferred to the state-run co-operative at fixed prices. Furthermore, grain was used – in many but not all cases – to pay the yearly remuneration (*mizaniya*) of such traditional craftworkers as the hairdressers, including the one who cuts the donkey's hair. At the end of the harvesting season, the religious tax (*zakah*) is paid in kind, not in quantities described by the Koran and the shari'a, but rather in terms of a symbolic act of mercy to those villagers who have no relatives and are unable to sustain themselves fully by their own means.

The subsistence crops cultivated to remunerate the permanent workers on the farm (2) serve as a subsistence base to these workers' households. The extent to which these crops are transformed into marketable produce or kept for direct consumption depends on the extent to which the needs of the households are tied to market exchange and consumer goods.

On the other hand, of course, not all the produce earmarked for market exchange (4) actually goes to the market. Occasionally, extra payment in kind for the daily wage labourers (*anfar*) and for the daily paid children and young women (*ayal*) is taken from crops, mainly fruit and vegetables when they are being harvested. Also, the trustees find occasion when some parts of these crops can be appropriated for their own benefit.

Finally, the produce of the land leased for loyalty purposes (3) may be partly consumed by the leaseholder (who in most cases is a small peasant) and it may (instead or also) be handed over to the *'izba* farmer for sale on urban markets (depending on the leasing terms).

**Different uses of the labour force**

In general, the *'izba* involves five various types of productive activity and correspondingly uses different types of labour force:

- labour that is tied to the household of the *'izba*;
- labour that is exclusively ascribed to the supervision of the process of agricultural production and/or the use of agricultural technology;
- heavy labour for cash-crop cultivation, which is related only to specific seasons;
- children's and women's labour, which is tied to specific works and also related only to specific seasons; and
- occasional labour, which is tied to the maintenance of the animals and/or instruments of the farm.

In relation to the general types of labour employed, the *'izba* processes can be traced down to basically three different types:

1. internal household processes (supervisors, servants);

2. agricultural labour processes (agricultural workers); and
3. handicraft processes for the maintenance of the farm (crafts).

The forms in which these types of labour input are remunerated can also be classified in three different variations. Labour inputs attached to the internal household processes on the one hand, and to supervising and instructive functions in the agricultural labour processes on the other (1) are permanent labours that are remunerated in a sharecropping arrangement (called *ma'ash* in the local vernacular); labourers in this relation get a plot of land that they usually cultivate for their own subsistence. This labour relation is basically associated with reproductive functions in general: the supervisional and instructive workers are: the *khauli*[7] who is the super-instructor of all working processes on the farm and the chief 'negotiator' between owner and workers; the *rayyes*, who supervises a group of hard-working day labourers and who disposes of the appropriate agricultural know-how; and the *kallaf*, who deals with all functions attached to the maintenance of the livestock, including the rearing and feeding of animals, and the hard work attached to the natural fertilization process. Household labourers (*shaghala*), children, women, and men (the latter as cooks and servants) are employed on the household management of the farm and waged within the sharecropping arrangements.

Daily wage labour (2) is basically involved with the processes of cash-crop production on the fields. Children, women and men are employed in different operations with different wages: men basically for hoeing and cutting processes, and women and children for the strewing, gathering and picking processes, with wages between 25 and 75 piasters.

**The functional structural apparatus of the agricultural farm**

The structural apparatus of the big farm can be best illustrated by looking once again at the distribution of the cultivable land of the big agricultural unit. The farm is generally divided into four parts: the subsistence part for the owners' household, the subsistence part for the permanent workers, the cash-crop production part, and the part rented to loyal villagers.

The owners' subsistence part includes the feed for the livestock, a part of which legally is to be delivered to the state co-operatives against cash, and a part which is to be distributed as *zakah* (religious tax) among the very poor in the village. This category also includes the *mizaniya*, the in-kind remuneration of craftworkers employed to repair and to maintain livestock and agricultural implements.

I have said that cash-crop production also entails some type of subsistence for the workers themselves, not only in the form of wages but also in the form of gifts taken during the harvesting times. And here again, of course depending on the type of crops, legal regulations must be observed concerning the delivery of a part or the total of the crop to the state co-operative.

If we further analyse the four parts of the farm, taking into consideration the quantity of labour inputs, the way labour is marketed and the labour conditions, we will certainly find that there is a structural difference between these four parts of the land. It may seem surprising that even on the micro-level of a single farm it is possible to show the structural differences between the various factors entering the production process. In this respect the subsistence parts, irrespective of their diverse purposes, constitute a specific unit of production. The labour input in subsistence products is much smaller than in the market crops. Most of the field work (ploughing, fertilizing, even harvesting) is carried out by the permanent workers who get their remuneration through this type of crop itself.

The labour input to the cash crop is considerably more extensive, and here wage labour is the usual type of employed labour. Women and men are deployed in different labour processes, and the permanent labourers function as instructors and foremen and as mediators between capital and labour, even if they only handle the machinery. The piece of leased land is subject to leasing stipulations and the position of the leaseholder himself. In general, the leaseholder himself cultivates the land partly for his own consumption and partly for the market, where his crops are sold along with the produce of the landowner of a big farm. The leaseholder, as I have already noted, has a specific strategic function for the farm in terms of maintaining loyalty structures inside the village.

The internal processes and functions can thus be associated with the specific functions they gain in the external, social involvement of the farm in total, as shown in Table 5.1.

**Table 5.1**
**Internal Functions and External Involvement**

| A | B | C | D |
|---|---|---|---|
| workers' subsistence | household subsistence | cash crops | rented land |
| supervision, mediation between capital and labour | holders' consumption | market | rent |
| permanent workers *khauli/rayyes* | *zakah*/poor *mizaniya*/crafts trustees | wage labour | relatives/dependents |
| power relations | | capital (economic) relations | power relations |

## Labour-force formation and the privatization of reproduction

The small peasants possess only small and simple means of production all tied closely to the household of the peasant family or to the immediate use of the individual (Stauth, 1983). All other production means, often even the plough and working animals, are controlled by the *'izba* and so in most cases are the objects of production – land and water. To gain access to these preconditions of production, the small peasant has no other way than by selling his own and/or his unit members' labour. It is therefore both on the level of their preconditions of existence on the one hand, and on the level of social relations in meeting everyday needs – that is, on the level of monetarized inputs – on the other hand, that the small peasant household is totally dependent on the big agricultural farm. This dependence can be best visualized by comparing the internal structure of the familial unit of production and reproduction of the small peasants with the structure of the *'izba*, which I have described above.

As in all agricultural operations here, access to land, the distribution of produce and the allocation of labour input are of structural importance.

**Property relations**

The unit of the small peasant household is the family nucleus. Landless peasants and proprietors of one *feddan* and less tend to separate their households from their larger families, even if because of lack of opportunity they still share the house with their relatives' families. Independence and liberty, as they say, are more important than working for the wealth of others. On the other hand this separation between the household units of the small peasants leads to a lack of solidarity that can be seen in often long-lasting quarrels among relatives and close neighbours. In such cases of conflict, the *fellahin*, since they tend to leave their *'aila*, are concretely unable to match the strength of the big owners, who permanently symbolize their property and power in strong kinship relations. Those who share kinship with the big owners, but have no access to the property trusts, remain symbolically tied to the politically and economically forceful power group centred around the big farmholders, in many cases with only little in return. The non-property kinship groups within the village are of little or no (i.e. purely symbolic) importance for those who want to stand up against the dominance of the propertied, powerful kinship groups. In most cases, the kinship groups of the landless and small peasants are not even known by name to many of their members.

**Allocation of produce**

Subsistence crops are the same for rich and poor in the Egyptian village; there are no other crops for the rich to live on than those that feed the poor (of course, their diets are different). The poor, however, never or only exceptionally sell produce from the field; almost all produce is processed through the peasant household. It is men's work to care for the raw inputs from the fields; it is women's work to transform them into consumption goods. The small peasants sell their women's products (not their own): cheese, butter, milk, fat and poultry. The share of these products that is sold determines what is bought for consumption within the household. If there are marketable surpluses they derive from these goods in the main, even if there is some commodity production within the small peasant unit; marketable surpluses derive typically from products prepared in the house, like baskets, wool and knitted products (these also involve men's work), never, or very rarely, from the production of cash crops.

**Labour relations**

The small peasants, as we have seen, possess limited means of production, including land and water, their access to which is reached through selling their labour. The allocation of their labour in agrarian farms is intended to subsidize the small family unit of production; the forms of allocation of the labour force are represented in four domains:

1. wage labour;
2. subsistence agricultural labour;
3. subsistence household labour; and
4. small commodity production.

The variations of labour forms in each single domain differ strongly. We shall concentrate on the most important ones. The labour force of the small peasant unit of production is sold in wage-labour relations in the cash- and government-crop spheres of the agrarian farm, and so men's, women's and children's work is materialized in the cash crops deriving from the big agricultural farms.

Another form of wage-labour relations is *tarahil* labour, which is contract labour subject to seasonal migration; it is used today basically in the urban sectors for state-run projects for construction and communication. The historical equivalent of this type of labour is the so-called Asiatic form of forced surplus labour extraction. Subsistence wage labour, in the form of traditional sharecropping arrangements, is deployed in household services and in supervisory and instructive work for the farm production. Here, the wage gives access to the production of subsistence means; it thus gives the possibility of the reproduction of the alienated labour force, but it does not cover the actual reproduction of this labour: subsistence means have to be processed and transformed within the unit itself. This holds true as well for the structural conditions in which the cash wages for the daily labourers are delivered and consumed. To understand fully the importance of the various forms of labour relations, one should take into account that field labour (whether wage- or subsistence-oriented), household labour and small commodity production within the household constitute an integrated unit of production for the means of consumption by the producers themselves. These producers themselves decide whether to allocate their labour to self-contained and self-sustained forms or to alienate their labour power within the systematic realm of the cash-crop production of the big agricultural farm. The decision on whether production is orientated for self-consumption or allocated for the production of market produce depends on the extent to which the small units of production have access to means of production (land, animals, etc.).

It also becomes clear that the attachment of the *fellahin* to the normative orientation of all social organizational forms of subsistence production is by no means reactionary. It is a rational decision to defend and to protect the known channels of organizing for survival; on this level, peasant behaviour reflects a rather rational attitude. If there were other options, given this basis for enhancing the chances of survival, the peasants who depend on subsistence production would give it up readily in favour of new means. But, all things considered, the reproduction of the social organization of labour within the subsistence-orientated small peasant unit is dependent on the continuity of production relations within large-scale agriculture. On the other hand, the fact that small peasant producers can safeguard their reproduction within the framework of large-scale agriculture, with its different labour and production conditions, means that all exploitative means lie in the hands of the big-farm owners and the trustee families.

With these various labour relations, the *fellahin* maintain the set of preconditions of their cycle of reproduction. The opportunities offered to them to maintain their life-cycle within the framework of the *'izba* system are structured in such a way as to exploit a cheap labour force, which is cheap only because it provides for the cost of reproduction (within the household unit) by itself – that is, by its own subsistence production for direct consumption. To defend their lifestyles and to maintain their control of the modes and functions of immediate reproduction, the *fellahin* become enslaved and tied to the *'izba* system by the necessity of gaining monetarized household inputs. For the small peasants *wage income pays for the social possibility of maintaining their lifestyles*. For the apparatus of accumulation, the big agricultural farm, this form of separation of production and reproduction serves to externalize the costs of reproduction of the exploited labour force. *This economic separation and exclusion of the modes and styles of making a living* from the systematic integrative and regulative forces of the local accumulation system, the *'izba* system, has to be substituted by non-economic forms of social integration, which I will now describe.

## The power system of social and private relations

It was shown above that the types of valuation of the *fellahin*'s labour force determine the general social preconditions of a reproduction which basically remains subsistence-oriented, and therefore does not include (or includes only to a very small extent) the production of means of consumption. This part – the very real, *necessary* part, so to speak – of the social process of production is left to the private control of the individual worker. It is not directly subject to the systematic integrative and regulative forces of the economic apparatus of the big farm, but remains organized as a contradictive force in local communal spheres of households and household-networks. On the basis of their large extent of subsistence and use-value production, the households maintain their traditional moral ties by which they judge and struggle against a hostile, capitalist world.

The economic apparatus of the big farm therefore performs no functions of social integration outside the working processes on the farm itself. If this is so, how does the *'izba* system maintain its dominance over the local-communal milieux of the moral economy and their structural subsumption to it?

The lack of social integrative and regulative forces on the economic level is compensated within the *'izba* system by frequently coercive power relations. Without these power relations, the reproduction of the big-farm system in Egypt would be impossible. As a result, the local power structures are tied to the economic apparatus of the *'izba*. No other institution of power can be allowed to establish itself on the local level. This, of course, affects the functioning of the local agencies of the central state apparatus as well as the socio-political processes by which the social milieux of reproduction form a potential unit of political will and constitute a proper base of moral and political unrest. The local power structure is therefore one of the principal sources of momentum for the *'izba* system itself.

The political mechanism of the big-farm apparatus operates on three different levels:

1. On the level of the labour process on the farm itself, a rigid hierarchy of coercive mechanisms has to compensate for the lack of 'work commitment' of a labour force that has to replace machines, but remains tied to the experience of its own self-contained and self-sustained production. The protection of the valuation process of this labour force is only possible by coercive means.
2. A constitutive element of the *'izba* system is the economic separation between production and reproduction: that is, on the one hand the economic apparatus entails the necessity of extorting cheap labour from the *fellahin* and of imposing lower costs of reproduction and, on the other hand, of stipulating a household network where the larger portions of income are taken from the production for self-use. On this level, the weakness of integrative forces in the economic part of the system means that the political part has to control the symbolic means of potential moral and political defence of lifestyles exercised within the social milieux of reproduction. This control covers the various fields in which the morality of production for the generation and regeneration of the people is expressed, and the linkages of sustenance, everyday practice and lifestyles are formed. In other words, the normative apparatus that is based on the subsistence redoubt of the small peasants' households is to be occupied and determined by the accumulative apparatus of the *'izba* system. The members of the big-farm family trusts exert an initial influence over the definition and judgement of religious practices and tradition of

lifestyles, the forms of exerting legal sanctions, and the organization of peasant labour, whether it is officially stimulated (as in Nasser's time), or initiated on religious or other traditional grounds.

3. On a third level of political interference between the state and the peasants, the *'izba* system has to exempt the central state apparatus from its inherent obligations for a general application of laws, administrative regulations, and socio-political benefits, since all of these would contradict strongly the actual and possible forms of protecting the valuation of the *fellahin* labour force within the *'izba* system itself.

**Coercive mechanisms of the labour process**

The small peasant household employs various modes of securing the reproduction of its members' labour force. Subsistence production coincides with petty commodity production, daily wage labour with sharecropping arrangements. The basis of reproduction remains the subsistence redoubt of the household; the only occasional and/or seasonal commodification of the labour force fosters little 'work commitment' among agricultural labourers. Today, now that the professional agricultural worker (*nafar*) who seeks daily employment all during the year has become rare, the working discipline is considered weak; the work of women, children and old and/or occasional workers remains committed to the sphere to which they normally are attached: subsistence–reproduction labour inside the household unit.

There are no machines that could dictate the working rhythms in a way similar to the anonymous objectification exerted by the rule of capital when it has truly subsumed the labour process to its realms.

Instead, there is a coercive apparatus by which the big farm governs the labour process. The regimentation of workers begins with the contracting for the work (*'amula*) and ends with strict obedience to orders and to the rules of the work *(nizam ash-shughel*).

The *'amula* starts with the orders of the landholder (*muzari'* – the trustee member of the owners' league) to one of his permanent workers (whom he terms, according to the *'izba* regime of the old days, '*khauli*' and sometimes simply '*rayyes*') to hire a specific type and number of labourers for a specific task. For the hoeing of rows (*khutut*) of several *feddans* of cotton, potatoes or green beans, for example, he would need a group of males; the size of the group varies according to the size of the land, the available labour and the calculations of the *muzari'*. (Eight men hoe one *feddan* in one day – a tiring stint, as one can tell from just a half an hour of participation – eight hours of work under a burning sun with temperatures up to 35°c in the shade.) The *khauli* would not himself contract the labourer but rather contracts another *rayyes*, who functions here as a contractor (*mu'awil*) for a group of workers – in most cases relatives, friends and/or members of the neighbourhood. The contractor guarantees the appearance of a specific number and a specific quality of labourers on the field for the next day, and he is normally paid in advance.

Labour-contracting is one of the most important events of everyday public life in the Egyptian village. The evenings between seven and eight o'clock are reserved for this undertaking, and at this time of the day one can see the men walking around in the village to see their clientele. The small *mu'awil* has to see his labourers to tell them where to go the next day, and he will contact the men either in the coffee bar or at their homes. At the least, he will then be offered a cup of tea. Should it be women or children that are needed and contracted, his own wife and children will be sent off to tell them, or, should he want a chat, he will go himself to talk with the men of the house.

The small village contractor normally will participate in the work on the field as a type of foreworker and remain close to the group of workers. In addition to his own 'wage' he makes about five piasters for each of the contracted men. *Rayyes* never participate in the work of women and children (*ayal*), but only supervise this work; for this, he gets about 2.5 piasters per head.

A permanent worker on a big farm (*khauli*, *rayyes*) sometimes – depending on the work season and the needs of labour input on the farm – appears as contractor on his own: in case of a labour shortage in a neighbouring village, the *khauli* of the big farms there would come and ask his help to send workers to the fields in his village. The biggest farms in an area of three to five villages, for example, have well-established systems of contracting labour from neighbouring villages; these contractors often do not join the labourers in the fields, but take only contracting as their business and pay better wages to the *rayyes*, who would have to lead the groups contracted through him.

The normal village-based big farm (between 20 and 40 *feddan*) never hires more than 12–15 male workers (*anfar*), or 30 women and children (*ayal*), even in the height of the season. In exceptional cases of traditional *'izbas* still in operation, however, sometimes hundreds of *anfar* and *ayal* might be hired.

The working order on the field (*nizam ash-shughel*) depends, of course, on the number of workers employed in a given process, and also on the type of instruments used and on the necessary skills. Hoeing, for example, requires higher skills than the seeding of cotton, which is done by children. The hoeing of cotton rows requires a specific technique to cut and scratch the thick and hard crust of soil, dried by the sun after irrigation, without spoiling the plants. The *mu'awil* and/or the *rayyes* of the hired daily workers (*anfar*) assure the quality of the work, and because skilled labour is required only skilled labourers are allowed to work. Work commitment in this case is relatively high since both the *mu'awil/rayyes* and the worker follow 'professional' rules and both commitment and performance can be judged individually. In other cases, small groups of workers led by a single *mu'awil/rayyes* require only slight supervision from the farm's employees, and the *muzari'* and the *khauli* might pass by no more than once or twice during the day to share a few words with the *rayyes*.

**Non-economic dominance over the peasant community**

A hierarchical power-structure is important for the supervision and instruction of the labour process, but the system must also control the spheres of organizing and producing everyday life and ensure a strict operation of these spheres on the economic level. The basic mechanisms with which the big landholding trusts of the *'izba* system interfere in the moral milieux of use-value production by the small peasantry and their life-styles are the traditions of the community (*taqlid al-qariya*). These traditions vary from region to region and sometimes from community to community, and they depend on the socio-ecological conditions of the communities themselves. These traditions prescribe a specific symbolic and obligatory framework which, as a result of historical struggles between the central state and religious/legal orthodoxy on the one hand and the villagers' lively practices, culture and symbolic defences on the other hand, form the specific boundaries of social practice in the village.

This framework as a whole remains bound to the ritual and argumentative protection of the known and given modes of securing subsistence. It thus entails specific local and traditional patterns of defence of peasant lifestyles.

Wherever the tradition of the village gains a specific importance within the communal public, it is exactly on that level that the landowning group of the village has to interfere:

- they interfere in decisions over what is allowed for by religion and tradition;
- they impose their morals as they exercise public power within the community in arbitrating between the parties in cases of conflict and criminal acts;
- they infiltrate the modern and traditional socio-political organizations of the peasantry.

The basic institutions of such interference are the village headmanship (*'umdiya*), the membership in a sort of arbitration committee (*lagna al-musallahat*), and (in exceptional cases, depending on the local importance of the *sufi* orders) the membership in a family mosque, symbolizing the importance of the lineage.

To settle a personal dispute between members of the same household unit (relatives in the broad sense of neighbours and friends) by arbitration is a task that normally is given to one of the big owners, the *kubar al-'aila*, who is recognized as the religious man; disputes on working conditions, wages, and so forth between the *kubar* and the labourers are settled by what is known as a modern-thinking (Nasserist) authority. (Such a person might, in Nasser's time, have organized local labourers' unions. He would still be a person of political influence in any of the various 'government parties' thereafter and, of course, remain one of the *kabir* of the village with his own big holding.) Disputes over construction, traffic and irrigation are arbitrated by a university-educated *kabir*, who manages his farm dynamically, paying the best wages and owning modern agricultural machinery, but who otherwise is weakly placed in the kinship structure of the village. Religious matters (including disputes over inheritance) are arbitrated by the *Azhar* graduates among the *kubar*. And, finally, in political and legal matters – but also possibly in all the other matters mentioned – the *'umda* is the competent authority.

The unity of ruling family trusts governing the *'izba* system is evident in discriminatory practices in daily social interactions: for example, no small peasant would dare to greet a member of the *'umda*'s family while still sitting on his donkey, or to remain sitting as one of the *kubar* entered the room. As long as the *kubar* stands, the others must also. (But of course, the reverse is not true; a family trust member is not supposed to stand up to greet one of the small peasants.) If one does not observe this tradition, it is *'aib*, a disgrace or a shame. This is an implicit means of imposing loyalty (*'asabiya*) and exerting political power by the *kubar* families.

The normative idealization of kinship and its symbolic defence – a necessary element of the organization and production of survival in the milieux of reproduction of the small peasantry – is one, but only one, instrument of binding the small peasantry to the systematic and institutional framework of the big farm. The maintenance of strong kinship ties, as we have seen, is imperative for the *'izba* trust membership; kinship is not, however, the sole and automatic guarantee of access to this privileged class. Furthermore, there is a strong social differentiation among this stratum of the landowning class.

An analysis of the 25 richest landowners in a village of 5,000 inhabitants, situated in the centre of the Nile Delta, suggests that only three (all of them the managing trustees of different owner-groups of four to six members) keep regular contact with each other, both within the village and in their external relations to the urban centres of Tanta and Cairo. And only by doing so do they really represent the system. The regularity, exclusivity, and hierarchization of these relations are essential for the distinct formation of this group and for their political dominance of the village.

The background, means and type of these relations may be summarized as follows:

1. The direct patriarchal origin of the group includes the village's founders: the forefathers, grandfathers, and fathers who had established the most significant political and religious functions in the village;
2. The regeneration of kinship relations within the main branch of the family has created vague relations of land ownership between the three families: every one of these three large owners claims to have the right to possess (*hiyaza*) parts of the other owner's land;
3. They share common characteristics of cultivation and economic behaviour; market-oriented cultivation of profit-producing crops, 'clever-

ness' with labourers and common contact with traders;
4. They share kinship relations and have similar interactions with the respected and influential members of the family in Cairo and with other esteemed and distinguished friends of the family;
5. Most of them have middle school or high school education;
6. The maintenance of diverse religious and traditional rules and laws is binding for this group and respected by the other villagers, although the underlining and maintaining of these norms have demonstrative, formal character;
7. They acquire urban-, middle- and upper-class consumption articles such as modern furniture, cars, television sets and refrigerators; the purchase and repair of these items create mutual contact and communication; and
8. Informal, limited reciprocal relations determine several forms of friendly and interactive behaviour among members of the group.

One or more of these characteristics are shared by the rest of the big landowners in the village, but their relations are not so strong as in the case of the three village leaders. The form of relations among the members of the rich strata of *'aila* (families) reflects at the same time the form of relations that a particular family has with members of poorer families. Both the strict maintenance of religious and traditional rules and demonstrative show of modern urban wares are ways of asserting economic and social status in the village. So because of the practice of village tradition, in the form of submitting the village population to the power of the ruling stratum, the acquisition of modern wealth is becoming the real means of social differentiation.

Should these means fail to establish a strict hierarchical order of power in the village, the *taqlid al-qariya* mechanisms possess a still wider range of means to impose power and to exert it.

## Pauperization of milieux of reproduction

Today, the Egyptian peasantry is systematically integrated by an economic and power apparatus. The set of mechanisms through which this apparatus operates *vis-à-vis* the small peasantry is called the *'izba* system – that is, the farming system applied by the landowning class in Egypt.

This system only exists through the employment of the labour of the peasant. The specific *type* of valuation of the labour of the peasantry leads to the continuation and creation of subsistence- and use-value orientated networks in and between households – networks whose interaction mechanisms are moral and symbolic rather than economic. The creation of these disintegrated milieux of a moral economy is a consequence of a specific *type* of the essential *interaction* between the small-peasant household and the cash-crop orientated production system: the valuation of the basically subsistence-reproduced labour force.

The example clearly shows how a market sector creates and structures a household sector that it is unable to supply or to integrate socially through modern, civic means: the market system in its periphery creates the subsistence modes of living which then are only governed by pure non-economic and coercive means. It is the form of transactions between the two sectors that creates a specific form of social interaction.

The system has its own rules and mechanisms, its internal and expansive regulations. It exists separately from the necessary means of survival of the rural population, and hence these are the necessary preconditions of its own existence. It is this systematic, organized, regular, public production that is considered as social, i.e. surplus production. It is the individual, specific, direct, use-value orientated work for reproduction that is considered as 'personal' and 'private'. Marx's classical separation between necessary and surplus labour implied the necessity of surplus for the society as a whole. The crisis of growth reminds us of the value of the necessary. The real crisis of today, which becomes even more apparent in the core–periphery relations, is underdevelopment of the necessary and not the crisis of growth.

## Notes

1. Raising the problem for earlier stages of capitalist development Laslett and Wall (1972) might serve as an example; see also Flandrin (1979: 50–111). For a recent discussion see Smith, Wallerstein and Evers (1984).

2. *'Izba* today has two meanings in rural Egypt. First, it refers to the big estate that was owned by the 'state-class', which had its base of wealth and status in the military administrative ranks of the capital rather than social ties with the rural communities. This class was more or less destroyed by the Nasserist Revolution and the legal and regulative structures it brought forth. This class was replaced then by the class of village headmen and notables (*kubar*) who relied upon strong social ties to the village population. The institution of the *'izba*, with few exceptions, vanished. But the specific system of use of labour that it entailed was employed on the fields of villages' upper strata, who for long had struggled to put their feet on the paths of the old Pasha and foreigner class. Second, the old *'izba* often provided some huts for the labourers who were permanently employed on a sharecropping basis. With the changes mentioned above, these 'labour camps' increasingly turned into small villages. Today, they dispose of their 'own' land; however, in administrative terms, they form no separate unit from the old villages.

Big domains and latifundia have a long history in Egypt, which will not be elaborated here. Becker is still a most prominent resource (1924), as is Shaw's annotated translation of a source from the late Mameluk time (1964). Property relations have been extensively studied by Gabriel Baer (1962), especially in his articles on the 'village community' and the 'shaikh' (1969). For a critique and amendments to Baer's studies, see Disuqi (1975).

The term '*'izba* system' here, refers to a specific type of farm management and labour employment, regardless of whether it applies to the traditional *'izba* or – as today – mainly to the big holdings of the village upper social class. Thus, it could be easily compared with similar production systems in agriculture, like the hacienda (see, for example, Richards, 1979).

3. Small peasants in Egyptian statistics, are those who possess less than five *feddan*. The tremendous splitting of landholdings in the last years and the decrease of productivity even in the subsistence sphere do allow us (for the regions observed in the delta of the Nile) to define all holdings between one and five *feddan* that do not employ the one or the other variation of the system described above as the *'izba* system (see also Radwan 1977), and all holdings of less than one *feddan*, as belonging to this category.

4. I use this term 'moral economy' here in the way introduced by E. P. Thompson (1974), to refer to a mechanism of social integration in milieux of use-value production, surrounded otherwise by a capitalist world.

5. For a detailed evaluation of the socio-economic and political structures of the *'izba* system when applied in the big village-based capitalist farms, see Stauth (1983: chapter 5).

6. Nasser's land reform policies – which in dissolving the economic base of the ruling classes of the *ancien régime* were quite rigidly applied – led to new types of estates: politically loyal family groups of the old class divided their lands according to the new laws. The urban branches of these families had three options: to rent the land, to have it cultivated by a local agent (*khauli*), or to leave it in the hands of a relative who remained in the village. Both the division of land and the new forms of management led to a reintegration of the villages.

On the other hand, the old village-based classes of the *'umda* and *shaikh* families strengthened their positions by fully taking advantage of the new educational and administrative system. In general, one could claim that Nasser's policies led to a new unification of the rural élites. However, due to the essential importance of kinship relations (and their local strength in quality and quantity), there are big differences to be observed in applying the *'izba* system even from one village to another. For an intensive appraisal of the state-class relations of the dominant state in rural Egypt, see 'Auda (1979). On Nasserism and land reform, see Abdel-Malik (1968), Radwan (1977) and Zaki (1977).

7. This and the following functions were already exercised on the old domains of the late Mameluk era; see Shaw (1964: pp. 146f).

## References

Abdel-Malik, Anouar, 1968, *Agypten: Militärgesellschaft*, Frankfurt am Main: Suhrkamp.

'Auda, Mahmud, 1979, *al-Fallahun Wa'l-Daula*, Cairo.

Baer, Gabriel, 1962, *A History of Landownership in Modern Egypt, 1800–1950*, London: Oxford University Press.

——— 1969, *Studies in the Social History of Egypt*, Oxford: Oxford University Press.

Becker, C. H., 1924, *Islamstudien*, vol. 1, Leipzig.

Disuqi, Asim, 1975, Kibar Mullak al-Aradi al-Zira 'iyya wa-Dauruhum fi'l-Mujtama' al-Misri (1914–1952), Cairo.

Feder, Ernest, 1977, 'Agribusiness and the elimination of Latin America's rural proletariat, *World Development*, vol. 5, pp. 5–7, 559–71.

Flandrin, Jean-Louis, 1979, *Families in Former Times*, Cambridge: Cambridge University Press.

Goldschmidt-Clermont, Luisella, 1982, *Unpaid Work in the Household: a review of economic evaluation methods*, Geneva: International Labour Office.

Laslett, Peter and Wall, Richard (eds.), 1972, *Household and Family in Past Time*, Cambridge: Cambridge University Press.

Radwan, Samir, 1977, *Agrarian Reform and Rural Poverty: Egypt, 1952–1975*, Geneva: International Labour Office.

Richards, Alan R., 1979, 'The political economy of *Gutswirtschaft*: a comparative analysis of East Elbian Germany, Egypt and Chile', *Comparative Studies in Society and History*, vol. 21, no. 3, pp. 483–518.

Shaw, Stanford, 1964, *Ottoman Egypt in the Age of the French Revolution*, Cambridge: Cambridge University Press.

Smith, Joan, Wallerstein, Immanuel and Evers, Hans-Dieter (eds.), (1984), *Households and the World-Economy*, Beverly Hills, CA: Sage.

Stauth, Georg, 1983, *Die Fellachen im Nil-Delta. Zur Struktur des Konflikts zwischen Subsistenz und Warenproduktion im ländlichen Ägypten*, Wiesbaden: Franz Steiner.

Thompson, E. P., 1974, 'The moral economy of the English crowd in the 18th century', *Past and Present*, no. 50, pp. 76–136.

Zaki, M. G. D., 1977, *al-Qanun al-Zira'i*. Cairo.

# 6. Commoditization and the Small Peasant Household in Egypt[1]

*Kathy Glavanis*

The purpose of this chapter is twofold: first, to try to establish how far commoditization has proceeded amongst small peasant households in rural Egypt and to determine the factors hindering its further development; and second, to compare small peasant household production in Egypt with simple commodity production in agriculture within the context of advanced capitalist society. The latter comparison will be made in order to highlight the specificity of the productive enterprise in Egypt and the constraints on its transformation into simple commodity production or capitalist agriculture. Here I would like to indicate my heavy reliance on the work of Friedmann (1978a; 1978b; 1980a; 1980b; 1981) on the process of commoditization and on the nature of simple commodity production within advanced capitalism.

According to Friedmann, in order to determine the extent to which commodity relations have penetrated the productive process, it is necessary to look at the 'proportion of goods purchased at market determined prices for productive and personal consumption over time', as well as the extent to which there is mobility of labour and markets in land, other means of production, and credit (Friedmann, 1980b: 174, 160). Related to the above process and premised on it is the process of monetization, which 'in the aggregate tends to lead to commoditisation' (Friedmann, 1980b: 177).

Friedmann elaborates upon the process of commoditization as it relates to household production by indicating factors which she sees as either contributing to or resisting the further commoditization of the cycle of reproduction. Turning first to those factors which lead to the generalization of commodity relations, Friedmann states:

> Commoditisation occurs to the extent that each household is severed from direct reciprocal ties, both horizontal and vertical, for renewal of means of production and of subsistence, and comes to depend increasingly on commodity relations for reproduction. The process of commoditisation ultimately implies the individual status of each

> household. It becomes an enterprise, where relations to outsiders progressively take the forms of buying, selling, and competition. (Friedmann, 1980b: 162–3)

Despite generalized commodity relations at the national or international levels, Friedmann underlines the possibility of household reproduction resisting commoditization.

> Whatever the level of specialisation in production of commodities, if household reproduction is based on reciprocal ties, both horizontal and vertical, for renewal of means of production and subsistence, then reproduction resists commoditisation. If access to land, labour, credit, and product markets is mediated through direct, non-monetary ties to other households or other classes, and if these ties are reproduced through institutionally stable reproductive mechanisms, then commodity relations are limited in their ability to penetrate the cycle of reproduction. (Friedmann, 1980b: 163)

We thus need to ask: 1) to what extent is household production amongst small Egyptian peasants based on reciprocal ties, both horizontal and vertical, for renewal of means of production and subsistence; and 2) to what extent is access to land, labour, credit and product markets mediated through direct, non-monetary ties to other households or other classes? Or, looking at the small peasant household in Egypt from the opposite end of the spectrum, to what extent, first, have direct reciprocal ties been severed, and, second, has the household taken on an individual status, where its relations to outsiders take the forms of buying, selling and competition? In the discussion which follows, I will attempt to examine within the framework outlined by Friedmann the extent of commoditization of the reproduction cycle amongst small peasant households in Egypt.

## Productive consumption

By productive consumption I mean the tools, land, animals, seed, fertilizers, machines or other means of production necessary for the renewal of the peasant household. To what extent, then, does the small peasant household purchase these goods at market-determined prices?

### Tools

The most basic tool of the small Egyptian peasant is the *fas* (hoe). This multi-purpose tool is used for digging out the *zariba* (animal pen), for spreading *sibakh baladi* (traditional fertilizer, urine-soaked dirt) in the fields, etc., in addition to hoeing. Virtually all peasants own one. It can be purchased in district centre markets for the relatively small sum of £E3.00

for the locally produced version,[2] or for the slightly larger sum of £E5.00 for the imported types.[3] Usually there is no need to buy more than one hoe in a lifetime, and often they are inherited.

The second most basic and essential tool of the small peasant is the *sharshara* (sickle). This is primarily used to cut clover twice daily during the winter and spring months, to harvest wheat in May and to cut unripened maize stalks. Again, virtually all peasants own a sickle, but sometimes borrow a second from a neighbour or relative in time of need. Like the hoe, the sickle is produced by urban craftsmen and is sold in district centre markets for the small sum of approximately £E0.30. Sickles are usually bought once in a lifetime and are often used long after the teeth on the blade have disappeared.

The main tools used traditionally for ploughing and land preparation are the *mihrat* (two-animal wooden plough), the *loh* (wooden plank attached in place of the plough used for levelling the ground), the *'asabiyya* (wooden box-like instrument used to level ground by hand), the *batana* (triangular-shaped wooden instrument attached in place of the plough for making ridges within a field for irrigation purposes), and a second instrument called a *loha* (flat wooden instrument with handle and rope used by two people to make irrigation ridges). These tools are usually required by the peasant between four and six times per year. Traditionally these tools are jointly owned and used. They are usually attached to a given area of land which is irrigated by a single water wheel. The ownership of the tools is determined by the traditional method of theoretically dividing them into 24 qirats[4]. These rights are distributed amongst the peasants proportionately, depending on the amount of land held. The tools rotate amongst the group of peasants cultivating within this given area, but are under the charge of the *mu'allim* (master) who is selected from amongst the peasants themselves. He is responsible for making sure that these tools are used according to the priority of peasant requests without conflict. Likewise, if any tools need repairing, the master must arrange for it and collect the necessary sum from each peasant. Most of these tools are rarely replaced, however, but even the most expensive item, the plough, which costs £E15.00–20.00, would not be terribly burdensome when divided amongst ten or more households.

Three other traditional agricultural implements are essential for the small peasant: the *ghabit* (canvas donkey sack), the *shi'b* (forked stick used to support the donkey sack), and the *ma'taf* (woven palm basket). These three items are primarily used for the traditional method of fertilizing the land: urine-soaked earth from the animals' pen in the village and fields is dug up, placed in a basket, dumped in the donkey sack, and transported to the field. *Ratsh* (extra dirt which is removed to the end of the field when it is levelled) is used to refill the donkey sack and taken back to the animal pen where it is spread on the floor to begin once again the process. This is a very time-consuming process and precedes the ploughing of all land.

As necessary implements for the carrying out of one of the most important processes of peasant agriculture, almost all peasant households own these three implements. Donkey sacks can be purchased from district centre markets for the relatively small sum of £E2.00 and are usually replaced every few years. Supporting sticks are usually prepared by the village carpenter from the peasant's own wood or purchased from the carpenter for a small sum. A certain number of woven baskets are still produced within Egyptian villages by men who have this specialist skill. Some sell their craft production and others merely produce for their own consumption. Otherwise these baskets can be purchased from district centre markets. In 1976–7, a basket could be bought for approximately £E0.30. These also are usually replaced every few years.

**Land**

The majority of small peasant households acquire land through inheritance. Officially, inherited land needs to be registered in the name of the new owner at *al-Shahr al-'Aqari* (Land Registry Office), but many small peasant households fail to do so as they are required to pay a fee of £E1.00 on every £E100.00 of value.[5] Annually they are obliged to pay a series of taxes on the land, but Law 51, 1973 exempted all owners of three and fewer *feddans* from these taxes[6] (al-Najjar, 1974: 195). Thus, the bulk of small peasant households who cultivate their own land are not required to make cash outlays in order to ensure the annual release of the land for cultivation.

The ability to expand this inherited land base through the purchase of other land is usually limited. Agricultural land costs have become extremely high in relation to rural incomes, and no saving and credit facilities are available for such purchases. In 1974–5, the average annual income in rural areas was about £E65.00 (Ikram, 1980: 48); the cost of a *qirat* of good agricultural land had risen to approximately £E300.00 whilst land bordering on the builtup residential area of villages could be purchased for approximately £E1,000.00. Thus, purchases on the open market are not common for small peasant households. Other reasons for these limited purchases are land fragmentation and traditional agricultural technology, both of which will be discussed later.

Some small peasant households do manage over the years to buy an additional one, two, or three *qirats* of land. Usually these purchases primarily take place between the family or relatives, and often they take the form of a brother buying from his siblings their shares of the inheritance. More accurately, this process can be described as 'paying off'. In many of these cases, the market value of the land does not determine the price paid by the brother or relative as it is said to be 'within the family'. This phenomenon is especially true for sisters and other female relatives. Sometimes this can mean that a sister is only paid one third of the going rate within the particular village. Another strong tradition amongst small peasant households is the transference of one or two *qirat*s of land from the sisters' shares to the cultivating brother without payment. This is said to be a sister's recognition of her brother's greater need as head of a household and a way of assuring greater security in the future in the event of problems with her husband or in-laws. Finally, amongst the majority of small peasant households, sisters withdraw all of their rights to inheritance in order that their brothers' holdings may be more viable. All of the above mechanisms allow many small peasant households to reconsolidate the father's holding as it was on his death. Not all peasant households, however, are successful in their attempts at reconsolidation and hence further fragmentation takes place. This is usually the case where there is more than one brother who cultivates.

A traditional form of mortgaging[7] provides some small peasant households with an additional means by which to obtain a permanent extension of their land base. Given the lack of official credit facilities within the countryside, sometimes the only possibility for a landowner to obtain cash quickly is to mortgage his land. The exact nature of these types of mortgage contracts varies within the countryside, but usually the landowner receives half the negotiated value of his land, which is agreed to be repaid in a given period of time. From limited comparative data, however, it would appear that this type of mortgaging usually leads to the permanent alienation of land from its owner. It is not without significance that this type of mortgaging is sometimes called *gharu'a* (drowning). The prevalence of this form of mortgaging is difficult to ascertain in that the land officially remains the property of the owner and is therefore registered in his name in the co-operative records. Needless to say, the ability of most small peasant households to fund such a loan is limited, but the possibility of obtaining permanent usufruct rights to additional land through this method of delayed payment can be enticing.

To gain temporary access to a larger land base through various forms of rental arrangement is far easier for most small peasant households than is purchasing land. But land rented at the officially low rate is becoming less and less common (Stauth, 1979: 24). Where this kind of tenancy arrangement pertains, it would appear that there is a great likelihood that kinship relations between the tenant and landowner play an important role (Stauth, 1979: 24). Likewise, rents of this sort do not usually involve more than one fourth or one half a *feddan*.[8] In many areas, these rental rates have in practice already been raised. Moreover, those landowners wanting to rent out their new land are highly unlikely to choose this form of rent, which ensures a small return and a long-term sitting tenant.

As a result of the above process, the two main forms of rental arrangements which appear to be available to the small peasant household are short-term cash rents and unofficial sharecropping arrangements. Known by various names throughout the countryside,[9] short-term cash rents are far above the legal rate and have no security. The duration of tenancy usually varies from half to a full year. Most peasants can only afford to rent a few *qirat*s at a time in this way, with a very few managing to afford more than half a *feddan* (Stauth, 1979: 24). From limited comparative data, it would appear that there is a high degree of uniformity between short-term rental rates, both within a given village and between villages, at least within the Delta.[10] This situation seems quite different from that which pertains to land prices, which seem to vary widely both within a given village and between villages. Nevertheless, certain structural factors act to limit the feasibility of this kind of rental arrangement for small peasant households, namely land fragmentation and traditional agricultural technology. These factors appear to be less significant for renting than for its purchase. This aspect will be discussed later in this chapter.

Turning now to sharecropping, both the official and the unofficial types, this form of tenancy agreement would appear to be far less important than cash rents within the Egyptian countryside as a whole, and in particular amongst small peasant households. Although up-to-date statistics are unavailable, data from the Fourth Agricultural Census (1961) give us at least some idea about the extent of sharecropping, even if this data refers to a much earlier period. In 1961, sharecropping and other types of leases represented only 8% of all rented holdings, occupying 12% of all rented land (Abdel-Fadil, 1975: 21). The distribution of this type of tenancy within the category was likewise skewed. For small peasant holdings of less than 3 *feddans*, sharecropping tends to be negligible (Abdel-Fadil, 1975: 21).

Of course, the above data refer to the official type of sharecropping and no data are available on the extent of more disadvantageous forms, i.e. where the peasant pays more than half the costs of production and takes less than half of the produce. From limited comparative field data, it would seem that the exact conditions of this form of tenancy vary greatly, even within a very limited geographical area, and the ability of any given landlord to contribute less and take more is often based upon the historically determined social relations between the two parties, i.e. non-market forces.

However, recent data, although on a limited scale, would indicate a possible change in the nature of some sharecropping arrangements. With the increasing profitability of certain kinds of vegetable crops, sharecropping of the official, and even more so of the unofficial varieties, has become more profitable than even short-term rents. This reality is perhaps echoed in Section 33 of Law 67, 1975 on the 'organization of the relationship between tenants of agricultural land and its owners', which allows for the substitution of sharecropping for a cash tenancy if both parties agree. Such a form of sharecropping might thus be seen within the context of increased commoditization for a small peasant household, unlike the more traditional form which tended to inhibit this. Of course, the ability of a peasant household to sharecrop non-subsistence crops is dependent upon whether it has usufruct rights to another plot of land or not, on which the traditional subsistence crops can be grown.

Another form of temporary access to land for some small peasant households is called land exchange, *tabaddul* or *badl al-ard*. The primary forces leading to such exchanges would appear to be: 1) the government-imposed triennial cultivation of cotton on most agricultural land; and 2) the government policy of maintaining low cotton prices despite the increasing cost of inputs. As a combined result of these policies, sometimes two peasant households arrange informally between themselves to exchange land in order to lighten the burden of cotton cultivation for the peasant whose land has fallen within the cotton-designated area. As a condition of this exchange, the two households agree to reciprocate with a similar exchange the following year. Through such exchanges, which would appear to be based quite often on strong kinship ties, small peasant households are able to reduce the degree of commoditization over the long term, as none will have to be totally dependent upon the cultivation of cotton, which precludes the cultivation of wheat and maize, the two most important subsistence crops. The extent of the importance of such exchanges is difficult to determine as they are not recorded in the co-operative files. However, Stauth's research (1979: 26) and my own would indicate that it is a phenomenon in need of further research.

Finally, another means by which small peasant households can obtain a temporary extension of their land base is through various forms of labour service. Known throughout the countryside by various names,[11] this system is based upon the exchange of a peasant's labour for the usufruct rights of a designated piece of land. The exact amount of land to be exchanged is negotiated between the owner and the labourer, who is often a small peasant landowner; in some areas the amount seems to have varied according to the age and skill of the labourer (al-Bahi, 1955: 19–42). The extent of labour service in the Egyptian countryside is unknown, but there are some indications that it is waning as a form of agricultural labour (Stauth, 1978: 12–13). Other research suggests that it still has some vitality as a form for organizing labour and land within certain areas of the Delta at least.[12] Where this form does exist, it would seem to be based on close kin and social relations which bind the small peasant to the landowner over a long period of time (Stauth, 1978: 11–12). Thus, as a form of access to an extended land base, it generally acts to inhibit the commoditization of the reproduction cycle of the small peasant. On the other hand, if the small peasant household already possesses a plot of land, then it is possible that production on the labour service land can be of a non-subsistence nature, e.g. vegetables, and therefore can lead to the increased commoditization of the reproduction cycle of the peasant household.

**Animals**

Animals have traditionally played a crucial role in small peasant households in rural Egypt. The most important of these for the successful reproduction cycle of the small peasant are the *gamusa* (female water buffalo) and the donkey, and all strive to obtain access to this minimum. As far as agricultural production is concerned, the female water buffalo provides draft power for ploughing and irrigation, as well as with the most important source of fertilizer. On the other hand, the donkey provides the major source of transportation which is particularly crucial for the traditional method of fertilizing the land, a highly intensive animal and human operation for small peasant households.

Prices for animals are generally determined in the large weekly livestock markets of district centres, and sometimes the more distant governorate capitals. Even if an animal is going to be sold within a village or to someone in a neighbouring village, the common practice is for the animal to be taken to one of these larger markets for assessment to ensure a fair price. The majority of small peasant households obtain their animals in one of these large markets.

Animal prices in Egypt have risen dramatically over the last 10 to 15 years, due to the government's policy of protecting meat prices from international competition. In 1976–7, a three- to four-year-old female water buffalo cost between £E300.00 and £E400.00, while a cow of a similar age cost between £E200.00 and £E300.00. These prices should be contrasted with the average annual income of rural areas of about £E65.00 for 1974–5 (Ikram, 1980: 48). By 1981, the price for a three-year-old female water buffalo had risen to between £E400.00 and £E600.00.

Given the large disparity between the cost of a three-year-old water buffalo and the average annual rural income it is not surprising that most small peasant households cannot afford to buy their own animals. As a means of gaining access to such an animal without having to find the necessary cash, many small peasant households are incorporated into partnerships with better-off villagers or non-resident relatives. These partnerships, usually called *shirk*, seem from limited comparative evidence to vary in detail within villages and within regions (Stauth, 1978: 13–14; Hopkins, 1980: 69). Despite these differences in the forms of partnerships, a common aspect of nearly all such arrangements is the lack of freedom on the part of the small peasant household rearing the animal to sell it without the approval of the investing partner (Hopkins, 1980: 69). The timing of the sale and purchase of these animals is crucial to the successful reproduction of small peasant households and hence such decisions are often the source of dispute between the two partners (Hopkins, 1980: 69).

The exact extent of partnerships in animal ownership amongst small peasant households is hard to determine, but limited comparative research would indicate that a very large percentage of these households have access to animals through a partnership. This seems to be especially true of Delta villages (Stauth, 1978: 13–14; Hopkins, 1980: 69). In Hopkins's study of Zawiyat Ghazal in the province of al-Buhaira, about half of the animals were owned on a sharing system (1980: 69). However, if these data were disaggregated, this percentage would almost certainly be higher amongst small peasant households. Unfortunately, most data on animal production in Egypt do not include this kind of information, as those carrying out the surveys assume that the peasant who raises an animal owns it (Fitch and Soliman, 1983: 46–9). Thus, it would seem that while small peasant households obtain animals at market-inflated prices, in actuality through the non-market mechanism of a partnership the majority only pay a part or none at all of the purchase price of the animal which they raise.

Many small peasant households obtain temporary access to animals for ploughing and irrigation through informal co-operative relations. A large percentage of these households have regular access to only one large animal, while the traditional plough requires two. Many households must therefore continuously arrange for the borrowing of another animal in order to carry out the basic processes of land preparation. The exact extent and nature of these informal co-operative arrangements are difficult to ascertain. However, Stauth suggests that these kinds of co-operative arrangements for ploughing are on the wane and have been replaced by mechanized ploughing, for which the peasant must pay cash (1978: 15). Nevertheless, where they exist such relations would seem to help inhibit the commoditization process amongst small peasant households.

**Seed**

Amongst small peasant households, seed for the sowing of the main subsistence crops of clover, wheat and maize is usually provided for by part of the previous year's crop. If small peasant households have insufficient quantities of seed for sowing, usually they will borrow from a neighour or relative and repay in kind at the next harvest.

Certain kinds of seeds are obtained from government co-operatives. Due to the government's efforts to introduce various varieties of dwarf wheat in Egypt, high yield variety wheat seeds were distributed through the co-operatives at prices per *kila*[13] above the market prices of wheat in rural Egypt. It would appear from limited comparative data that many small peasant households refused to plant these kinds of wheat even though they were forced to buy this wheat seed from the co-operative because their allotment of fertilizer for clover was tied to its purchase. Cotton seeds must also be purchased from the co-operative since they are specially selected for each region. The same is true for rice and other compulsory crops such as lentils. All such purchases from the co-operative must be repaid after the harvesting of cotton at the end of the agricultural year, usually in the month of November. Some small peasant households purchase a variety of other seeds, in particular vegetable seeds, from specialized seed shops in district centre markets.

**Fertilizers**

Most small peasant households rely heavily upon the use of traditional natural fertilizer obtained from their own animal pens. If all labour is unremunerated, such a method of fertilizing the land avoids a cash outlay. But although this method is very effective, it is also very labour-intensive; each *qirat* of land requires approximately 30 loads to be considered adequately fertilized. Children's labour is often used for this tedious task, but if the small peasant household is unable to muster the necessary family labour, then someone needs to be hired. In 1981, a young boy of 13 could be paid between £E1.00 and £E1.50 per day at the height of the fertilizing season.

Another and more common strategy adopted by small peasant households who are unable for various reasons to devote the necessary labour to this process but who are unwilling to spend cash on wages is to reduce the number of loads per *qirat*, sometimes by half. This under-fertilization in the long-run has negative effects on the productivity of the land, but momentarily acts to inhibit the commoditization of the reproductive system of the small peasant household. The exact extent of the adoption of this strategy is difficult to assess given the lack of data on the use of natural fertilizers in rural Egypt.

In addition to natural fertilizer, small peasant households also use a considerable amount of chemical fertilizer, a practice which has increased substantially since the establishment of co-operatives at the village level. This trend is indicated at the aggregate level, where the quantity of fertilizers advanced to agricultural producers through the co-operatives on a short-term loan basis between 1956 and 1967 increased over 300% (Abdel-Fadil, 1975: 149). Fertilizers for clover, wheat, cotton, maize and other compulsory crops, depending on the area, are distributed amongst all cultivators whose land holdings are registered in the co-operative records. This method of distribution of course excludes all illegal forms of tenancy from the right to co-operative fertilizers, etc., at least directly. The amount distributed is proportional to the size of the landholding and its division according to the officially determined crop rotation pattern. All this means that those who do not have officially registered landholdings or those who deviate from the official crop rotation scheme, for instance by growing more clover and less cotton, have to buy fertilizer from the district centre markets at a rate higher than that of the co-operative.[14]

On the average, according to one estimate, most small peasant households annually take short-term credit for fertilizers and seeds from the co-operatives that amounts to between £E10.00 and £E20.00 per *feddan* (Stauth, 1978: 15). However, the use of fertilizers is not obligatory and peasants can avoid the outlay if they want. Thus, to a certain extent they have the ability to control the extent of commoditization of this part of the reproductive cycle.

**Pest control**

Traditionally, cotton pests were the responsibility of the individual household and were fought with family labour on small peasant holdings. With the establishment and generalization of government co-operatives, however, pest control passed out of the hands of the individual households and into the hands of the co-operative. This process led to a further extension of the monetization of the reproductive cycle of small peasant households. The local co-operative became responsible for organizing teams of young children, who were paid a wage, to pick off the infested leaves during the hot summer months. When needed, the co-operative organization would also oversee the use of pesticides on infected cotton. All of the above costs are calculated and proportionally charged to all cotton cultivators. As a result, given the government-imposed triennial crop rotation of cotton, all landholders incur these costs at least every three years. One practice of small peasant households which leads to an intensification of this cycle is their delay in planting cotton which is done in order to be able to gain another cut or two from their clover. The likelihood of pest attacks goes up significantly with this delay.

Over the period 1961–76, pest control charges have increased steeply as compared to the nearly stable prices paid to the producers for cotton (Ikram, 1980: 265). As a result, small peasant households failed to plant the required amount of cotton, but most could not escape cultivating some.

Another, but indirect, negative side-effect of government policy is that small peasant households to a large degree seem to have stopped interplanting their cotton with vegetables such as onions because of their inability to control the teams of children who often destroy or steal their additional crops. This has indirectly led to an additional decrease in the subsistence production of many small peasant households, and has contributed to an increase in the extent of monetization of the reproductive cycle and/or a deterioration in the household diet.

**Machines**

Mechanization in the Egyptian countryside has proceeded rapidly since 1952, in particular over the last 10 years. Several recent studies have shown that this process has incorporated not only the larger agricultural producers but many small peasant households as well (Radwan and Lee, 1980: Chapter 4 19; Richards, Martin and Nagaar, 1983: 25; Hopkins, 1983: 186–7; Hopkins, Mehanna and Abdelmaksoud, 1982). Radwan and Lee's survey, carried out in 1977, of a random sample of 1,000 households in 18 villages found that even in the smallest categories of landholdings, for example, between 3 and 6 *qirat*s, 36% of holdings used machinery. In the category 6 to 12 *qirat*s, 52.7% of holdings used machinery (Radwan and Lee, 1980: Chapter 4 18).

That is not to say that the process of mechanization has proceeded evenly for all small peasant households. On the contrary, a recent comparative survey on agricultural mechanization in Egypt emphasizes the uneven impact of this process on small peasant households[15] (Hopkins, Mehanna and Abdelmaksoud, 1982). Comparing the surveyed Delta villages with those surveyed in the province of al-Minya in Middle Egypt, large gaps existed between the level of mechanization for levelling, furrowing, irrigation and winnowing, while the levels of mechanization for ploughing and threshing were very similar.

Despite the differences, it is possible to generalize, based on comparative data, that ploughing, threshing and, to a lesser extent, irrigation have been mechanized to a very high degree (Hopkins, 1983: 186–7; Hopkins, Mehanna and Abdelmaksoud, 1982: 100; Richards, Martin and Nagaar,

1983: 25). Based on the above studies one can conclude that the main characteristic of

> mechanization in Egyptian agriculture is that certain operations are mechanized for all relevant crops, and others are almost never mechanized for any relevant crops. Each crop therefore has certain operations that are mechanized and others that are not, and so each farmer's practice will be a combination of mechanized and non-mechanized operations. (Hopkins, Mehanna and Abdelmaksoud, 1982: 92)

Another major conclusion from the above study is that mechanization on the whole is based not on ownership but on rental arrangements.

> Relatively few farmers own their own tractors. The number who own pumps is slightly more. Therefore mechanization in general in Egypt means that the farmer rents in the services of a tractor or a pump. . . . The farmer may choose to rent from a cooperative instead of a private farmer, but most take the latter course, even where a cooperative tractor is available. Questions of cost, schedule of payments, and tips become important. (Hopkins, Mehanna and Abdelmaksoud, 1982: 93)

This finding coincides with my own research in 1981 where one *qirat* was being ploughed twice for £E0.30, with an additional charge of £E0.05 for tractor for ploughing would appear to be fairly consistent throughout the countryside. In the survey by Hopkins, Mehanna and Abdelmaksoud, the most common price listed was £E0.25 per *qirat* per two turns (1982: 122). This finding coincides with my own research in 1981 where 1 *qirat* was being ploughed twice for £E0.30, with an additional charge of £E0.05 for levelling and another £E0.15 for furrowing for cotton cultivation. These charges include an implied government subsidy: 42% for a 60–65 h.p. tractor hired from a co-operative and 22% for the same tractor hired from a private party (Cuddihy, 1980: 76). On the whole then, mechanization of ploughing has further monetized the reproduction cycle of the small peasant household although at a deflated rate, but many still use the traditional plough as a means of avoiding this unnecessary cash outlay.

Irrigation, as was earlier stated, has to a large extent been mechanized, although to a lesser degree and less evenly than ploughing and threshing. In the Delta village surveyed by Hopkins *et al.*, 74% of landholdings had mechanized irrigation as compared to only 34% of the villages surveyed in al-Minya (Hopkins, Mehanna and Abdelmaksoud, 1982: 100). Unfortunately the survey does not provide the same comparative detail for the cost of renting irrigation pumps as it does for tractors. However, based on fieldwork in 1981, a pump could be rented for £E0.50 per hour, with an estimated three hours needed to irrigate one *feddan* of land in not too dry a state. Stauth mentioned for the earlier period of 1977 the cost of £E10.00

per *feddan* per year for the renting of an irrigation pump (1978: 15).

The many small peasant households who have not mechanized the irrigation process, however, must rely upon one of the many traditional forms of irrigation such as the water wheel in its many varieties, the Archimedes screw, etc. The most common of these traditional methods is the water wheel (Hopkins, Mehanna and Abdelmaksoud, 1982: 125). Water wheels are usually the joint property of a group of peasant producers whose land is irrigated by the same wheel. Each water wheel is theoretically divided into 24 *qirat*s which are distributed proportionately amongst the small peasant households depending on the amount of land they hold. These rights do not automatically pass on to a new owner or tenant, and these must negotiate their right to access when land is rented or purchased. Repairs and upkeep of the water wheel are the joint responsibility of all owners, and any costs incurred are divided proportionately. The peasants select from amongst themselves a representative who is supposed to be generally responsible for the upkeep and operation of the water wheel. He arranges for the water wheel's annual inspection by the carpenter and the collection of the carpenter's fee. Traditionally, the *misaniyya* (annual fee) was always paid in kind. Although it is likely that this fee in kind is now paid in cash in most rural regions, it was still being paid in kind in an area of the Delta in 1977. At that time the fee for each *feddan* was one *kila* of maize and one *kila* of wheat.[16] Thus, for a relatively small payment in kind or its equivalent in cash, the small peasant household was assured of access to a means of irrigation. However, the replacement of a traditional water wheel or *sa'ya* is much more expensive, costing up to £E350.00 in 1974–5 (Morsy, 1978: 91).

Threshing has also become intensively and uniformly mechanized within rural Egypt. This is evident from the survey by Hopkins *et al.* which found that 85% of the Delta sample and 86% of the al-Minya sample used mechanized threshing (Hopkins, Mehanna and Abdelmaksoud, 1982: 100). The incredible speed by which this process took place is not revealed by these static statistics. My own fieldwork found that in 1977 a large percentage of the small peasant households used the *norag*, the traditional animal-drawn thresher, while in 1980 nearly the entire village used mechanized threshers. Despite the cash outlay, which amounted to approximately £E0.60 per hour or approximately £E1.80 to £E2.10 per *feddan* in 1981, small peasant households along with larger ones turned *en masse* to this kind of threshing, abandoning the more time-consuming *norag*.

This rapid transition from using a traditional method requiring no money to one which does, and moreover requires a work team of at least three persons, can be partly explained by the extreme labour intensity of the month of May. During this month wheat is harvested, threshed, winnowed and stored, land is fertilized and ploughed, maize is sown and irrigated, cotton is hoed and irrigated, and in the rice regions of Egypt rice is planted.

In terms of access, the traditional locally produced thresher was owned by most extended families and was kept within the family over the years, whereas mechanized threshers often tend to originate outside the village and are thus beyond the control of the small peasant household in terms of setting its own work schedule. As a result of these new developments, the process of commoditization has been extended almost uniformly amongst small peasant households.

Unlike threshing, winnowing has not become motor-mechanized. From the Hopkins *et al.* study, it would appear that hand-driven winnowers predominate in all regions of the countryside (Hopkins, Mehanna and Abdelmaksoud, 1982: 100). These machines tend to be jointly owned and operated by village partnerships. Instead of cash, the owners take a given portion of the winnowed wheat as their *agna* (payment). In 1977, in one area of the Delta this amounted to one *kila* for every three *ardebs*[17] of wheat winnowed, but by 1981 it had increased to one *kila* for every two *ardebs*.[18]

## Personal consumption

According to Bernstein, 'when food needs are satisfied on a regular basis by purchase this signifies that commodity relations have developed to a higher level' (Bernstein, 1979: 429). In the average Egyptian small peasant household there is considerable reliance upon the purchase of food. In 1976–7, items purchased in the weekly local market usually averaged around £E0.50 to £E0.80. Common purchases were rice, macaroni, lentils, tomato paste, salt and spices, as well as small quantities of fruit and vegetables not grown by small peasant households, such as oranges, cabbage and potatoes.

Part of the monthly expenses of the small peasant household are spent on subsidized goods obtained with a *bataqat tamwin* (ration card). A limited amount per family of rice, sugar, tea, oil, horse beans and soap is bought monthly. For the average family of five, in 1976–7 these costs ran in the region of £E4.00 per month.

The small peasant household also depends upon the purchase of other necessary items such as kerosene, tobacco and matches. Kerosene is usually bought from itinerant merchants, while tobacco, tobacco papers and matches are usually bought from village shops. Additional tea and sugar are also purchased from these. It is important to note that although prices within village shops are higher than prices in the weekly markets, which are in turn higher than prices in district stores, small peasant households tend to buy locally as they only infrequently leave the village and also because many shop-owners provide them with short-term credit.

For the average peasant household cultivating one *feddan* of land, there is usually no need to purchase wheat or maize. The peasant cultivating less than one *feddan*, however, often needs to purchase wheat and maize to provide for the basic subsistence of the family. Besides relying heavily on maize and wheat bread within their diet, small peasant households depend upon their home-produced cheese and upon a few green vegetables from the fields such as chicory, *mulukhiyya*[19] and *khubbaizi*[20] during the winter and tomatoes, cucumbers, aubergines, watercress and okra during the summer. Vegetable production amongst small peasant households is small and seems to be decreasing; in winter, clover has become much more important and has expanded in acreage, while in summer, double- and triple-cropping amongst cotton bushes seems to have declined, as was mentioned earlier.

One new phenomenon in terms of personal consumption amongst small peasant households is the purchase of subsidized American wheat flour. These purchases free women from the jobs of washing and drying the wheat and having it milled in order to bake bread. This trend is still undeveloped amongst small peasant households, who must still grow wheat for the by-product, straw. Most small peasant households therefore have wheat to use for home consumption. Ironically, American white flour is seen as being healthier by the peasants, for whom it has become a status symbol.

In order to meet the daily, weekly and monthly expenses of the household, many small peasant households rely heavily upon the selling of home-produced milk and animal products. Although the exact extent to which home milk and animal production amongst small peasant households is commoditized varies according to different accounts (Stauth, 1979: 14–15; Hopkins, 1980: 68, 71; Fitch and Soliman, 1983: 52–5), it seems misleading to underestimate the importance of these transactions for the successful reproduction of the small peasant household. This reliance is not new but has traditionally been the major means by which small peasant households gain access to market goods. In addition to the above, small peasant households will occasionally sell a *kila* or two of wheat or maize within the village or at the weekly market. The likelihood of such sales increases for the small peasant household when its milk-producing animal is dry due to pregnancy which thereby eliminates an important source of daily cash for the household.

Besides the need to purchase regular consumption items such as food and fuel, small peasant households occasionally need larger sums of cash to purchase more substantial items such as clothing, household utensils or furniture, although the average small peasant household rarely replaces or even mends such items. An even bigger sum of money, perhaps some £E200.00, may have to be obtained if a son in the family is going to be married.[21] In such cases, small peasant households may sell a small animal or a share in a larger one in order to meet these costs.

An important condition for the successful reproduction of the small peasant household is the successful impregnation of its large female water buffalo or cow on an annual basis. Not only does pregnancy provide the household with a calf which can be sold, but with each additional pregnancy the milk productivity of the animal increases significantly. Men with this specialist skill called *gassas* visit most villages two or three times per year and have traditionally been paid an annual fee in kind, which in

1977 amounted to 1 kila of maize per peasant household.

Most other services within Egyptian villages have been monetized, such as tailoring and carpentry. However, in some parts of rural Egypt there are some services which are still paid for by an annual fee in kind. The Quranic reciter and the village barber are sometimes paid in this way. Finally, it is worth noting that barter still exists in parts of rural Egypt to a certain extent, with small village vendors of vegetables and fruits accepting payment in ears of maize, bread, or cheese. This is true for only the poorest of local traders. The persistence of the above non-monetised services and relations contributes to the inability of commodity relations to become generalised.

## Mobility of land, credit and labour

As already discussed, the mobility of land ownership within the Egyptian countryside is extremely limited. Land rarely comes for sale on the open market because extreme fragmentation and, to a lesser extent traditional technology limit the possible buyers for most small strips of land. Small peasant households, when they can, try to consolidate their often divided holdings and are uninterested in obtaining several *qirat*s of land in some part of the village far away from their other holdings. Likewise, purchasing land distant from its own water wheel rights and traditional co-operative relations would also be problematic for the small peasant household.

The evidence indicates that there seems to be a lively short-term cash rental market in rural Egypt; the previously mentioned inhibiting factors for purchasing land operate also for tenancies, though to a lesser degree. However, the other forms of tenancy would appear to be encased within a multitude of non-monetized, non-commodity relations, which act to inhibit the further growth of the commoditization of land. Relations between tenants and landowners are often not purely market relations, and the very forms of these tenancies are based to a large degree on the production of use values.

Credit, institutionally tied to co-operatives, is limited to short-term loans in kind. Long-term cash loans are extremely limited, and small peasants do not qualify due to their lack of collateral (Abdel-Fadil, 1975: 147). Short-term cash loans are usually gained through personal ties within the village, while larger sums of money can be obtained only through the selling of a large animal or land, either of which can be extremely detrimental to the peasant household in the long run. Informal mortgaging arrangements often lead to a permanent loss of the peasant's land.

With regard to labour mobility within the agricultural sector, it is important to emphasize that a major percentage of Egyptian peasant landholdings are less than five *feddans*, with nearly 40% of the total landholders cultivating less than one *feddan*. Likewise, recent data seem to indicate that the phenomenon of landlessness has decreased and a 'labour shortage' problem in rural Egypt has appeared. All of these factors together indicate that a sizeable mobile labour force does not exist, that while perhaps 30% of the total landholders may need to seek outside employment, they do so only to supplement their total household product. Daily agricultural wages have risen sharply since 1974, and this has contributed to the fact that while a landless labourer's income is less than that of a small peasant household it is nevertheless not very much below it (Richards and Martin, 1981a: Radwan and Lee, 1980).

From the preceding discussion it is clear that within the reproduction cycle of the small peasant household in Egypt there has been considerable development and intensification of commodity relations over the last two and a half decades. However, it is likewise evident that non-commodity relations are essential to the reproduction of the peasant household and that some of these relations are not mere remnants of the past but have emerged out of a given conjuncture of new forces, e.g. the phenomenon of *tabaddul*.

The issue remains of the transformation of the small peasant form of production in Egypt into simple commodity production. Here, Friedmann's discussion concerning the development of simple commodity production in North American wheat production is enlightening. As Friedmann points out, simple commodity production in wheat production arose due to a conjuncture of forces – namely the availability of land, credit, and correct technology – which created the right conditions for the emergence of simple commodity production. Once this form of production arose, it was able, due to its internal organization, to undermine capitalist production of the same commodity in times of falling world prices.

Given the above historical specificity of the development of simple commodity production in wheat production, what appear to be the major constraints on the development of simple commodity production within Egyptian agriculture? What immediately emerges is the severe lack of markets in land and credit, which is related to the overall development of the Egyptian economy and the nature of the state. It would seem that Friedmann's emphasis on the relation of simple commodity production as a form of production to the larger economy is important, and it could be hypothesized that the emergence of simple commodity production within Egyptian agriculture is dependent upon the overall transformation of the Egyptian social formation, and specifically the further development of capitalist relations.

However, as a concluding remark, I think it necessary to add that despite the above, peasant production in Egypt does not entirely coincide with Friedmann's notion of a form of production unresponsive to price changes due to a lack of markets in labour, credit and land. On the contrary, as Ikram has pointed out, Egyptian small peasant producers are highly affected by price changes and have consistently changed their strategies in what and how much they grow of various crops.

> On a rotational basis for a fully commercial farm, the most profitable mix would be a combination of those crops having the highest gross margins per feddan per unit of time subject to technical restraints, such as the need to follow cotton by berseem. This would lead to expansion of areas of long-season berseem, wheat, and maize, and a contraction of areas under cotton, rice and short-season berseem. This is what was happening in the 1970s. (Ikram, 1980: 197)

Given the above, I think it is necessary to re-evaluate the kinds of notions Friedmann presents in terms of peasant production as they relate to simple commodity production. Perhaps there are more similarities between simple commodity production and the form of peasant production described for Egypt. In particular, I think her notion of competition as it pertains to simple commodity production, as well as her emphasis upon the individuality of the enterprise, needs to be rethought. As is clear from her own analysis, simple commodity producers were able to continue to produce wheat despite a loss of returns. Thus it would seem that the crucial factor for the viability of simple commodity producers is in the nature of the internal organization of the productive unit, as it is for small peasant producers in Egypt.

## Notes

1. The central argument of the following essay was originally presented in a paper prepared for the Rural Middle East Workshop, University of Durham 25–27 September 1981. It was elaborated more fully in 'Non-capitalist Relations and the Small Peasant Household in Rural Egypt', unpublished Ph.D. thesis, University of Hull, 1984, upon which the following is primarily based. Part of the material was subsequently published under the title, '"Historical Materialism or Marxist Hagiography?" A Response to a Positivist Critique', *Current Sociology*, 34(2), 1986: 173–98.

The data presented in the analysis was collected during my periods of fieldwork in Egypt, January 1976–September 1977, and March–April 1981, or is based on my general knowledge of Egypt. Prices refer to April 1981 unless otherwise specified. The transliteration of Arabic words have been done in accordance with the local dialect of the Delta governorate of al-Minufiyya, and specifically the village of Mit Qamar (pseudonym), where most of my fieldwork was carried out.

I would like to take this opportunity to express my appreciation to the Department of Sociology and Social Anthropology, University of Hull, and the Centre for Middle Eastern and Islamic Studies, University of Durham, for the financial support which made my research possible.

Finally, it is impossible to express adequately my deep appreciation of my husband, Pandelis M. Glavanis, from whom I have received support and encouragement since the inception of my project on rural Egypt.

2. Egyptian hoes are made not within the village but by urban craftsmen.
3. In 1976–7, the price of a hoe was considerably lower at £E2.00. Stauth mentions a price of £E4.00–5.00 (1978: p. 15).
4. A feddan (4200,833m$^2$ is divided into 24 *qirat*s (175.035m$^2$).
5. Information obtained from the *sarif* (tax collector) for the village of Mit Qamar, November 1976.

6. Implementation of this law was delayed for several years. During the autumn of 1976 when village taxes were being collected, peasants complained about the non-implementation of the law. In the summer of 1977, Sadat reaffirmed its validity and it would now seem to be enforced in the countryside.

7. The following information on the practice of mortgaging is derived from my own fieldwork and that of Stauth (1978: p. 13).

8. Both Stauth's research (1978, p. 24) and my own found that this was the case.

9. Amongst the names I have seen used for short-term cash rentals are: *sagil* (from my own fieldwork in Mit Qamar); and *igar bi'l-zira'a* ('rent by agriculture').

10. Stauth, basing himself on fieldwork carried out during 1977–8 in two Delta villages (1978: p. 11), states that the short-term rental rate was £E7.00 per *qirat* per annum. This finding coincides with my own fieldwork in another area of the Delta. Concerning uniformity within a given village, my fieldwork indicated a variation of only £E0.50 per *qirat* per half year.

11. In Mit Qamar, where I carried out research, it was known by the villagers as *igar bi'l-muzara'a* ('rent by cultivation'), whereas Stauth (1978) uses the term *ma'ash* (subsistence) similar to al-Bahi (1955).

12. During my period of fieldwork several new labour service arrangements were established.

13. A *kila* is a dry measure equivalent to 16.72 litres.

14. Stauth suggests that the market rate for fertilizers is sometimes double the co-operative rate (1978: p. 11), although my own research suggested a difference of approximately 50% for the year 1976–7.

15. 80% of all households surveyed by Hopkins, Mehanna and Abdelmaksoud possessed less than three *feddans* (1982: p. 75).

16. This is an example taken from my fieldwork in Mit Qamar in 1976–7.

17. An *ardeb* is a dry measure used for wheat, maize, etc., equivalent to 198 litres.

18. This information is from my own fieldwork in Mit Qamar, 1976–7 and 1981.

19. *Mulukhiyya* is a variety of winter mallow. Its scientific name is *Corchorus olitorious*.

20. *Khubbaizi* is a variety of winter mallow.

21. In 1981, peasants estimated that the *mahr* (bride price) of the poorest peasant was about £E200,000 for the village of Mit Qamar.

## References


Abdel-Fadil, Mahmoud, 1975, *Development, Income Distribution and Change in Rural Egypt (1952–1970)*, Cambridge: Cambridge University Press.

al-Bahi, 'Abd al-Fattah Ibrahim, 1955, *al 'Amal al-Zira'i wa'l-Batala fi Qariya Misriyya-Ghamrain Minufiyya* ('Agricultural Labour and Unemployment in an Egyptian Village – Ghamrain Minufiyya'), Report 133, Sirs al-Layana, The International Centre for Basic Education in the Arab World. (Typescript).

Bernstein, Henry, 1979, 'African Peasantries: A Theoretical Framework', *The Journal of Peasant Studies*, 6(4): 421–443.

Cuddihy, William, 1980, *Agricultural Price Management in Egypt*, World Bank Staff Working Paper 388, Washington, World Bank.

Egypt, The General Organisation for Official Publications, 1976, *Qanun Ragam 67 li-Sanat 1975 li-Tanzim, al- 'Alagat bain Musta'jirin al-Aradi al-Zira'iyya wa-Mullakiha (Law No. 67 for 1975 Regarding the Relationships Between Tenants of Agricultural Land and its Owners)*, Cairo.

Fitch, James B. and Ibrahim A. Soliman, 1983, 'Livestock and Small Farmer Labor Supply' in *Migration, Mechanization, and Agricultural Labor Markets in Egypt*, ed. by Alan Richards and Philip L. Martin, Boulder, Colorado, Westview Press: 45–78.

Friedmann, Harriet, 1978a, 'Simple Commodity Production and Wage Labor in the American Plains', *The Journal of Peasant Studies*, 6(1): 71–100.

_______ 1978b, 'World Market, State, and Family Farm: Social Bases of Household Production in an Era of Wage Labour', *Comparative Studies in Society and History*, 20(4): 545–586.

_______ 1980a, 'Economic Analysis of the Postbellum South: Regional Economics and World Markets', *Comparative Studies in Society and History*, 22(4): 639–652.

_______ 1980b, 'Household Production and the National Economy: Concepts for the Analysis of Agrarian Formations', *The Journal of Peasant Studies*, 7(2): 158–184.

_______ 1981, 'The Family Farm in Advanced Capitalism: Outlines of a Theory of Simple Commodity Production in Agriculture', Toronto, University of Toronto. (Unpublished MS.)

Glavanis, Kathy R. G., 1981, 'Commoditisation and the Egyptian Peasant Household', paper presented at the Rural Middle East Workshop, University of Durham, 25–27 September.

_______ 1984, *Non-capitalist Relations and the Small Peasant Household in Rural Egypt*, unpublished Ph.D. thesis, University of Hull.

Glavanis, Kathy and Pandeli Glavanis, 1986, '"Historical Materialism or Marxist Hagiography?" A Response to a Positivist Critique', *Current Sociology*, 34(2): 173–198.

Hopkins, Nicholas S., 1980, 'Animal Husbandry and the Household Economy in Two Egyptian Villages', Report of the Rural Sociology Segment of the Project on 'Improved Utilisation of Feed Resources for the Livestock Sector, Phase I', Cairo, Catholic Relief Office.

_______ 1983, 'The Social Impact of Mechanization', in *Migration, Mechanization, and Agricultural Labour Markets in Egypt*, ed. by Alan Richards and Philip L. Martin, Boulder, Colorado, Westview Press: 181–198.

Hopkins, Nicholas S., Mehanna, Soheir and Bahgat M. Abdelmaksoud, 1982, *The State of Agricultural Mechanization in Egypt. Results of a Survey: 1982*, Cairo, Ministry of Agriculture.

Ikram, Khalid, 1980, *Egypt: Economic Management in a Period of Transition*, The Report of a Mission sent to the Arab Republic of Egypt by the World Bank, Baltimore and London, The Johns Hopkins Press for The World Bank.

Morsy, Soheir Amin, 1978, *Gender, Power and Illness in an Egyptian Village*, unpublished Ph.D. thesis, Michigan State University.

al-Najjar, 'Abd al-Hadi 'Ali, 1974, *al-Fa'id al-Iqtisadi al-Fa'li wa-Daur al-Dariba fi Ta'bi'tihi bi'l-Iqtisad al-Misri (The Real Economic Surplus and the Role of Taxation in its Mobilisation for the Egyptian Economy)*, Cairo, al-Hai'a al-'Amma li-Shu'On al-Matabi' al-Amiriyya.

Radwan, Samir and Eddy Lee, 1980, *The Anatomy of Rural Poverty in Egypt, 1977*, World Employment Programme, Geneva, International Labour Office.

Richards, Alan and Philip L. Martin, 1981, 'Changes in Rural Real Wage Rates: A Review of the Evidence and of Demand Side Pressures', Economic Working Paper No. 9, Agricultural Development Systems Project, Arab Republic of Egypt, Ministry of Agriculture and University of California.

Richards, Alan, Martin, Philip L. and Rifaat Naggar, 1983, 'Labor Shortages in Egyptian Agriculture', in *Migration, Mechanization, and Agricultural Labor Markets in Egypt*, ed. by Alan Richards and Philip L. Martin, Boulder, Colorado, Westview Press: 21–44.

Stauth, Geörg, 1978, 'Subsistence Production in Rural Egypt: Strategies for Development', paper presented at the International Conference on Strategies of Development in the Arab World, Louvain-La-Neuve, 11–14 December.

——— 1979, 'Dissolution and Peripherilization of the Small Peasantry: The Case of the Fellahs of the Nile Delta', Universityof Bielefeld. (Unpublished MS.)

# 7. Household Production and Capitalism: A Case Study of South-eastern Turkey

*Zülküf Aydin*

Within the pages of the *Journal of Peasant Studies* there has been a recent growth of interest in the structural transformations taking place in the Turkish countryside (Margulies and Seddon, 1984; Keyder, 1983a, 1983b; Hann, 1985). The issues addressed were also the subject of an earlier debate, widely known as the Boratav–Erdost debate. Although both Boratav and Ersdot closed their controversy in the early 1970s without arriving at any conclusion, I think a reconsideration of their theoretical positions and the political implications of these is absolutely necessary as they already have had some serious repercussions. In this contribution I shall question some of the premises of the arguments put by the contributors in the debate and hope that this will clarify some of the issues concerning the Turkish agrarian question.

Political developments amongst the Turkish Left in the late 1960s and early 1970s were very closely related to the debate on the Turkish agrarian question. The debate was important in two senses. First of all, it contributed to the understanding, or misunderstanding, of the nature of the transformation undergone by the Turkish countryside. Second, its theoretical conclusions were used in an uncritical fashion in the construction of political strategies by various sections of the Turkish Left, which believed in the unity of theory and practice.

In this chapter I shall attempt to show that the arguments put forward in the debate were theoretically unsound and empirically unfounded; the positions taken in the debate were based on a misunderstanding of the concept of the mode of production, and the political strategies drawn from these positions were largely responsible for the so-called 'tragedy of the Turkish Left' in the 1970s and 1980s.

## The debate

Although there were some other minor contributions to the debate, the two major contributions came from Korkut Boratav and Muzaffer Erdost.[1] In a short article published in *Emek*, the journal of the Turkish Workers' Party, Korkut Boratav summarized the arguments in his book *Gelir Dagilimi* (Income Distribution).[2] He argued that three distinctive relations of production could be observed in Turkish agriculture: petty (simple) commodity production, capitalist production, and feudal and semi-feudal production. Of these the most widespread was simple commodity production, which is subject to the exploitation of merchant and usurer capital. Boratav considered the relations of exploitation between simple (petty) commodity production and merchant and usurer capital as primitive forms of capitalist exploitation. The fact that the largest part of agriculture is under the influence of primitive capitalist relations leads one to the conclusion that a primitive capitalist mode of production is dominant in Turkey. In *Gelir Dagilimi* Boratav tries to show the insignificance of feudal and semi-feudal relations in Turkey by way of statistical data. In his view it is possible to say that feudal and semi-feudal relations of exploitation, which occur either in sharecropping form or in more pure and rigid forms, are intensified in the cases where an *aga* (landlord) owns one or more villages. According to the Village Inventory Surveys carried out by the Ministry of Village Affairs, which covered 22,047 villages in 43 provinces, the number of villages totally owned by a landlord, family or dynasty is 71, and that only constitutes 3.2% of the total. This ratio is higher in eastern provinces but still does not exceed 11% of the total number of villages in the provinces of Tunceli, Agri, Hatay, Mardin, Erzurum, Diyarbakir, Siirt, Urfa and Gaziantep. The conclusion may be drawn that feudal and semi-feudal relations are extremely limited, and cover little more than 10% of villages in some of the eastern provinces.

Another criterion put forward by Boratav to show the limits of feudal and semi-feudal relations is the number of landless peasants working as sharecroppers. The Village Inventory Surveys for 43 provinces show that landless sharecroppers constitute only 2.6% of total farming families. If the number of small landowners who also work as sharecroppers is added to this percentage, the figure increases considerably. The 1963 Agricultural Census states that the percentage of sharecropping families out of the total is 15%. But in order to be considered as a semi-feudal relationship, sharecropping will have to be in the form of smallholdings. If the number of peasants working as sharecroppers for small landowners is excluded from the calculation, the number of peasants sharecropping for landlords who own 500 *donums* or more of land would be about 90,000 (2.6% of total farming families).[3] Boratav maintains that if the boundaries of *agadom* were to be extended to 200 *donums* of land, then only 3.3% of farming families could be classified as sharecroppers.

It is clear that Boratav uses the following three criteria to denote the nature and extent of feudal and semi-feudal relations of production: the number of landless families, the number of sharecropping families working for a large landowner, and the number of villages whose lands belong to an individual, a family or a dynasty. He thus arrives at the conclusion that feudal and semi-feudal relations of distribution constitute only an insignificant part – a mere 2.6–3.3% – of Turkish agriculture. But Turkish agriculture is not purely capitalist either: since only 10% of farming families work as wage labourers, this relation of production cannot be considered dominant in the Turkish countryside. The most common or predominant relation of production is based on small ownership, which embraces 75–80% of the rural population.[4] Since in Turkey small producers lose their surplus product not to the feudal element but to merchant and usurer capital, Boratav argues that a backward capitalism is dominant in Turkey.

Boratav may be right to argue that the type of capitalism existing in Turkey is not a fully developed capitalism, but his method of identifying the backward nature of capitalism in Turkey is extremely dubious.

Boratav's use of the size of landholding as a criterion in identifying capitalism and feudalism is erroneous. The identification of sharecropping arrangements with semi-feudal relations of production is not very convincing either. A number of recent Latin American studies have shown that the use of sharecropping arrangements by large landlords is not a sign of feudalism but a result of profitability calculations made by the landlords.[5] My own research in southeastern Anatolia, where landlord–sharecropper relations are most widespread, has also revealed the fact that it is much more beneficial both economically and politically for the landlords to use sharecroppers rather than wage labourers in certain cases.[6] Capital accumulation is one of the basic features of capitalism, and the landlord's decision-making is affected by his concern for capital accumulation.

In deciding whether capitalism or feudalism is dominant in a particular country it is extremely misleading to look at the relations of production or the immediate process of production in single units of production. Boratav has made the mistake of confusing a mode of production with the immediate process of production and relations of exploitation. It is wrong to identify sharecropping with semi-feudalism and wage labour with capitalism. Boratav's empiricist method leads him to a static definition of modes of production. His concept of mode of production is read off from relations of production and his definition of relations of production is read off statistical data (the validity of which is doubtful).

Lenin warned against too stereotyped an understanding of capitalism in rural areas in his *Development of Capitalism in Russia*.[7] Kautsky also argued that the development of capitalism in agriculture does not have to follow the same path as industry. Peculiarities of agriculture present some obstacles to the separation of direct producers from their means of production:

> To study the agrarian question according to Marx's method, we should not confine ourselves to the question of the future of small scale farming; on the contrary, we should look at all the changes which agriculture

> experiences under the domination of capitalist production. We should ask: is capital, and in what ways is capital taking hold of agriculture, revolutionizing it, smashing the old forms of production and poverty and establishing the new forms which must succeed?[8]

In order to be able to talk about capitalist domination in agriculture we should then ask Boratav: is it really necessary to have a predominance of the wage labour relation that could be counted empirically? Taking capitalism as a world system, Wallerstein argues that wage labour is not a necessary labour form but only one of the possible labour forms to be used in capitalism.[9]

In his explanation of the nature of Turkish capitalism Boratav comes very close to the concept of articulation of modes of production, without using the concept. He argues that within a social formation there exist various relations of production side by side or inside each other. One of these relations of production is dominant, however, while others are subordinate. The relations of production which are congruent with the superstructure of the society are the dominant relations of production.[10] We already know how Boratav uses statistical data to identify the existence of certain relations of production (and modes of production). The dominance of one mode of production over others within a social formation does not mean, in Boratav's writings, that they are subordinate to the laws of motion of the dominant mode of production. The way he treats the statistical data suggests that the dominance of one mode of production is tantamount to its percentage being greatest compared with the ratio of other modes of production (or relations of production). Therefore the capitalist mode of production based on wage labour constitutes 10% of the social formation, feudal and semi-feudal relations of production based on sharecropping constitute about 5–10%, and simple commodity production based on small holdings constitutes 75–80%.[11] But if the statistical definition of modes of production provided by Boratav is accepted, there is no dominant mode of production in the articulationist sense, rather a coexistence of several modes of production, one of which happens to be the most widespread. This kind of approach has been criticized by Banaji, who argues that individual enterprises in an economy can show different relations of exploitation of labour. The important point is that these enterprises are subject to the laws of motion of that economy. For Banaji, to identify the mode of production with the form of exploitation of labour is to engage in vulgar Marxism. He maintains that relations of exploitation such as wage labour, sharecropping, etc. are simple categories since they can occur in different modes (epochs) of production. The concept 'mode of production' cannot be deduced from the survival and reproduction of different forms of exploitation in individual enterprises or branches of the economy. In an economy where capitalism is dominant, 'pre-capitalist enterprises, contrary to formal appearances, are in essence capitalist since they are subordinated to capitalist laws of motion'.[12] In the same vein Bernstein argues that capitalism has become universal and has destroyed the conditions of reproduction of other modes, even when forms of subjugation of labour units of production typical of these modes have only been partially transformed.[13]

As I stated earlier, Boratav's contention that a backward, primitive capitalism is dominant in Turkey may be right, but his statistical formulations and empiricist definitions do not warrant such a conclusion. The nature of the agrarian structure cannot be understood by focusing solely on the number of wage labourers, on the amount of land owned or by studying agriculture in isolation, independently of the whole mechanism of social production.

Boratav's analysis was adopted by the Turkish Workers' Party (TWP) in sketching out their tactics and political strategies. Writing in the journal of the TWP several writers reiterated Boratav's argument that a kind of capitalism was dominant in Turkey and that therefore the revolutionary struggle should be channelled into the fight for socialism.[14] For them, both in industry and in agriculture a working class who could lead a struggle for socialism had emerged. The development of capitalist relations had proved detrimental to small and middle peasants and pushed them to unite with the working class, giving them a revolutionary potential. Therefore, conditions for a fight for socialism were now ripe. The appearance of Boratav's article in *Emek* no. 6 attracted severe criticism from those who believed in the dominance of feudal and semi-feudal modes of production in Turkey. The most aggressive reply came from Erdost, who attacked Boratav's interpretations of statistical data and his theoretical position.[15] Erdost criticized Boratav for using unreliable statistics as he arrived at the conclusion that the extent of feudal relations was 5% of the total rural structure.

Erdost's criticism could have been accepted had it not been for the fact that he calculated the extent of feudalism and semi-feudalism as constituting 46% of the total structure.[16] In doing so, Erdost falls into the same trap as Boratav by using the amount of land as a sufficient criterion for a definition of feudalism or semi-feudalism. Second, it is not possible to identify a mode of production with the relations of production within a single unit of production. Agrarian structure cannot be identified as feudal, semi-feudal, or capitalist by focusing solely on a household or a village, or even a region in isolation from the context of larger structures like a social formation or the capitalist world system. The number of workers or sharecroppers in these units, or the amount of land owned, cannot be used as the only criterion for the identification of a mode of production.

Erdost differentiates between patriarchal, semi-feudal, feudal and capitalist production very categorically. Among the 9 million production units in Turkey, only 600,000 production units employ wage labour and therefore the capitalist mode of production, he argues, cannot be considered a dominant mode of production. He admits that capitalist relations do exist in Turkish agriculture, but says they are in no way dominant. He maintains that in a country like Turkey, where small peasant holdings are predominant, one cannot speak of the dominance of capitalism. On the contrary, one can hold that pre-capitalist relations of production are dominant in agriculture.[17] One of the most crucial denominators used by Erdost to show the dominance of pre-capitalist relations of production in the Turkish countryside is the extent of the production of commodities. Simple commodity production should be separated from capitalist production. Production of commodities for the market in order to be able to buy some necessities such as salt does not aim at a profit. Indeed, it is absolutely different from the production of commodities for profit. If the producer produces commodities by the use of wage labour in accordance with the formula m–c–m, then there is a capitalist commodity production. Since small peasant holders do not sell most of their products in the market, their exploitation by capitalism is very limited. The rate of capital exploitation of small producers can be measured by the amount of commodities offered for sale in the market. This does not exceed 10% of the total wheat crop, which is the largest crop produced by small producers.[18] The logical conclusion of Erdost's argument is that capitalist relations of production constitute 10% of total agrarian relations.

This is highly misleading, because 'once commodity relations are incorporated in the cycle of the peasant household as an economic necessity', as Bernstein argues, 'the question of how much of its resources are devoted to the production of use-values and of commodities is secondary, though still important'.[19] Today capitalism has acquired a universal character; the pre-capitalist appearance of the family farm should not lead us to believe that this constitutes a mode of production. Capital controls the conditions of reproduction of the peasant family farm. The problem should be posed not in terms of whether or not capitalism exists in the countryside, but in terms of how capital comes into relations with the household and through which mechanism capital exercises its dominance over the household.

In the paragraphs which follow, I shall try to indicate some of the mechanisms through which capital extracts surplus from household producers in south-eastern Anatolia, and I shall argue that capital does not have to use wage labour in order to accumulate. In both small peasant household production and large landlord estates, peasant family labour plays an instrumental role in the accumulation of capital. Marketing, credit systems and price control by the state are the basic mechanisms of surplus extraction from the peasant household in south-eastern Anatolia.[20] Retention of certain aspects, such as the use of family labour and ownership of the means of production, may lead one to think that household production is a pre-capitalist survival, blocking the development of a fully capitalist relation of production. But household production cannot be treated as merely a pre-capitalist survival for, despite its formal appearance, the conditions of household production have dramatically changed in the course of its life history. Although the formal appearances of a household production unit in the Ottoman Empire and in modern Turkey may reveal similarities, the relations of production engaged in by the household unit are totally different. In today's Turkey the capitalist mode of production is dominant and the conditions of reproduction of the household as a unit of production are determined by this mode. The concepts of real and formal subsumption of labour by capital seem to be applicable in the transformation of Turkish agrarian structures. The concept of formal subsumption implies that capital can achieve effective control of the production process without undertaking its immediate organization or dispossessing the direct producers. If this assumption is tenable, then the focus of attention becomes not the future proletarianization of the peasantry under the dominance of capitalism but the relationship between family-based household production and the activities of different forms of capital.

The development of capital accumulation requires a transfer of surplus from the labouring classes (workers, peasants) to a non-working class. This transfer can take place between agricultural and industrial sectors. The transfer of a surplus from agriculture to industry presupposes a commodity market. Therefore the commoditization of the peasantry becomes necessary for capital accumulation. The process of incorporation of the peasantry into commodity production will also illuminate the forms of extraction and appropriation of surplus labour.

In south-eastern Anatolia two types of production unit have coexisted side by side for centuries: small peasant households and large landlord estates. The historical roots of large landownership in the area can be traced back to the 16th century. Being unable to extend its control over the remote eastern parts of the empire, the central Ottoman authority granted large areas of land in return for military service to Kurdish tribal leaders, especially those engaged against the Persian threat in the east. Unlike people under the *timariot* system, the Kurdish notables and tribal chiefs enjoyed complete dominance over the land, without the fear of losing it, since the right of inheritance was a part of the deal between them and the central authority. With the weakening of centralized authority from the 17th century onwards, the Kurdish notables consolidated their control over the land and with the promulgation of civil law, which accepted private ownership in land, they became *de jure* owners. The rest of the state lands in the area were worked by small peasant families who had usufructory rights over the land. With the acceptance of private property in land in 1926 the *reaya*s (peasants) who could produce an official document proving that they were the users of the land became the formal owners of the land to which previously they had only had the right of use.

Given the low level of technology, human labour was an absolute necessity for the cultivation of land. Therefore, most peasants had access to land through various forms of sharecropping arrangements.[21] Because of rivalry and feuds between local landlords, all the sharecroppers of the same landlord would be inhabitants of the same village, owned by the landlord, where the centre of the landlord's farmstead would be situated. On the other hand, the cultivators of the rest of the state lands would live in villages relatively independent of landlord control. This is the historical factor behind the two types of village settlement in today's south-eastern Anatolia: peasant villages and landlord villages. For this reason the choice of individual villages as units of study can be justified.

I studied the villages of Gisgis and Kalhana in Ergani district, in south-eastern Anatolia, in the belief that the study of representative villages of both the peasant and landlord type might give some clues to the understanding of the process of transformation of agrarian structures. Before going into the features of the transformations taking place in the countryside, exemplified by the cases of Gisgis and Kalhana, it is important to sketch out the rural structure existing in the area up to 1950. I take the date 1950 as a stopping point because from that year onwards, as a part of the European Recovery Programme, the bulk of external funds were poured into Turkish agriculture, facilitating a technological change which had a direct bearing on the labour requirements of the large landlords.

Our knowledge pertaining to the relations of production in eastern Anatolia before the Republic (1923) is extremely limited; there has been virtually no research done on this subject. Given the backward nature of agricultural technology and production that existed even up to the late 1940s, it seems clear that the relations of production had not changed with the declaration of the right to private property in land in 1926. What happened with the acceptance of private property in land was that *de facto* private ownership in land was confirmed by law.

Writing in 1934, I. H. Tokin stated that in the 1930s in the eastern and south-eastern provinces the land and other means of production used by the peasant were the property of the tribal leaders, *bey*s and *aga*s, and despotism lay behind landlordism.[22] In the provinces of these regions peasants not only cultivated the land but also lived on the land of the *bey* and served as corvée labour.

In the early 1950s the peasants who worked on the landlords' land were called *maraba* or *azab*. The *maraba* was a direct producer who obtained a share of what he produced. Although in some places the *maraba* may have had his own land, he could not benefit from it. This was because either his land was not fertile, or he was indebted to the *aga*. In most cases the *maraba* did not own any means of production: the *aga* owned both the land and the implements, and the *maraba* only had one *rubu* (one fourth of the crops). For their part *azab*s may be said to be agricultural labourers. The nature of relations of production engaged in by the *azab*s was described by Aras in the 1950s:

> Agricultural labourers in Southeast Anatolia are generally devoid of both land and capital. In other words, they are poor people without any house or farm. For this reason the whole family prefers to take shelter on

> a farm than to find a temporary wage job. They would undertake the work given to them as a family (male, female and child members who are able to work will work together).[23]

Aras suggests that rural workers were family labourers rather than individual labourers. This was very convenient for the landlords, who faced difficulties in finding a labour force.[24] *Azab*s were not sharecroppers but were more or less temporary wage labourers who were employed by the landlords under arrangements similar to sharecropping arrangements. *Azab*s would not only work in agricultural work, but would also personally serve the landlord who supplied them with board and lodging. They were generally paid in kind, and sometimes they were allowed to cultivate a small plot of land on their own account, using the implements of the landlord, in lieu of receiving any payment. This way of cultivating the land on the workers' account was called *ikramiye* (bonus) or *se'ere* in the local dialect.

In addition to the *azab* labour form several types of sharecropping arrangements existed in the area, such as *yaricilik*, *icare*, *cariyek* and *marabacilik*, which differ from each other in terms of the amount of inputs supplied and products shared.

Despite the variety in types of arrangements between the direct producers and the landlords, one thing that emerges is that both in *azab* arrangements and in sharecropping arrangements the peasant's household is the basic unit of production. The household, in order to reproduce itself, takes part in various relations of production. It is the level of development of productive forces which enforces the above-mentioned relations between the landlords and the peasants. Due to the low population density in the area, the landlords, who also held political power, mostly resorted to force to keep the peasants on their lands.

Following the establishment of the Republic, the rural economy was still to a large extent a closed economy, based on self-sufficiency, with very few relations with the market. In 1927 only 5–6.5% of Turkey's total land area was under cultivation.[25] The relation of the peasants to the market was only tied to the purchase of necessary consumption goods, such as sugar, paraffin, tea and coffee.[26] However, I. H. Tokin points out that despite the dominance of a self-sufficient closed economy in eastern, south-eastern and some parts of central Anatolia, in western and coastal parts of Anatolia which had a continuous relation with the world market and which were equipped with railway networks, the producers produced not for their own consumption but for the market.

In the period 1923 to 1950 not only small farms but also large farms were technologically backward. Large holdings used only 5–10% of their lands as cultivated fields, the rest being used for pasture.[27] Keyder's study implies that this is true of the periods when agricultural prices declined in the world market.[28] In the periods of economic boom landlords used as many sharecroppers as they needed to cultivate their idle lands. The mechanisms used to bring peasant families into sharecropping arrangements were debt bondage and usury. For Keyder, the 1926–46 period was one of decline in agricultural prices in the world market. Therefore it is understandable that most of the large landlord holdings were kept idle until just before the 1950s. But in the 1950s Turkish agriculture underwent a tremendous structural change. This was mainly due to the priority given to agriculture in Turkey's development efforts. Her integration into the capitalist world economy as a peripheral country necessitated her taking her place in the world division of labour as a producer of agricultural goods. The number of tractors and combine harvesters increased drastically. For instance, the number of tractors in Turkey rose from 17,000 in 1950 to 42,000 in 1960, 116,100 in 1971 and 243,000 in 1975.[29] With the state's help, middle and large landowners started to use agricultural machinery on their farms and to expel some sharecroppers from their lands. Technological change resulted in the enlargement of the cultivated areas, increased productivity of labour, the introduction of new crop varieties and a rise in the number of unemployed peasants.[30]

Yet, despite these changes, the household as an economic unit, a unit of reproduction of the peasant family, persisted in south-east Anatolia. The persistence of peasant family farms in south-eastern Anatolia has to be explained in terms of the combination of historically specific conditions and the peasant household's reaction to these changing conditions.

The introduction of a multi-party system and of agricultural machinery took place more or less at the same time. All of a sudden, tribal Kurdish notables found themselves a part of the power bloc in Turkey in the 1950s. Their tribal affiliations and their control of land in the region gave them a tremendous peasant backing in the elections. Once they became influential figures in local and national politics, they were able to use their political influence to gain access to credit facilities, improved seeds, technological aids, fertilizers, insecticides etc.

The maintenance of dependent small family producers was an important factor enabling the landlords to translate their political power to economic gains. It is therefore not surprising to find landlords in south-eastern Anatolia still keeping some of their sharecroppers and not using their agricultural machinery to the optimal level. On the other hand, small peasant producers react to the effects of unfavourable market conditions, merchant and usurer exploitation, and a hopeless labour market, by sticking to a plot of land, diversifying their activities and increasing their labour input.

But what are the actual processes of production organized in peasant and landlord villages? What kinds of production relations exist between the two, and how do various forms of capital operate in the villages?

Gisgis and Kalhana villages are in the Ergani district of Diyarbakir province, which is about 958km south-east of the capital city, Ankara. Both villages are on the stabilized road that runs between Ergani and

Cermik district centres. The distances from Kalhana and Gisgis to Ergani are 6 and 18km respectively.

## Gisgis

The history of Gisgis dates back to early times, though it is not known when exactly it was established. Gisgis is one of the villages that landlords were not very interested in, owing to the hilly, stony and infertile nature of most of its lands. The land is divided more or less equally amongst the inhabitants, though there are a fair number of landless people in the village. As a result of the inheritance system the land has been continually fragmented. The average area of land per household is about 33 *donums* – too small to maintain an average-sized family. The use of chemical fertilizers and machinery in the hilly and stony fields is very limited. The productivity of these fields is low. However, in the pockets of irrigated fields on small plateaux scattered among the village lands and used as fruit and vegetable gardens, the productivity level is comparatively high.

Wheat, lentils and barley are cultivated in the less fertile lands, basically for family consumption, whilst fruit and vegetables are cultivated entirely for the local market. There is thus a high degree of commercialization in the village. Market-orientated fruit and vegetable gardening is a fairly new event. It began in the late 1950s with the improvement of the transport system. To a lesser extent sheep-rearing is another commercially orientated economic activity. Several households derive most of their income from sheep-rearing. However, agriculture and animal husbandry are not the only sources of livelihood in the village. About 40% of the families in the village derive the main part of their livelihood from work other than agricultural. In some families agriculture is a secondary source of income: either direct involvement of some members of the family or indirect involvement of the family as a whole in agriculture constitutes a secondary source of income. In the former case the head of the household may work outside agriculture, as a civil servant, labourer, grocer, teacher or such like, while his wife and children cultivate the land. In the latter instance the lands of the household may be given to sharecroppers.

Given the uncertain employment possibilities outside agriculture, peasants always try to have access to a piece of land from which they can earn a living or at least part of a living. If they have insufficient, or no land by which to secure their livelihood they engage in various relations of production. Wage labouring, sharecropping and tenancy are the main types of relations the peasants may engage in. The members of a household may engage in all of these relations either at the same time or at different periods.

Landlessness is a fact of the last 60 years of the history of Gisgis. In the 1920s there were no landless families in Gisgis, though some families did not have any licence for the land they farmed. Several factors facilitated the alienation of land from the peasants, including excessive taxes imposed on farmers during World War Two, indirect taxation later, and today usury, unfavourable price mechanisms, indebtedness and the high rate of population growth.

Bad harvest years, crop failure, the wedding of a son or the purchase of a piece of land for a newly married son to set up a farm are the most common causes of indebtedness amongst peasants. Merchants, usurers, landlords and the Agricultural Bank are the agents from whom money is borrowed. Since the credit extended by the Agriculture Bank is obtained in accordance with the amount of land owned, its significance is negligible for the small peasants.

Once a peasant becomes indebted it is very difficult for him to be able to repay in time, since the farm does not produce enough surplus. Therefore the search for supplementary income becomes an integral part of the survival process of the peasant family farm. This supplementary income is obtained through seasonal or permanent migration. At the time of my study, every household in the village had one or more members who had migrated outside the village. Permanent migration has basically been towards the industrialized centres and the Cukurova and Agean regions, where a large labour force is required for the cultivation of commercial crops such as cotton, tobacco, etc., which are grown for the world market. Those who have left for other areas keep contact with their families by sending money home or by obtaining some of their foodstuffs from the village. The survival of the household production unit is therefore supported by the supplementary income provided by the migrant members of the household. On the other hand, the existence of the household as a safety valve enables the migrant worker to sell his labour power at a lower rate than its market value.

As well as long-term permanent and seasonal migration, daily commuting to nearby town centres or to landlord villages at the peak of harvest time is another aspect of mobilization in the search for supplementary income. While young male members of the household work on building sites in town centres, some female members go to Kalhana village, either for hoeing or for cotton picking in different seasons.

In short, under unfavourable conditions the peasant household opts to diversify its activities and lengthen its total working time in order to be able to survive.

## Kalhana

The history of Kalhana is as old as that of Gisgis, but in contrast to Gisgis, Kalhana is a landlord village. While 10 families in the village own land, most of the lands around Kalhana are owned by just two families. The rest of the 46 households do not own land but have access to very small pieces of land through sharecropping arrangement. The majority of land is irrigated. Until the 1950s, because of the scarcity of labour the landlords allowed the peasants to have access to the land on a more or less equal basis. Various kinds of sharecropping arrangements, *azab* and *maraba* types of labour, were in operation in the village. With the mechanization that took place in the 1950s sharecropping and other types of arrangements between landlords and peasants lost their significance in quantitative terms. Having to a considerable extent lost their access to land, peasants occupied the lands and damaged the landlords' machinery. However, the landlords easily silenced the peasants with the help of the gendarmerie.

Today in Kalhana cotton and sugar beet are grown in irrigated lands. The cultivation of cereal crops such as wheat, lentils and barley takes place mainly in less fertile areas. Landlords employ a small number of permanent wage labourers to use the machinery and supervise the production. The landlords' farms are divided into two parts, one directly cultivated by the landlord himself, using wage labour, and the second cultivated on a sharecropping basis by a peasant family resident in the village or in a neighbouring village (Malan, Keydanevleri or Balahur). Consideration of their long-term interests leads landlords to allocate a part of their land to peasant families. The production of cotton requires a large labour force to be available at harvest time. This need forces the landlord to give a piece of his land to sharecroppers, who are thus tied to the farm by the arrangement. This system strengthens the landlord's position also in imposing his will on the labourers with regard to payment. For instance, labourers are paid in kind when they are employed in cotton picking. The amount of remuneration depends on the amount of cotton picked but a healthy worker could only earn the equivalent of TL60–70 in the labour market in cotton during a 10-hour working day, whereas in 1977 the daily wage of a worker was about TL150–200. Thus by tying sharecroppers and landless peasants to the farm, landlords decrease their total costs in production, although in a simple sharecropping arrangement taken alone it may be the landlord who appears to be on the losing side.

Sharecropping arrangements are considered beneficial by landlords and the rural poor alike. From the point of view of the rural poor, the sharecropping arrangement provides a basic source of income and sometimes also a place in the village to live in, if they come from elsewhere. Furthermore, since the amount of land sharecropped does not necessitate year-round labour from the household, some male members of the family are also able to seek supplementary income outside the village.

It is beneficial from the landlord's point of view, in the long run, to give some land, especially the relatively infertile parts, to the landless poor or to poor peasants with little land, for this keeps a high number of potential workers in the village, at the same time as it enables him to a certain extent to impose his will on the sharecroppers. For instance, he may give lands to those who guarantee a certain number of people to work in peak seasons as cotton pickers.

Total land enclosure, denying the peasants any access to land, would risk undermining the basis of the political power of landlords. Using the economic dependence of their sharecroppers in the village, landlords have been able to mobilize according to their own interests the votes of bonded peasants. The landlords also use their political influence to obtain economic benefits such as easy access to government credits, fertilizers and machinery, etc.

It therefore seems that the existence of peasant household units is vitally important in the functioning of landlord farms that are basically aimed at profit maximization. Given the concrete historical, political and economic conjuncture in Turkey, the subsistence-seeking mentality of the household as a unit of production and reproduction plays an instrumental role in the profit maximization of large landlord farms.

The important thing for the household is to be able to obtain that amount of product which is necessary for its reproduction. The amount of labour spent in obtaining this product is not assessed in monetary terms. It is this patriarchal way of cost calculation that marks the viability of the household under conditions where an enterprise based on rational calculations could not survive. In the profit-maximization process large farms in south-eastern Anatolia internalize this non-rational calculation of labour cost by the household. It is therefore possible to argue that wage labour is not the only form of labour to increase profitability in agriculture. Accordingly, in suggesting political strategies one has to be very careful, otherwise the consequences may be quite tragic.

## A typology of Turkish farming

Capitalism can dominate agriculture without actually establishing wage-labour/capital relations. The capitalist domination of agriculture should not be confused with the existence of capitalist relations of exploitation. In what follows I shall attempt to develop a farm typology indicating the heterogenic nature of the transformation undergone by the countryside.

### Large estates 1

These exist basically in the Cukurova region. Land enclosure is complete. These farms are totally market-orientated. Cotton is produced for the world market by the use of wage labourers. The farm employs a small permanent labour force, including tractor drivers, overseers, labour-recruiting officers and clerks. Most of the labour-intensive work is done by seasonal migrant labourers, mostly coming from the east and south-east.

### Large estates 2

These are predominant in south-eastern Anatolia. Land enclosure has not been taken to its full extent because of specific economic and political factors. Production again is geared to the market: depending on the availability of irrigation either cotton, sugar beet or wheat is produced as the main crop. Irrigated lands are cultivated by the landlord: a small team of wage labourers, basically technical staff, works along with low-paid families of sharecroppers. The wages of seasonal labourers are paid in cash for irrigation and hoeing work, but in kind for cotton picking. In non-irrigated marginal lands wheat and some other grains are grown by sharecropping families. If the farm constitutes mainly non-irrigated lands the most productive parts are cultivated by machinery and wage labourers, whilst sharecroppers are doomed to use the least fertile lands.

**Capitalist farms based on tractor ownership**
A recent trend is for a tractor owner without land either to rent land for cultivation or, in certain cases (generally merchant or usurer tractor owners), to become a sharecropper. In either case the decisions about the type of crop, fertilizers etc. are taken by the tractor owner. In the latter case costs of seeds and fertilizers are shared between the parties, and the product is also shared at the end of the harvest. The first type has been gaining momentum all over Turkey.

**Satellite subsistence family farm**
These exist mainly in the east and south-east as appendages to large estates type 2. The peasants' access to land depends entirely on the landlords' need for the labour of the peasant family and on his political and economic interests. The peasant households cultivate their plots of land in return for a rent in kind and in the form of cheap labour. In certain cases the peasant household is forced by the exigencies of market conditions to produce commodities such as sugar beet and cotton, but in general in small plots peasant households opt to produce their staples and animal fodder. In the production of both commodities and consumption goods the household operates with the aim of subsistence. Since the farm is not big enough to provide for the maintenance and the reproduction of the family, a supplementary income is needed. This is obtained by working on the landlord's estate for very low remuneration.

**Independent family farms**
This is the most widespread form of production unit in the Turkish countryside. The household has enough land to reproduce itself by using basically family labour. An insignificant number of wage labourers may be employed in the process of production. This type of production unit has a highly unstable nature. Under unfavourable market conditions the household may be able to continue its production by over-exploitation of its members. In a long-lasting crisis, however, it always faces the risk of losing its land. Under favourable market conditions it may be able to accumulate capital and transform itself into a large estate type 1.

**Independent dwarf family farms**

These are also very widespread in Turkey. In the east and south-east ex-sharecroppers run most of these farms. In the rest of Turkey, demographic pressure and inheritance laws coupled with limited employment opportunities outside agriculture can be considered the most important factors underlying the existence of this type of farm. The small amount of land owned by the family does not ensure the reproduction of the household. Supplementary income requirements for the household's reproduction are met by diversification of the economic activities of the household members (as wage labourers, craftsmen, tradesmen, etc.). The members of the household are able to offer their labour power at lower than market rates since a part of their reproduction needs is met by their household production. Dwarf farms therefore constitute a cheap labour reserve for capitalist enterprises. It is a very common practice among 'dwarf' farmers to cultivate another 'dwarf' landlord's land on a sharecropping basis.

**Landless workers**

These are the rural inhabitants who have lost their lands or their access to land in various ways but nevertheless have remained in the villages. They work on large farms as seasonal wage labourers. In most cases the wages received from agricultural work are too low to maintain a family, due to considerable competition from 'dwarf' farmers. As a result the head of the family may leave the village for seasonal work elsewhere, while the rest of the family remains in the village.

It should be noted that my classification, which is based on class relations within and between various holdings, differs to quite a considerable extent from that of Caglar Keyder.[31]

Keyder produces four descriptive village case studies, then reduces them to two basic categories: villages dominated by petty commodity production and capitalist villages. This differentiation is further given a spatial dimension when Keyder argues that capitalist villages characterize the most backward region, while the rest of Turkey comprises villages under a petty commodity production of some sort. There are many theoretical problems in Keyder's analysis. First of all the village is taken as a unit of analysis in explaining the paths of rural transformation that have taken place in the Turkish countryside. An immediate implication of this is that each village is a homogeneous unit. This completely ignores the class relations that exist within each of these units. A second aspect missed by this approach is inter-village relations. Particularly in south-eastern Anatolia, villages where small peasant ownership is dominant (Keyder's petty commodity type) exist in clusters around each landlord village, and landlords take advantage of these cheap labour sources. In other words, the existence of peasant villages is absolutely vital for the functioning of the landlord economy. Keyder's spatial differentiation thesis does not reflect the fact that there is a considerable number of the so-called 'petty commodity' villages in Keyder's 'most backward' and 'properly capitalist' region.

Keyder uses the term 'capitalism' very loosely and it is not clear what he means by 'proper capitalist' relations. In his other writings Keyder seems to have subscribed to the Wallerstein understanding of capitalism.[32] If this is so, the 'properness' or 'improperness' of capitalist relations would simply disappear. As is well known, Wallerstein takes capitalism as a world system and holds that various labour forms are possible under capitalism: according to circumstances they can take the form of wage labour, sharecropping or even slave labour.[33] Therefore there are no 'proper' capitalist relations of production.

It is again incomprehensible why 'under the domination of capitalist national and world economy' each village would 'submit to a transformation and adaptation'.[34] Why should two villages three or four kilometres apart show different paths of transformation? A possible answer may be in terms of the class structure of the region. Then the question becomes one concerning the impact of capitalism on the rural structure as a whole, rather than its impact on villages, since class relations and structural relations are not restricted by village boundaries.

In the end, Keyder reduces his village types to two class relations: petty commodity and capitalist, but this completely undermines his theory of transformation based on village typology.

## Notes

1. Some of the contributions to the debate appeared in Boratav, 1969a; 1969b; 1970a; 1970b; Erdost, 1969a; 1969b; 1969c; 1969d; 1970; Kardam, 1970; Kutlay, 1970a; 1970b.
2. Boratav, 1969a, and 1969b.
3. Boratav, 1969a, pp. 108–10 (page numbers for *Gelir Dagilimi* refer to the 3rd edition, published in 1976).
4. Boratav, 1969a, pp. 112–13.
5. See Martinez-Alier, *Haciendas, Plantations and Collective Farms*, London: Frank Cass, 1977.
6. Aydin, unpublished, 1980.
7. V. I. Lenin, *Development of Capitalism in Russia*, Moscow: Progress Publishers, 1964.
8. J. Banaji, 'Summary of selected parts of Kautsky's *The Agrarian Question*', *Economy and Society*, vol. 5, no. 1, 1976.
9. I. Wallerstein, *The Modern World System*, New York: Academic Press, 1974.
10. Boratav, 1970a, pp. 178–80.
11. Ibid., p. 211 and Boratav, 1969a, p. 113.
12. J. Banaji, 'Modes of production in a materialist conception of history', *Capital and Class*, vol. 3, 1977.
13. H. Bernstein, 'Notes on capital and peasantry', *Review of African Political Economy*, no. 10, 1977, pp. 60–73.
14. See *Emek*, June 1969 and April 1970, especially articles by Selik and Culhaoglu in repsective issues. Also see Kutlay, 1970a; 1970b.
15. Erdost, 1969c.
16. Ibid., pp. 39–40.

17. Ibid., p. 40 and Erdost, 'Turkiye'de feodalizm var mi?' ('Does feudalism exist in Turkey?'), *Turk Solu*, no. 80.

18. Erdost, 1969c, pp. 44–6.

19. H. Bernstein, 'African peasantries: a theoretical framework', *Journal of Peasant Studies*, vol. 6, no. 4, July 1979, p. 426.

20. Material concerning south-eastern Anatolia was collected in 1977 as a part of my doctoral research.

21. For a detailed account of various sharecropping arrangements existent in south-eastern Anatolia before the 1950s, Aydin, 1980, chapter 5, pp. 255–60.

22. Tokin, 1934, pp. 176–7.

23. A. Aras, *Guneydogu Anadolu'da Arazi Mulkiyeti ve Isletme Sekilleri* ('Types of Landownership and Agricultural Management in South-east Anatolia'), 1956, pp. 24–5.

24. Keyder argues that one of the features of the Turkish agrarian structure has been the abundance of land and the scarcity of labour ever since the 16th century. Since the maintenance of the Ottoman state was based on its alliance with the independent peasantry, the enserfment of peasants had not taken place in the Empire. See Keyder, 1983a.

25. P. Zhukovsky, *Turkiye'nin Zirai Bunyesi* ('Agricultural Structure of Turkey'), 1951, pp. 128 and 131.

26. Tokin, 1934, pp. 22–3.

27. K. Koylu, *Turkiye'de Buyuk Arazi Mulkleri ve Bunlarin Isletme Sekilleri* ('Big landed estates and their management in Turkey'), 1947, pp. 120–1.

28. Keyder, 1983a.

29. See State Institute of Statistics, *Summary of Agricultural Statistics* for the relevant years.

30. Y. Kanbolat, *Turkiye Ziraatinde Bunye Degisikligi* ('Structural change in Turkish agriculture'), 1963, p. 42.

31. Keyder, 'Paths of rural transformation in Turkey', *Journal of Peasant Studies*, vol. 11, no. 1, 1983b.

32. See especially Keyder, *Definition of a Peripheral Economy: Turkey 1923–1929*, London: Cambridge University Press, 1981, pp. 1–2.

33. I. Wallerstein, *op. cit.*, pp. 125–8.

34. Keyder, *op. cit.*, 1983b, p. 36.

## Selected bibliography

Aksit, Bahattin, 1967, *Türkiye'de Azgelismis Kapitalizm ve Köylere Girisi* ('Underdeveloped capitalism in Turkey and its penetration to villages'), Ankara: ODTO Ög. Bir. Yay.

——— 1985, *Köy Kasaba ve Kentlerde Toplumsal Degisme* ('Social change in villages, towns and cities'), Ankara: Turhan Kitabevi.

Aras, Ali, 1956, *Güneydogu Anadolu'da Arazi Mülkiyeti ve Isletme Sekilleri* ('Types of landownership and agricultural management in South-east Anatolia'), Ankara: Ankara Üniversites: Yayini

Ayden, Zülüküf, 1980, 'Aspects of Rural Underdevelopment in South-eastern Anatolia: The Household Economy in Gisgis and Kalhana'. Unpublished Ph.D. Thesis, Durham University.

——— 1986, *Underdevelopment and Rural Structures in Southeastern Turkey*, Ithaca Press, London.

Banaji, Jairus, 1976, 'Summary of Selected Parts of Kautsky's The Agrarian Question', *Economy and Society*, vol. 5, no. 1.

——— 1977, 'Modes of Production in a Materialist Conception of History', *Capital and Class*, 3.

Bernstein, Henry, 1977, 'Notes on Capital and Peasantry', *Review of African Political Economy*, no. 10

——— 1979, 'African Peasantries: a Theoretical Framework', *The Journal of Peasant Studies*, vol. 6, no. 4.

Boratav, Korkut, 1969a, *Gelir Dagilimi* ('Income distribution'), Istanbul: Gerçek Yayinevi.

——— 1969b, 'Tarimda Feodal Oretim Iliskileri Feodal Kalintilar ve Basit Meta Oretimi' ('Feudal Relations of Production, Feudal Remnants and Simple Commodity Production in Agriculture'), *Emek*, No. 6, July.

——— 1970a, 'Tarimda Oretim Iliskileri Ozerine' ('On the relations of production in agriculture'), *Proleter Devrimci Aydinlik*, no. 1/15, January.

——— 1970b, 'Gecikmis Bir Uyari' ('A belated warning'), *Proleter Devrimci Aydinlik*, no. 20, June.

Erdost, Muzaffer, 1969a, *Türkiye Sosyalizmi ve Sosyalizm* ('Socialism and Turkish Socialism'), Ankara: Sol Yayinlari.

——— 1969b, 'Türkiye'de Feodalizmin Bugünkü Durumu Ozerine Bir Taslak' ('A Sketch on the Position of Feudalism in Turkey Today'), *Aydinlik Sosyalist Dergi*, no. 5, March.

——— 1969c, 'Dogu Anadolu'do Hayvanciligin Feodal Niteligi' ('The Feudal Nature of Animal Husbandry in Eastern Anatolia'), *Aydinlik Sosyalist Dergi*, no. 8, June.

——— 1969d, 'Turkiye Tariminda Hakin Oretim Iliskisi Ozerine' ('On the Dominant Relations of Production in Turkish Agriculture'), *Aydinlik Sosyalist Dergi*, no. 13, November.

——— 1970, 'Yeni Opportünizmin Elestirisi' ('Critique of the New Opportunism'), *Aydinlik Sosyalist Dergi*, no. 19.

——— 1984, *Kapitalizm ve Tarim* ('Capitalism and Agriculture'), Ankara: Onur Yayinlari.

Hinderink, Jan and Kiray, Mübeccel, 1970, *Social Stratification as an Obstacle to Development: A Study of Four Turkish Villages*, New York: Preager Publishers.

Hann, C. M., 1985, 'Rural transformation on the East Black Sea coast of Turkey: A Note on Keyder', *The Journal of Peasant Studies*, vol. 12, no. 4.

Kanoblat, Yahya, 1963, *Türkiye Ziraatinde Bünye Degisikligi* ('Structural change in Turkish agriculture'), Ankara: SBF Maliye Enstitüsü.

Kardam, Ahmet, 1970, 'Milli Demokratik Devrim ve Köylü Meselesi', ('National democratic revolution and the peasant question'), *Aydinlik Sosyalist Dergi*, no. 24, October.

Keyder, Caglar, 1981, *Definition of a Peripheral Economy: Turkey 1923–1924*, London: Cambridge University Press.

——— 1983a, 'The cycle of sharecropping and the consolidation of small peasant ownership in Turkey', *The Journal of Peasant Studies*, vol. 10, nos. 2 and 3.

——— 1983b, 'Paths of Rural Transformation in Turkey', *The Journal of Peasant Studies*, vol. 11, no. 1.

Köylü, Kazim, 1947, *Türkiye'de Büyük Arazi Mülkleri ve Bunlarin Isletme Sekilleri* ('Big landed estates and their management in Turkey').

Kutlay, M., 1970a, 'Geri Kapitalizm' ('Backward capitalism'), *Emek*, vol. 3, no. 2, July.

——— 1970b, 'Türkiye'de Geriligin Gelismesi' ('The development of backwardness in Turkey'), *Emek*, vol. 3, no. 3, August.

Lenin, V. I., 1964, *Development of Capitalism in Russia*, Moscow: Progress Publishers.

Margulies, Ronnie and Seddon, David, 1984, 'The Politics of Agrarian Question in

Turkey', *The Journal of Peasant Studies*, vol. 10, no. 4.
Sirman-Eralp, Nükhet, (work in progress), 'Female Labour in Commodity Production: A Study of Household Formation and Composition in a Cotton Producing Village in Western Turkey', Ph.D. Thesis, University of London.
State Institute of Statistics, *Summary of Agricultural Statistics*.
Teklei, Ilhan, 1977, *Kirda ve Kentte Donüsüm Süreci: Bagimli Ketlesme* ('Process of Transformation in the Countryside and in the City: Dependent Urbanisation'), Ankara: Mimarlar odasi Yayinlari.
Tökin, Ismail Hürev, 1934, *Türkiye Köy Iktisadiyati* ('Village Economics of Turkey'), Istanbul: Kadro Mecmuasi Nesriyati.
Wallerstein, Immanuel, 1974, *The Modern World System*, New York: Academic Press.
Zhukovski, P., 1951, *Türkiye'nin Zirai Bünyesi* ('Agricultural Structure of Turkey'), Ankara.

# 8. Women and Household Production: The Impact of Rural Transformation in Turkey

*Deniz Kandiyoti*

The resilience and continued viability of household-based forms of rural production have been a recurrent theme in recent writing on agrarian relations in the Middle East.[1] At a more general level, there has been a clearer recognition that a differentiation of peasant households is one possible but not necessarily exclusive outcome of the intensification of commodity relations in agriculture.[2] At a time when even international development agencies are promoting the support or even re-creation of forms of organization of labour mimicking the smallholder peasant sector, the value of households as vehicles for less costly and more flexible forms of labour control and reproduction seems self-evident.[3] Against this background, it would appear that the internal workings of peasant households that could provide us with substantial clues concerning their viability have remained relatively undertheorized and unexplored.[4] Specifically, the effects of agricultural commoditization on processes of household formation and their impact on age/gender hierarchies within households deserve far more attention than they have received so far.

The evidence seems to suggest that beyond some general tendencies, the precise forms that household organization and dynamics will take cannot be automatically read off from processes of capital penetration. This is not only due to the fact that such penetration may take a multitude of forms and produce a wide variety of outcomes, but also because it builds upon already existing patterns of kinship and production. The history of productive relations between the sexes prior to capitalist incorporation has a direct bearing on the specific forms that subsequent division of labour takes and possibly sets limits to its variability. Thus, the female farming system of sub-Saharan Africa meant that exclusive male recruitment for work in plantations, mines and public works at below subsistence wages could proceed with women's subsistence production ensuring the support of children, the sick and the aged.[5] In those parts of Asia, on the other hand, where full familial participation in agricultural tasks prevailed, colonial patterns of labour recruitment affected the entire household where both men and women had to intensify subsistence production and work in the export sector to meet new cash demands.[6] In the Jamaican plantation economy the emergence of a 'semi-committed' proletariat engaged in intermittent, uncertain and poorly remunerated wage labour resulted in little commitment on the part of men to support a family, which in turn reinforced a matrifocal family organization and a high involvement of women in productive activities as the main agents of family maintenance.[7] In Latin America, as households start losing access to land, women tend to take on subsistence farming when their men start working for wages,[8] whereas in small family units producing cash crops the viability of the enterprise is based on the male household head's ability to mobilize unremunerated family labour, which in practice often means the labour of women.[9]

It would thus appear that changes in the sexual division of labour are mediated both by the nature of pre-existing relationships between the sexes and by the modalities of capital penetration in rural areas. Clearly, both the internal and external factors that determine the options that households have in organizing production and reproduction need to be given careful consideration. Only when the abstract category of 'household labour' or 'unremunerated family labour' is actually broken down into different categories of concrete labourers can the mechanisms accounting for survival be fully elucidated. A large number of studies have shown that household-level adaptations and strategies for survival build upon the generic subordination of women, which actively shapes and informs labour deployment options and patterns.[10] These are evident in the internal allocation of tasks (subsistence vs. market-orientated, mechanical vs. manual, remunerated vs. unremunerated), in decisions regarding which household members are to be 'freed' for wage work, whose education will be invested in, which household members will become temporary or more permanent migrants, and what portion of the income they generate will be under the continued control of the household.

Many have argued that capital penetration in agriculture actually accentuates sexual divisions by introducing deeper cleavages between market-orientated and subsistence-orientated activities, as well as disparities in access to extra-household agencies and institutions (to obtain credit, access to land, new technology and other agricultural inputs and marketing outlets) which gain a new and crucial significance in the reproduction of peasant households. The task of this chapter will be to illustrate the complex and often contradictory effects that capital penetration in rural Turkey has had on household formation and dynamics in general, and on the place of women in peasant households more particularly. Our discussion will start with an examination of the 'ideal-typical' peasant household, which constitutes the most important nexus of patriarchal relations. This will be followed by an analysis of different processes of rural transformation and the differing outcomes these represent in the determination of women's productive and reproductive roles. Even though the case materials referred to throughout the text are drawn exclusively from rural Turkey, they can be seen to have a broader relevance for the whole 'patriarchal belt' extending from Morocco to Bangladesh.

## The social organization of the Anatolian peasant household

As is the case in many agrarian societies, the Anatolian peasant household represents a clear-cut instance of 'classic' patriarchy.[11] Anthropological accounts of this virilocal and patrilineal household draw attention to its domestic cycle involving wealth dispersion (land and livestock) after the father's death among the sons who divide property equally among themselves (daughters do not inherit) and reaccumulation in the individual households of sons, which in turn go through a phase of extended patrilocality until further division through inheritance occurs.[12] Both the relatively primitive level of productive forces (ox and plough technology) and the operation of the domestic cycle create an 'equalizing' dynamic at the level of the village which stands in contrast to the sharp age–sex hierarchies within the households themselves. The social and sexual hierarchy within the household also corresponds to a hierarchy in the labour process. Command over labour is an absolutely critical feature of production and accumulation of wealth especially in the case of abundant cultivable land, a condition that obtained in many parts of rural Turkey. Both the organization of production and the social organization of the patrilineage depend on the reproduction of males, giving women the critical role of being the agents of reproduction of the group. Sons ensure the continuity of the lineage while daughters are exchanged at a very young age to ensure the reproduction of another lineage. This exchange may or may not be accompanied by the payment of *baslik* (bride price) but in all cases we see the complete appropriation by the patrilineage of women's production and reproduction.[13]

Women's key reproductive role, which together with advancing age constitute the main ingredients of women's status, should not lead us to overlook their productive role and their value as labour. The suggestion that women's status drops with advanced agriculture as opposed to more primitive forms of subsistence because of greater incompatibility with child-rearing, leading to the withdrawal of women's labour from production, is simply not borne out by the Anatolian case where going back to work after a brief post-partum period was not an uncommon occurrence. If anything, it is in fact post-menopausal women free of child-bearing duties who participate least in agricultural production and act as overseers and co-ordinators of fertile brides. And therein lies one of the most striking facets of village patriarchy, where hardest work is always associated with youngest age, female sex and lowest status:

> ... daughters are less important than sons, as any patriarch will aver, because at an early age they marry out into another family: yet the most hardworking labour input within the family (which largely determines living comfort) comes from daughters-in-law, brought in from other families who have conditioned them to be submissive and hence a valuable and economical labour force, precisely because of their undervaluation.[14]

The labour productivity cycle of a women in a peasant household will closely parallel the domestic cycle of the household itself. The in-marrrying bride will be at the very bottom of the age–sex hierarchy and work very hard indeed both in agricultural production and at the heavier household chores such as carrying water and fetching firewood. Her status improves with her ability to produce male offspring and as she gains seniority. She reaches the apex of her influence when her married sons in turn bring her brides. Not only does her workload become much lighter but she may even be involved in the more managerial aspects of production such as the allocation and co-ordination of tasks among the younger women. Despite obvious built-in sources of tension within this system, its cyclical nature ensures its relative stability under subsistence or semi-subsistence conditions since the willingness to provide for the elders ensures a future guarantee towards similar services in one's old age. Ozbay draws our attention to demographic factors such as higher mortality rates and shorter life expectancy of household heads, which limit and curtail the life span of the extended household, thus averting prolonged friction and serious imbalances in the producer/consumer ratio within households.[15]

The division of labour within the peasant household is related to every facet of its social organization. The spread of commoditization of agriculture, which may take a wide variety of forms and exhibit varied outcomes, has a decisive impact on household organization and women's productive roles. This impact may take the form of direct consequences for women's work through the allocation of new tasks or reallocation of old ones to women in a manner that totally breaks with the rhythm, intensity and life-cycle pattern discussed previously. Or it may have more derivative effects making themselves felt over a longer period of time and stemming from the gradual dissolution or transformation of the traditional peasant household and its domestic cycle. Finally, more than one mechanism may be operating simultaneously, sometimes producing contradictory effects. There are a number of possible outcomes for women's productive and reproductive roles.

## Rural transformation in Turkey: its implications for women

The transition to production for the market and agricultural commoditization has advanced at different speeds in different regions of rural

Turkey. The fertile plains of western Anatolia – the Smyrna region – already cultivated export crops at a time when the now cotton-growing plains of the south, the Chukurova, were still malaria-infested. The central Anatolian plateau, a bastion of subsistence economy and nomadic existence, has only become truly integrated into the national market in the late 1940s and 1950s. Although rural transformation in Turkey has been the subject of numerous studies,[16] a direct and comprehensive analysis of its implications for women is a task that yet remains to be achieved. Our analysis will of necessity be based on incomplete and fragmentary evidence, mainly on case studies, and the discussion will be of a suggestive rather than conclusive nature.

It is widely acknowledged that changes in rural women's productive roles cannot be abstracted from the agrarian structures in which they are enacted and that capital penetration may create a considerable heterogeneity in the sexual division of labour. Clearly, the historical circumstances related to capital penetration, the type and size of tenure, the nature of the crop, the position of any particular household in terms of rural stratification will not only determine the amount, type and intensity of women's participation in production but will also be closely related to ideologies pertaining to women's place in general. However, the simple application of a typology of rural transformation and the insertion of women into a matrix of varied types of labour demand or non-demand may not render the full impact of change when our starting point is the patriarchal peasant household. We will therefore discuss rural transformation from two distinct yet interrelated angles, the first having to do with the transformation of village patriarchy, the second with women's changing roles in the production process.

**The transformation of village patriarchy**

The patrilocal extended family depends for its existence on common patrimony – namely land, animals or both. Therefore, any number of factors such as excessive fragmentation through inheritance and scarcity of cultivable land due to geographic constraints may theoretically impede its functioning and create pockets of rural labour surplus even under subsistence conditions. The fact remains that demographically speaking such labour surplus is a relatively recent phenomenon attesting to the irreversible and qualitative nature of the change brought about by production for the market. It therefore seems pertinent to ask in what ways incorporation into the market economy modifies the internal structure and functioning of peasant households. This question can be answered in a relatively straightforward manner where capital penetration has brought about either dispossession (as in the case of transition to capitalist farming where former sharecroppers rapidly become wage workers)[17] or the concentration of land and capital resources in fewer hands towards optimal holding size with the concomitant creation of a pool of marginal or submarginal villagers for whom land is a supplement to other income.[18] In these cases, the economic base of patrilocal extension is clearly eroded and the role of the father as the sole holder of economic resources is undermined. Only wealthier landed households are able to sustain extension as was shown by a national sample survey carried out in 1968;[19] while most farmers live in extended families, landless agricultural workers have the largest proportion of nuclear families. The proportion of nuclear families was found to be 44% among farmers, and 64% among sharecroppers, rising to a high 79% among agricultural wage workers. Thus, there is a clear correlation between size of landholding and family size and composition. Even among wealthier village strata, however, if developments go in the direction of greater diversification of income sources (such as branching out into non-agricultural commercial activities) despite the maintenance of powerful economic ties among brothers, or father and sons, residential extension loses its relevance.[20]

In fact, such economic ties often cut across the boundaries of village and market town. In the case of the family enterprise whose viability depends on its ability to command family labour, some built-in guarantees against further fragmentation through inheritance must be sought and relative affluence is often used as a means of educating children and orientating them towards non-agricultural occupations. Clearly, the tensions built into the patrilocally extended household come to a head when there is no viable patrimony, when the younger generation has independent sources of income or when the nature of what is to be shared changes dramatically. Thus, extendedness becomes a brief phase of the domestic cycle and a married son will generally set up a separate nuclear unit after he judges that he has contributed the cost of his wedding to the paternal household. In this respect early nuclearization rather than neolocality is still the rule but has specific causes and implications for familial roles.[21]

Modifications of the economic base of traditional village existence have had an important effect on authority relations between older and younger men in general, and fathers and sons in particular, as evidenced by a symptomatic decline in respect for elders and the assumption of leadership roles by younger married men. Although young men are still dependent on their fathers for the payment of their wedding costs, there is evidence that village bachelors are becoming increasingly freer of parental control in choosing a marriage partner.[22] Once married, a young couple looks forward to a certain amount of independence from their elders in terms of budget allocation and daily decision-making. It is not uncommon to find relatively young women with small children heading their own household at a time when they would normally be serving their mother-in-law. Conversely, the expectation of ageing in an extended household surrounded by subservient brides becomes increasingly remote.

In summary, it would seem fair to say that the decrease in patriarchal control is a direct function of the inability of the older generation to retain total economic control over the young. Although this development may at first sight seem to favour only the earlier emancipation of younger males, it does, through complementarity, have an effect upon women. However, those same processes that modify traditional family structure also modulate the demand for family labour and in particular the labour of women, so that the potentially liberating effect of patriarchal dissolution may be superseded by novel forms of exploitation.

Before addressing this question, an inherent paradox in this situation should be noted. The evidence suggests that larger landholdings bolster the extended family and prolong the existence of patriarchal controls. Yet it is those same households that are able to withdraw their women from the production process either because of their ability to use contractual labour or because they cultivate crops amenable to capital-intensive, labour-saving technology. The maintenance of a more patriarchal family structure here coincides with a significant alleviation of women's workloads. Small family farms on the other hand are heavily dependent on the labour of their women since the very viability of such enterprises depends on their ability to rely exclusively on family labour to the near total exclusion of contractual help. This is even more so among destitute landless families where every member of the family, including young children, has to contribute economically, generally through seasonal wage work. It would therefore seem that the very mechanisms bringing about the dissolution of the patriarchal household are those which at the same time make the increased and sustained input of women into the labour process absolutely critical.

**Women and changing rural production**

A clear distinction must be made here between women's domestic chores and their agricultural production, since capital penetration may have different and even opposite effects regarding these two spheres. Agricultural commercialization has contributed greatly to the expansion of the internal market in Turkey and home production has increasingly given way to the commoditization of consumption. Although many consumer goods, such as the transistor radio, have no appreciable impact on women's workloads, others clearly do. Thus, readymade clothes and store-bought foods, commercially distributed heating fuel, soap and detergent have made their entrance into villages, reducing considerably the labour that went into home production. The reduction of effort that went into home production of food and clothes is mitigated by a relative loss of control by women over resource allocation and the control of consumption within the household, in favour of the creation of a double standard of consumption between the sexes, a point to which we shall return later.[23] Nonetheless, the net impact of commercialization, in addition to better sanitation, has been to produce a relative alleviation of women's household chores.

As far as agricultural production is concerned the picture is far more complex. For the sake of simplicity, we shall schematically define outcomes as a relative retreat from production and labour intensification respectively, illustrating the different forms these outcomes may take by means of case studies.

The best examples of retreat from production may be found in the case of capital-intensive, mechanized cereal farming, a form of development that is particularly characteristic of central Anatolia in the Polatli, Eskisehir and Konya provinces. Here both the nature of the crop, which leaves no room for labour-intensive operations, and the labour-saving nature of the technology mean that women's contribution to production is restricted to very minor tasks. This situation tends to be fairly uniform throughout the village since whatever contractual relationships exist (such as land rent, tractor rent or seasonal help) take place between male villagers with sub-optimal plots and commercial grain farmers, or male wage workers from neighbouring villages.[24] A clear indication that agricultural labour brought no status under the 'classic' patriarchal system can be deduced from the distinct feeling of amelioration of status among women in such villages and the absence of any sense of loss of control; as suggested previously, labour did not bring any kind of resource control in its wake. It is not only that greater confinement to domesticity is a mark of status, but also that it very simply represents greater freedom from rural drudgery.

To talk about retreat from production in the case of large landholding families which have turned into properly capitalist enterprises would be quite inappropriate, especially when the capitalist farmers are former landlords who traditionally let their holdings out to sharecroppers. The women of such households were always confined to domesticity and enjoyed the help of servants; admittedly they represented a very small minority.

Finally, a less thoroughly explored case of retreat from production is that of the left-behind wives of migrants to EC countries who receive remittances from their husbands. Kiray[25] notes that these women manage the cash incomes they receive from abroad totally on their own and that independent households for the wife and children are established despite the fact that both the woman's and, more significantly, her husband's parents may be living in the same village. Abadan-Unat[26] discusses these women's lack of eagerness to 'toil in the fields' to an extent that may, in her view, cause 'neglect' of agricultural production. Clearly, such patterns must be subject to important regional variations, as well as to variations in the dependability and magnitude of remittance income, the nature of the subsistence base and demographic composition of the village.

Rather different patterns emerge in the case of small to medium family farms, the marginal or sub-marginal smallholders and landless agricultural labourers. A case study of cotton growing in the Söke valley of western Anatolia illustrates the dynamics of the small family farm.[27] Although the preparation of the soil and sowing are mechanized, cotton production requires successive hoeing operations to ensure proper spacing and successive harvests lasting up to two or three months, because of the irregular growth and maturation of the crop. This means that an adequate and timely supply of labourers to carry out those non-mechanized operations is absolutely essential. It appears that within this context agricultural enterprises small enough to be able to operate with the labour pooled within the family have a higher degree of viability than the larger estates, which are faced with management problems, particularly with respect to labour supply. The availability of a dependable and easily controlled female labour force for the labour-intensive processes of harvesting and hoeing is an obviously critical factor making for this viability. Typically, a female network activates a widening group of neighbours and kin who form work parties and enter into reciprocal harvesting arrangements so that labour is expended without exchanges of cash. For women, the transition to exclusive reliance on cotton production for the market has resulted in more intensive inputs into the labour process and a deeper cleavage in the sexual division of labour, whereby men become specialized in mechanized operations and bureaucratic/commercial dealings, whereas women are confined to unskilled, unremunerated manual operations.

The situation is further aggravated in the case of marginal or sub-marginal smallholdings. These are holdings so small that they cannot absorb the totality of available family labour so that other sources of income have to be sought to supplement income from land. These are the cases where the so-called 'feminization of agriculture' typically takes place, since it is the men who migrate temporarily or on a longer-term basis to seek alternative sources of income while the women remain totally in charge of agriculture. When this occurs in regions where labour-intensive crops such as tea, tobacco or hazelnuts are cultivated the fact that manual tasks are considered women's work anyway, means that men's failure to secure alternative sources of income and employment does not bring about a more equitable sharing of production tasks since the unemployed men will remain idle while their women carry out their habitual tasks. Similar observations may be made about village crafts, especially carpet weaving. In many villages of south-western Anatolia full-time, intensive carpet weaving by women constitutes the mainstay of village economy while men have erratic, seasonal incomes from tourism, fishing, sponge diving and small commercial endeavours. Typically, while women in times of need may be called upon to perform tasks which are considered men's work, the reverse is never true.[28] This may lead to extremes of quasi-parasitic dependence on women's labour, a dependence which far from giving women greater autonomy can only be sustained by means of harsher and more violent subjugation of women. It is within such contexts that men will uphold an ideology of their superiority with greatest force, although such defensive patriarchy must not be confused with its traditional form.

Ozbay[29] reports the case of a tea-growing village in Trabzon, in the Black Sea region, where men have withdrawn from agricultural production altogether. A few have permanent and many have seasonal jobs of a very short-term nature (several weeks a year) in a neighbouring tea factory. Since land is scarce and plots are small and overextended, possibilities of mobility within the villages are blocked so men seek opportunities for both higher education, which will give them access to non-agricultural jobs, and for migration to large urban centres; women are systematically denied such opportunities as evidenced in the particularly steep educational gap between the sexes in this situation.

Finally, in the case of landless agricultural workers, men, women and children all have to participate in seasonal wage work, such as cotton picking in the southern plain of Chukurova. Although there are no detailed studies of the exact labour input of each family member, there is little doubt that women's contribution is absolutely essential to the survival of the family. Typically a contract is entered into with the male family head who brings his whole family to work with him.

Whether the future holds further dispossession and marginalization of small producers or, on the contrary, the consolidation of the small family enterprise, the overall outcome would seem to be the continued involvement of women in agricultural production. Currently the diminishing numbers of women in the agricultural sector in Turkey,[30] as in many developing countries, are a function of major shifts in rural to urban population ratios; more women than men are now in the 'economically inactive' category in urban areas, while those who remain in rural areas are likely to be more burdened than ever, given the male bias in rural to urban migration until very recently.[31]

The continued access of rural households to their women's unremunerated labour, as well as to their wage work capacity, is an essential component of their viability and their reproduction under conditions of intensified commodity relations. Many studies show quite clearly that the centrifugal forces experienced by households that are in the process of losing direct access to the means of production are not spread evenly among household members. Typically, it is young, male labour which is lost to the household first. Even in cases where young, unmarried women do migrate for wage work, as in the case of domestic workers, the household retains control over a much larger portion, if not the totality, of their earnings. The fact that the generic type of patriarchy prevalent in rural Turkey was already predicated upon the total appropriation of the fruits of women's production and reproduction by the patrilineage, meant that the intensification of both their unremunerated and paid labour input and its continued control by the male-headed household was rendered relatively unproblematic, in contrast to regions in sub-Saharan Africa, for instance, where women traditionally retained some control over their own cultivation and marketing activities. In Turkey, the carry-over of traditional male privileges into the cash nexus is plainly apparent, giving men almost exclusive control over money even when they are not the ones who earned it. Thus not only do men often act as middlemen *vis à vis* their wives, daughters and sisters, marketing their goods and controlling the cash, but they also use this cash to their own advantage in matters of consumption. Recent studies on rural Turkey suggest that men eat more and better, spend more time and money on their leisure activities and indulge in conspicuous consumption more frequently than women.[32] At least at this stage of capital penetration in rural Turkey, the patriarchal control of women is prolonged and reinforced despite important transformations in household formation and dynamics.

## Notes

1. See for instance K. Glavanis and P. Glavanis, 'The sociology of agrarian relations in the Middle East: the persistence of household production', *Current Sociology*, vol. 31, no. 2, 1983.
2. H. Bernstein, 'Concept for the analysis of contemporary peasantries', *Journal of Peasant Studies*, vol. 6, no. 4, 1979, pp. 421–44 provides an excellent account of such processes.
3. See R. Galli (ed.), *The Political Economy of Rural Development*, Albany: State University of New York Press, 1981 and C. Payer, 'The World Bank and the small farmer', *Monthly Review*, vol. 32, no. 6, November 1980, pp. 30–46, for an account of World Bank policies. Also A. Conti, 'Capitalist organization of production through non-capitalist relations: women's role in a pilot resettlement in Upper Volta', *Review of African Political Economy*, vol. 15–16, 1979, pp. 75–91, for an interesting case study.
4. O. Harris, 'Households as natural units', in Young *et al.* (eds), *Of Marriage and the Market*, London: CSE Books, 1981, provides a thorough criticism of Chayanov's and Sahlins' attempts, as well as important clues regarding conceptual obstacles to the theorization of households. For other attempts see J. Smith, I. Wallerstein and H.-D. Evers (eds.), *Households and the World Economy*, London: Sage, 1984.
5. See E. Boserup, *Women's Role in Economic Development*, London: George Allen and Unwin, 1970; S. Young, 'Fertility and famine: women's agricultural history in Mozambique', in R. Palmer and N. Parsons (eds.), *The Roots of Rural Poverty*, Berkeley: University of California Press, 1977; M. Mueller, 'Women and men, power and powerlessness in Lesotho', in Wellesley Editorial Committee, *Women and National Development*, Chicago: University of Chicago Press, 1977.
6. A. Stoler, 'Class structure and female autonomy in rural Java', in Wellesley Editorial Committee, *Women and National Development*.
7. G. Standing, 'Labour force participation in historical perspective' (ILO, WEP 2021/W 50), Geneva: International Labour Office, 1977.
8. M. Leon de Leal and C. D. Deere, 'Rural women and the development of capitalism in Colombian agriculture', *Signs*, vol. 5, no. 1, 1979, pp. 60–77.
9. K. Young, 'Modes of appropriation and the sexual division of labour: a case study of Oaxaca, Mexico', in A. Kuhn and A. M. Wolpe (eds.), *Feminism and Materialism*, London: Routledge and Kegan Paul, 1978, pp. 112–54. See also C. R. Spindel, 'Oligopolic capital and rural production based on family labour: the economic and social role of the woman', paper prepared for 'Women and the working poor' Workshop, IDS, University of Sussex, 23–25 April 1980.
10. For a good dicsussion of household strategies in relation to migration decisions see L. Arizpe, 'Agrarian change and the dynamics of women's rural out-migration in Latin America', in *Women on the Move*, Paris: Unesco, 1984.
11. E. Wolf, *Peasants*, New Jersey: Prentice Hall, 1969.
12. P. Stirling, *Turkish Village*, New York: John Wiley and Sons, 1965.
13. D. Kandiyoti, 'Sex roles and social change: a comparative appraisal of Turkey's Women', *Signs*, no. 3, 1977, pp. 57–73.
14. J. C. Caldwell, 'A theory of fertility: from high plateau to destabilization', *Population and Development Review*, no. 4, 1978, pp. 553–77.

15. F. Ozbay, 'Transformation of the socio-economic structure and changing family functions in rural Turkey', in T. Erder, (ed.), *Family in Turkish Society*, Ankara: Turkish Social Science Association, 1985.

16. R. Aricanli and K. Somel, 'Observations on the nature of transformation of Turkey's land distribution and agriculture', Ankara: Economic and Social Research Institute, Middle East Technical University, ESA Working Paper no. 10, 1979. See also M. Cinar and O. Silier, *Turkiye Tariminda Isletmeler Arasi Farklilasma* ('Differentiation among enterprises in Turkish agriculture'), Istanbul: Bogazici University Publications, no. 165, 1979; C. Keyder, 'Paths of rural transformation in Turkey', in Asad and Owen (eds.), *The Middle East*, London: Macmillan Press, 1983; J.Hinderink and M. Kiray, *Social Stratification as an Obstacle to Development*, New York: Praeger, 1970; D. Kandiyoti, 'Social change and social stratification in a Turkish village', *Journal of Peasant Studies*, 1975, no. 2, pp. 206–19.

17. J. Hinderink and M. Kiray, *Social Stratification*.

18. D. Kandiyoti, 'Social Change'.

19. S. Timur, *Turkiyede Aile Yapisi* ('Family structure in Turkey'), Ankara: Sevias Matbassi, 1972.

20. D. Kandiyoti 'Social Change' suggests that some 'family enterprises' consist of a network of residentially nuclear families connected through their common contribution to a capital pool even though the actual productive activities they engage in may be different, i.e. some engage in full-time agriculture, others diversify into commerce and services. Even though each household is a separate consumption unit, it is not an autonomous production unit, and hence exhibits different patterns of authority relations when compared to fully nuclear households.

21. S. Timur, *Turkiyede Aile Yapisi*. Ozbay ('Transformation') further suggests that earlier neolocality is a solution to pressures brought about by demographic changes such as the relative reduction in the family's generation length (due to earlier marriages since the 1950s) and the increase in the life expectancy of the household head.

22. D. Kandiyoti, 'Bachelors and maidens: a Turkish case study', in J. G. Peristiany (ed.), *Kinship and Modernization in Mediterranean Society*, Rome: American Universities Field Staff, 1976.

23. M. Kiray, 'The women of small towns', in N. Abadan-Unat (ed.), *Women in Turkish Society*, Leiden: E. J. Brill, 1981, pp. 259–74.

24. D. Kandiyoti, 'Social Change'. See also F. Ozbay, 'Kirsal yörelerde kadinin statüsü, isgücüne katilimi ve egitim durumu' (Women's status, labour force participation and education in rural areas), *AITIA Yönetim Bilimleri Fakültesi Dergisi*, no. 1, 1979, pp. 201–24.

25. M. Kiray, 'The family of the immigrant worker', in N. Abadan-Unat (ed.), *Turkish Workers in Europe, 1969–1975*, Leiden: E. J. Brill, 1976.

26. N. Abadan-Unat, 'Implications of migration on emancipation and pseudo-emancipation of Turkish women', *International Migration Review*, vol. 11, 1977, pp. 31–57.

27. A. N. Sirman, 'Women and development – the changing position of women in an agricultural valley of western Turkey', paper presented at the Conference on Social Movements in Southern Europe, 24–25 May 1980, University College, London.

28. In such a village with high male unemployment, the suggestion by this researcher's husband that men may sit at the loom was greeted with general hilarity.

29. F. Ozbay, 'Kirsal yörelerde kadinin statüsü'.

30. In the case of Turkey the decline has been from an 81.5% overall participation rate of women in 1950 to 37% in 1975. See G. Kazgan, 'Labour force participation, occupational distribution, educational attainment and socio-economic status of women in the Turkish economy', in N. Abadan-Unat (ed.), *Women in Turkish Society*, pp. 131–59.

31. L. Erder, 'The women of Turkey: a demographic overview', in N. Abadan-Unat (ed.), *Women in Turkish Society*, pp. 41–58.

32. A. Baysal, 'Nutritional problems of Turkish women', in N. Abadan-Unat (ed.), *Women in Turkish Society*, pp. 107–21. See also Kiray, 'The women of small towns', pp. 41–58.

# 9. Gender Hierarchy in a Palestinian Village: the Case of Al-Balad[1]

*Analiese Moors*

Discussions of changing gender hierarchies in the Middle East have their specific problematics. As Sayigh (1981) has pointed out, the problem is not that women have been neglected; on the contrary, she speaks of a 'women complex'. Within the tradition of Orientalism women have been conceptualized as the symbol of a society seen as strange and threatening. Islam is considered as the fundamental ordering principle of these societies, and it is perceived as an all-embracing, unchanging and repressive institution. In line with this tradition, women in the Middle East have been defined as essentially Islamic, and therefore automatically as oppressed. An effect of the dominance of this approach has been that a lot of intellectual energy has been spent countering these claims, especially in the Middle East itself, as the extensive literature on 'women and Islam' bears witness.

Another obstacle in relating gender hierarchies to social transformation has been the dominance of one particular strand of feminist theory in studies of the Mediterranean area, the domestic/public perspective. The relations of women within the domestic sphere have been used to explain her subordination. From a different emphasis but within the same framework, attention has been directed towards the power of women in the domestic sphere and concepts such as 'informal power' have been developed. Both approaches have in common that they start from the separation of the world of women from that of men.

Rosaldo (1980) has shown that this perspective is rooted in dichotomous thinking, where presumably given differences between the genders are used as explanation and where men and women are seen in an essentialist manner. This emphasis on dichotomies prevents an understanding of the position of women in terms of relations between the genders. At the same time, it separates women from general social processes and leads to an inherently static and ahistorical approach.

A historical and holistic perspective is central to theories of structural dependency and modes of production; but in these theories gender is often not considered as a relevant category. It is often assumed that gender can be disregarded in discussions at high levels of abstraction such as those on the workings of modes of production. But it becomes problematic if gender is neglected in concrete analyses of the organization of production, when concepts such as 'peasants' and 'households' are used. All too often the gender neutrality of social categories such as peasants is presumed, while (implicitly) these are seen as male. The conceptualization of the household as a social and economic unit takes for granted, as Harris (1981) has pointed out, that the economic relations within the household are of a totally different nature (characterized by sharing and generosity) to those outside. Hierarchical relations between household members, however, are often neglected. Little attention is paid to the historical and social specificity both of household composition and of the nature of relations within the household. If within a certain community households are seen as units, and a discontinuity is asserted between intra- and inter-household relations, this certainly must be considered. It should not be taken as given, however, but should be analysed in order to avoid neglecting hierarchical divisions of labour and unequal rights to consumption within the household.

Transformations in the international division of labour and property relations form the framework within which changes in the sexual division of labour and the division of property along the lines of gender in Al-Balad will be discussed. This implies that the effects of external factors, such as the penetration of capitalism and colonization, will be considered. Changes in gender hierarchies are, however, not only determined by those external factors, but also by the nature of pre-existing gender relations. Furthermore, such an analysis cannot be limited to the 'economic' in a narrow sense. Kinship is also an important principle of organization, particularly for the reproduction of labour and in social reproduction (for example through inheritance systems). Moreover, the effects of cultural notions should not be disregarded; ideological constructs, such as the conceptualization of women's work, can influence directions of change. Using this perspective, changes in gender hierarchy will be analysed in the village of Al-Balad, taking as the starting date the end of the 1920s, when Al-Balad could still be considered a peasant village.[2]

## Al-Balad 1920-30: a peasant village

The village of Al-Balad is situated in the eastern part of the Djabal Nablus, a mountainous area with fertile plains, where dry-farming agriculture is dependent on irregular rainfall. At the end of the 1920s Al-Balad had approximately 500 inhabitants. The main fieldcrops were wheat and barley, which were rotated with summer crops such as sesame. Olive trees were planted around the village and livestock such as goats, sheep and cows were reared in large numbers. From the beginning of the century peasants from Al-Balad also started working irrigated land in the Far'a Valley, less than ten kilometres away, while continuing to live in the village. Later they built mudbrick houses in this region, which became the hamlet of Nazlat Al-Balad. The largely rocky, mountainous land between Al-Balad and Nazlat Al-Balad was used for herding goats. In early spring many households moved with their goats into the mountains, living in tents or caves.

The major political and economic developments affecting Palestine at this time did not leave Al-Balad unaffected. In 1922 the British had officially gained control over Palestine in a Mandate from the League of Nations. One of the clauses of this Mandate promoted the creation of a Jewish 'national home' in Palestine. As a result Zionist landbuying led in many cases to the expulsion of Palestinian peasants from their homelands. In the eastern Djabal Nablus, no Zionist colonization took place, but the effects of colonization elsewhere in Palestine made themselves felt as the economic centre was moving more and more towards the coastal areas.[3] The most important reason for the increasing landlessness of the peasantry in the Djabal Nablus was impoverishment due to high taxes and indebtedness, which forced them to sell their land.

During this period in Al-Balad there was a growing polarization in landownership. The influence of urban traders grew steadily in the village, and until the 1940s they increased their landholdings in the village by taking land from indebted peasants, which they then leased to sharecroppers. Also at this time within the Dar al-Shaykh, an influential village-based family, part of a larger landowning clan in the region, differentiation increased. Some family members moved into Nablus, where they engaged in trade and banking, while others were losing land. From the beginning of the 1930s onward, men from Al-Balad started to migrate temporarily to the coastal areas in search of employment. In most cases income gained from migratory labour was in addition to that from agriculture, which was still the main source of income. Most households had some land and goats, or had access to it as sharecroppers. As elsewhere, agriculture in the Djabal Nablus was still by and large directed towards subsistence production.

### Gender and property

Household property was mainly in the hands of older men. The extended virilocal household was the preferred form of residence, with sons living with and dependent on their father until he died, and daughters leaving the natal household at marriage to move in with their in-laws. In the rural areas of Palestine women generally did not inherit family property, even though according to Islamic law a woman should get half a man's share. The division of property along gender lines was legitimized by the ideology of the male provider. A man was considered financially responsible for his wife, children and unmarried female kin, while a woman was supposed to be provided for. Only in special cases, such as when a man only had daughters, did women inherit.

Yet women in Al-Balad were not totally excluded from control over (productive) property, although, in general, women owned less land and livestock than men. They did not acquire this property through inheritance, but rather received it either as gifts (mainly from a brother) or, more important, through transfers at marriage (the *mahr*). These transfers, in money or kind, were an essential part of the marriage contract, paid by the father of the groom to the father of the bride. Usually the bride's father gave one third of the total *mahr* to his daughter as the bride's share. This was the most important mechanism for women to gain access to property. Women protested if they did not get their 'bride's share' and this was one of the reasons why they resented *badal* marriages (exchange marriages where daughters and/or sisters were exchanged and no *mahr* was paid).[4]

Normally when the groom did not have the full amount of the *mahr* in cash, then it was paid in goods, livestock or land. In this way a bride could receive land registered in her name instead of money or gold.[5] It was difficult, however, for the bride to have real control over her land, especially if she was very young, as she often lived in the household of her in-laws, the former owners of the land. Only when she had her own household, and especially if she became widowed, did she gain full control over it.

Usually the greater part of the bride's share was used to buy gold (mostly coins, sewn on a long strip of cloth worn around her neck). The rest was spent on household goods, which also remained the bride's property. Women marrying in the 1930s and 1940s often sold their gold in order to buy productive property with it, be it a piece of land, a cow or some goats. In many cases these purchases were the start of a whole series of transactions. Women also used gifts from their male relatives to buy this type of property, over which women had almost full control. Only women in very poor households were sometimes forced to sell their gold in order to provide for the household.

### The sexual division of labour

Although most work of both men and women was directed towards subsistence, a division of labour existed along lines of gender. Domestic work was only under special circumstances done by men. It was the women who carried water from the well a few kilometres distant from the village, who collected wood in the neighbourhood of the village, who baked the bread, did the washing and cleaned the house. Gleaning grain, curing olives and preparing yogurt and butter from milk were also women's tasks. Most of this work was done outside the home, for until the 1940s most of the houses consisted of only one room. Women also took part in building houses by fetching water and carrying the stones; they made stoves from clay and mattresses and quilts from wool. During the winter months some households remained in Nazlat Al-Balad and in early spring many households with goats went with their tents into the mountains. In short, domestic work did not confine women to the house.

The sexual division of labour in agriculture was not very marked.

Women participated in most of the work tasks involved in growing winter crops, but the amount of male labour input was considerably greater than that of women. Women cleaned the seeds and helped with sowing, but ploughing was only done by men. Weeding, sometimes two or three times a season, was generally women's work. Harvesting was done by men and women together. Women collected the grain and piled it up in bundles. Threshing and winnowing were male tasks but women contributed by cleaning the sand off and sweeping the stalks away. Sieving was only done by women. Picking olives was the work of both men and women.

In growing summer crops, such as sesame and vegetables, the time input of women was larger, because planting and harvesting these crops was very labour-intensive. In animal husbandry, women's work was essential. While men herded the flocks, it was mainly women who milked the goats and cows; the processing of milk was exclusively women's work. Buying and selling smaller quantities of agricultural products in Nablus was also done by women, but men were responsible for larger amounts.[6]

Not all women in Al-Balad did the same work. What a woman did depended to a large extent on the wealth and prestige of the household involved. A characteristic of the lives of wives and female kin of large landowners, such as the Dar al-Shaykh, was seclusion. These women did not work on the land, nor were they involved in caring for the animals. They did not go to the well and neither did they collect wood. This was the task of the croppers' wives. Poor women in general, i.e. the wives of croppers or women not provided for by husband or male kin, contributed a significant amount of agricultural labour. They sometimes worked as harvesters for wages or gleaned the leftover grain. Also, as mentioned previously, the amount of time spent by women in agriculture was not only dependent on the access of the household to land, but also on the type of land (irrigated or non-irrigated) and especially on the family's access to livestock.

The main criterion for the division of labour between the women of the household was age. Since daughters generally married young, leaving the house, and married women had a greater responsibility for domestic work, it was the daughters-in-law who did the heaviest work with the least social status.[7] In this way the organization of work within the household was indirectly determined by wealth. Once the extended household broke up, mothers-in-law could not claim the labour of their daughters-in-law to the same extent as previously. The propertied households maintained the extended form of residence for a longer time and broke up later than the households of the less wealthy families. For men also, the allocation of labour within the household was organized on the basis of age: fathers controlled the labour of their sons. Although both men and women had control to a certain extent over their specific tasks, the relations between women and men was not symmetrical, for the dominant position of the oldest woman in the household was dependent on her husband's position. Once her husband died she lost most of her control.

**Control over income and consumption**

Control over income from male property was generally in the hands of the oldest man in the household. The rights to consume were distributed along the same hierarchical lines of age and gender that governed the allocation of labour. Furthermore, men had greater access to the market than women. The women most active in selling and buying were usually the poorest: the potential control of women was greatest when choices were most limited.

Men, however, were unable to dispose of the products of labour or income at will. A man was obliged to provide for his wife, children and dependent relatives. If her husband did not provide for her a woman could always take refuge with her father or brother, whose duty it was to care for her, for the relation between a man and his female kin, especially his sisters and daughters was lifelong. One of the reasons why a woman would not claim her inheritance rights was that this meant cutting her kinship relation with her brother.[8]

Women did not have any specific rights to the yields of their agricultural labour because men and women had jointly taken part in the production process; these products were used for the subsistence of the household. But when a woman had an income of her own from work that was not considered a duty, such as working at home as a seamstress, the effect of the definition of men as providers was that control over this income was hers, and she was not obliged to use it for the benefit of the household. The same was the case if a woman had her own property; she herself could decide for what purpose it was to be used.[9]

In the case of female wage labour, however, which in Al-Balad was limited to agriculture, the use of this income was already predetermined: women only did this type of work if they were destitute and had no male provider. They therefore had to use their income for the subsistence of the household. This was not socially recognized, however, as the basic assumption of the definition of men as breadwinners was that a woman was provided for and did not have to provide for others. In consequence, women's wages were considerably lower than men's wages.[10]

**Marriage organization**

Kinship was an important organizational principle for the reproduction of property relations and the allocation of labour. As the means of production were not very developed, the reproduction of human labour was very important. This gave marriage organization a central place in social reproduction.

Older men organized the marriages of sons and daughters. In the case of first marriages neither the groom nor the bride had much say in the matter. It was unlikely that a young man would have the means to finance his own marriage, so he was dependent on his father, who would house the new couple and pay the *mahr*, or give a daughter in exchange. Only when older men were marrying or remarrying did they arrange the marriage themselves. Choice of a marriage partner was also constrained by a system of historically instituted rules and practices. At its core was the construction of female sexuality as a threat to the social order and women as sexually irresponsible, ideas which legitimized a very young marriage age for women and her social seclusion.

Not all members of society shared these norms to the same extent. Girls preferred not to marry very young, and especially not to a man who was much older, because he would be too dominant. For a man, marriage was advantageous and necessary: he needed a wife for domestic work and to give him sons. For a young woman marriage had a different meaning. Even if a woman were to stay unmarried a male relative would provide for her, and as long as she was unmarried she did not have the responsibility of a wife and a mother for domestic work. More important was the fact that an unmarried woman continued living with her own relatives, with whom she structurally had a better emotional relation than with her in-laws. The same applied to the relation of a mother with her daughter, which was very different from her relation with her daughter-in-law.[11]

The views of women differed from the dominant ideology not only regarding marriage age; they also had different ideas about the preferred kin relation of marriage partners. Culturally, patrilineal endogamy was highly valued; ideally bride and groom were related through males only. In particular, men could claim their father's brother's daughter (*bint amm*) as a bride.[12] Young women, however, preferred marrying a man related through women, because then they would have their mother's sister as mother-in-law. Also, older women tried to consolidate their relations with their own kin by marrying their children to them. Men, on the other hand, were distrustful of their wife's links with her own relatives. This also became clear in the different stand of men and women towards village endogamy. In contrast to men, women strongly disliked being married to someone from outside the village as this severely hampered their contacts with their own relatives.[13]

In short, especially in the field of marriage organization, clearly antagonisms existed between the genders. The control of men over labour and property was to a certain extent limited, mainly because women had some autonomy over their own labour and a certain access to property. Also, the control of men over their own property and income was not absolute, for women could claim subsistence. The control of older men over marriage organization was, on the other hand, almost complete. At most, older women were able to have some influence due to strict social segregation.

## Depeasantization, migration and wage work

At present about 1,800 people inhabit Al-Balad.[14] There as elsewhere on the West Bank, the penetration of the capitalist market economy in subsistence agriculture has not led to capitalist production relations in agriculture itself (except for the citrus groves). The rapid expansion of opportunities for migration abroad from the mid-1950s meant that peasants were no longer forced to sell their land due to poverty.[15] With the Israeli occupation, land confiscations affected both the rich and the poor and nationality has become a determining criterion of access to land.

In dry-farming areas this, together with competition from subsidized Israeli agriculture, has resulted in a high increase in migration, wage labour in Israel and marginalization of agriculture. In Al-Balad these developments received a strong impetus when in 1970 a large fertile plain near the Far'a Valley, where wheat and barley were cultivated, was confiscated for a Jewish settlement. Most households still have access to some land, but dry-farming has become additional to wage labour, and production is directed towards subsistence. Also the size and number of flocks have dwindled because the mountainous lands have been declared a closed military area.

A different development took place in Nazlat Al-Balad, where about one quarter of the inhabitants of Al-Balad live most of the year. As in other areas where irrigation is possible, production has become market-oriented, with vegetables and citrus produce being sold as cash crops.[16] People from Al-Balad work there mainly as owner-operators and/or sharecroppers. Refugees and landless peasants from other villages work as wage labourers in the larger citrus groves.[17]

Implicitly or explicitly it is often stated that these changes in the social division of labour only touch the lives of men, since women still perform the same work their mothers and grandmothers had always done. Women in Al-Balad, just as previously, do not work outside the village and generally only work on the family lands.[18] But through analysing the changes in women's work and relating them to changes in men's work and to social change in general it becomes clear that even if women do the same work as generations of women before them, the meaning of this work has fundamentally changed.

**A new sexual division of labour?**

As previously, men rarely perform domestic labour; this remains women's work, but the organization of this labour has drastically changed. Most striking is its increased domestication. From the beginning of the 1960s cisterns have been constructed near the houses so that women no longer have to bring water from the well. Since the introduction of kerosene and butagas stoves for cooking and heating, only a few women collect wood. Women's domestic work is now almost exclusively done in or near the house. While at present there are great differences in the standard of housing, in general houses are larger than before, and have more furniture, which is no longer partly homemade but bought in Nablus.

The availability of water and fuel near the house has reduced the workload of women. On the other hand, demands made on housework have increased. The greater emphasis on hygiene has made tasks such as washing and cleaning more time-consuming, and cooking can be intensified almost without limits. Furthermore, the average household has more children, and mothers get less help from their daughters, who now usually attend school for at least four to six years.

This process of domestication is accompanied by an increased individualization of domestic labour. Women more often have to perform this work alone, since sons set up an independent household at an earlier age, especially when they work outside agriculture and have a higher income. This means an increased workload for older women, but less work and control for younger married women (daughters-in-law). In extended-family households there is still the same hierarchy in the division of labour between women as previously, but work requiring a lot of experience, such as baking bread, is now more often done by older women. Girls, especially those who attended school for a longer period, prefer not to acquire this knowledge.

The assumption that women take over men's tasks in agriculture when the latter migrate is not confirmed in Al-Balad. Ploughing, threshing, winnowing and to a lesser extent harvesting are still by and large done by men. If women are active in agriculture, they generally perform the same tasks as women in small peasant households did previously, with some minor changes. Processing butter and yogurt has been replaced by cheese-making, and the summer crop broom straw (*udra mkannis*) has taken the place of sesame. A larger variety of vegetables is grown in the valley and women also pick citrus, which has been cultivated since the 1950s.

The amount of labour input of men and women in agriculture has changed. While previously households often had access to different kinds of land (both dry-farming and irrigated) and to livestock, now many households only have dry-farming land, and very small landholdings have increased in number. There is a big difference between women's work in dry-farming households and in households which have access to irrigated land or which have large numbers of livestock. Whether women in dry-farming households work on the land is mainly determined by the social position and status of the household; not having women work on the land is still prestigious. But wealth and status are no longer determined by the amount of land owned. Most households with dry-farming land depend on wage labour, often migrant, while the products of the lands are an additional source of income in kind. To a large extent differences in income coincide with place of work: migrants to the Gulf States earn most, whilst labourers in Israel and most of those working on the West Bank earn considerably less.

Women in households of migrants to the Gulf States seldom work on the land. Because of their relatively high income these migrants can afford to limit women's work in agriculture, leasing the land or farming it with machinery and specialized male labour. Agricultural work of women is in this case also restricted because of the absence of father or husband. Since the woman's own family but especially her in-laws feel responsible for her conduct, they tend to restrict her freedom of movement as much as possible.[19] Furthermore, since men in the Gulf States do not stay away long, and are often working together with relatives, they are able to continue operating the farm themselves.[20] When men work in Israel or on the West Bank women more often work on the land. Because of the much lower income of these men the products of the land are still of importance, and as even most men working in Israel return at least twice a week, there is less family pressure on women whose husbands are still in close proximity to the household.

In dry-farming households both men and women now perform less agricultural labour in absolute terms. In terms of changes in the division of agricultural labour within the household this means a relatively increased labour input in agriculture for the older generation. Previously, younger men did the heavy work in agriculture; now they work outside agriculture and often outside the West Bank, which in turn limits their wives' participation in agricultural labour. The labour input of women, and particularly older women, has diminished less than that of men, since the impact of mechanization on men's work, in particular on ploughing, threshing and winnowing, has been much greater than on women's.

In households with access to irrigated land and/or a large number of goats, women still do a lot of agricultural labour. These households are usually extended for a longer period of time and daughters-in-law are still burdened with heavy, low-status work. Although less drastic than in dry-farming households, there have been some changes in male employment: young men do work (temporarily) elsewhere. This means either an increased workload for older men (if gender-specific work) or for women (if not). Since men's work is to a larger extent mechanized, the main workload now falls on women.

These transformations in the sexual division of labour have far-reaching consequences for the meaning of women's work. While previously men were already seen as providers, both men and women were still working for subsistence. With the rise of migration and wage labour, male and female labour have become very different. Men have been directly incorporated into the capitalist market economy – mainly as wage labourers – and a separate sphere of (unpaid) subsistence work, agricultural and domestic labour, has been created, less valued and to a large extent allocated to women. Within agriculture, a further differentiation has taken place. As mainly male work tasks have become mechanized (and mechanized tasks become men's work) the productivity of men's work in agriculture has increased much more than women's, resulting in a devaluation of women's agricultural work. In these ways differences between men and women have been emphasized. They are further reinforced by the increasingly unequal division of space. Previously both men and women were working in the village; at present men often work outside the village and even outside the West Bank, while women are increasingly restricted to their homes. At the same time the wage or cash form of men's income has strengthened the conceptualization of men as providers, with the effect that women now appear, on the whole, more as consumers than as producers.

**Diverging income and consumption**

With the shift from subsistence to a market economy and wage labour, the control of those active in the market sector has greatly increased. A much larger part of household consumption is bought in the market, which makes access to cash more important. This means that the autonomy of younger men in particular has increased considerably, while women have become more dependent, since their access to sources of income has decreased.

Women also have less control over the products of the labour of men, and consumption along lines of gender appears to have become increasingly unequal. Men's higher income makes it easier for them to fulfil on an elementary level their duty of 'provider' but, especially since this higher income takes the form of money, it does not automatically lead to an increased level of consumption for women. These problems are most pressing when men are working far away, in the Gulf States, and have a relatively high income. A large information gap occurs: women and older people in general lose sight of the labour and income of migrating men, whilst previously younger men were working within their eyesight. A young migrant's wife is in a particularly difficult situation, since her husband often sends his income to his father, and it is expected of her that she will postpone consumption until he returns home.

**Reduced access to property**

Impoverishment and partible inheritance have gradually reduced the access of men to land and livestock. The large-scale confiscations and closures of land accelerated this process significantly. This means that the power basis of older men – their control over the means of production – has been severely weakened. The access of younger men to wage labour, which contributes an increasingly important share to the total household income, has made sons less dependent on their fathers, and encouraged them to set up independent households. As nuclear households increasingly become the ideal, fathers pass on property, such as building land and financial support for building a house, to their sons earlier than previously.

The access of women to productive property has also lessened. Since the mid-1960s women no longer sell their gold (their bride's share) to buy land and only rarely to buy livestock. One reason is that women no longer have the opportunity to buy productive property with their gold because of the diminished value of the bride's share. In the division of property along gender lines, the value of what is passed on to young men and young women at or shortly after marriage has become more divergent. Compared to the value of houses and land, the relative value of the bride's share has diminished considerably.[21]

The lower value of the bride's share is, however, not the only obstacle to women's access to property. Male wage labour has also strengthened the concepts of men as providers and women as consumers. This in itself discourages independent property ownership by women. If a woman sells her gold nowadays, she usually does this to help her husband to buy a house, to set him up in a small business or to help him with the initial costs of migration. The result is that she loses control over her property. Although both men and women have less access than previously to land and livestock, this is more damaging for women, since only men have gained access to wage labour (and in a few cases to new forms of property such as shops or delivery vans).

### Marriage organization

Technological development – mechanization has been introduced even into subsistence production – has made human labour less important. And since wage labour instead of land has become the main source of livelihood, the patrilineal inheritance system has become less important. Marriage organization therefore has a less central place in social reproduction than previously, and in consequence the definition of women as sexually irresponsible is less emphasized.

The diminished control of father over sons implies not only more autonomy for younger men, but also an increased control over marriage organization by older women. Since social seclusion has not yet completely broken down, mothers have some control over arranging marriages. This is not only in the interest of this category of women themselves, but can also benefit younger women. As mentioned before, the interests of older and younger women coincide to a certain extent on points such as marriage age and choice of marriage partners. It has become easier for young women to refuse to marry their cousins, and to postpone marriage somewhat.[22] Also, mothers seem to succeed more often in arranging marriages of their sons and daughters to their own relatives instead of to in-laws.

## Changes in gender hierarchy: contrasts and contradictions

Al-Balad is no longer a peasant village with subsistence agriculture as its main source of employment and income, but a community where dry-farming agriculture has become additional to wage labour (mostly outside the West Bank) with a small minority of farmers producing cash crops on irrigated land.

In assessing the impact of these transformations for gender hierarchy, a number of contradictory trends are apparent. Generally speaking, it seems that age as a principle for hierarchical ordering has lost some of its importance to gender. The autonomy of younger men has increased because of their access to wage labour and the market, whilst women have become economically more dependent on men. But hierarchical relations and contradictory interests amongst women are also important. For older women the earlier disintegration of the extended household usually means a loss of control, while at the same time it means increased autonomy for young married women.

Nonetheless the increased economic dependency of women is not the whole story. For women the impact of these transformations has been complex. On the one hand, women have lost most of the control they had over labour and property, and women's work is less valued. But, on the other hand, these changes have afforded women some precarious advantages. As women are economically more dependent and marriage organization has become less central in social reproduction, ideological constructs legitimizing the subordination of women have become less important. This means that women are no longer defined as irresponsible in the field of sexuality to the same extent as previously. Since older men have concurrently lost some of their near-absolute control over marriage organization, women have gained more autonomy in this field. But this autonomy is precarious, for it is mainly based on the still existing social seclusion of women and while the economic seclusion of women has been strengthened, social seclusion appears to be breaking down.

The increased autonomy of women in marriage organization is one of the factors which explains why women do not perceive male domination as more marked. Another reason is that the self-images of women now fit much more closely with the way in which the dominant ideology defines them. While previously there was a clear contradiction between the ideology of the male provider and women's work, at present this contradiction is becoming much less apparent. Women's work has been made invisible and most women themselves do not define their subsistence labour as 'work'. This is related to the fact that there seems to be a consistently adverse relation between gender symmetry and social status. An autonomous gender position for women usually coincides with poverty and low social status. The diminished control of women over labour and property means a rising social status; individualization and domestication of female labour are prestigious social symbols and indications of increased wealth. Also, marriages which are socially advantageous for women (hypergamy) often imply a strong gender hierarchy. In short, the increased economic dependency of women is not only 'compensated' for by more space within the marriage system, but also by a higher place within the social hierarchy.

## Notes

1. Al-Balad is a pseudonym for a West Bank village where I did fieldwork from November 1980 until August 1981.

2. The end of the 1920s is also methodologically convenient as Granqvist's books are based on data collected in the village of Artas near Bethlehem in 1927. In this way the central problem of oral history – the influence of norms of the present on perceptions of the past – is to

a certain extent met.

3. An elaborate analysis of the peripheralization of the Djabal Nablus can be found in Graham-Brown, 1982.

4. See Granqvist, 1935, p. 226.

5. See Granqvist, 1931, p. 119.

6. A similar sexual division of labour in agriculture was observed in the beginning of this century elesewhere in Palestine (Dalman, 1964).

7. See Granqvist, 1935, pp. 149–50.

8. See Granqvist, 1935, p. 256.

9. See Granqvist, 1935, p. 239; 1931, p. 145.

10. Graham.Brown (1982: p. 147) mentions that in 1922 men earned PT15 plus food for picking olives, while women earned PT10 plus food.

11. See Granqvist, 1935, p. 146. The longer-term prospects of an unmarried woman are not so positive. If she marries when she is older this is likely to be a less prestigious marriage. If she remains unmarried after her parents have died she will live with her brother and his wife. Then the contrasts become apparent between herself as an unmarried childless woman and her sister-in-law as the mother of sons.

12. See Granqvist, 1931, pp. 66, 69, 76.

13. See Granqvist, 1931, pp. 93–4. Another pattern of marriage, taking account of the importance of kinship relations between women, was when two sisters married into the same household. The assumption was that as sisters get along well they would not stimulate their husbands to set up independent households.

14. Not included in this estimate are those who, together with their families, are living outside Al-Balad, some of them in Kuwait, but the majority in Jordan.

15. In Al-Balad men began migrating from the mid-1950s; in other areas, in particular the Jerusalem, Ramallah and Bethlehem regions, outmigration started at the beginning of this century, mainly to North and South America.

16. For an extensive study on irrigated agriculture see Tamari and Giacaman, 1980.

In 1984 the Israeli authorities published plans to widen the road from Nablus to the Jordan Valley. This road passes through Nazlat-Al-Balad. These plains, if implemented, will result in the destruction of the irrigation system, the confiscation of irrigated land and the destruction of houses (Law in the Service of Man, 1984). All this will severely damage agricultural development. Only 5% of West Bank agriculture is irrigated, largely concentrated in the Jordan Valley area.

17. Employment of the male labour force of Al-Balad (based on data on more than half the total male labour force) is as follows: 40% work outside the West Bank (17% in Israel, 5% in Jordan and 18% in the Gulf States, mainly Kuwait); 24% work as wage labourers or are self-employed on the West Bank, outside the agricultural sector; and 36% work in agriculture (23% have access to irrigated land and 13% have access only to dry-farming land; these are mainly older men).

18. In other villages some women do work as wage labourers, often in sewing workshops. This work has a very low status and is very badly paid (*see* for example Escribano and El-Joubeth, 1981, p. 155).

19. At the same time, while her husband is away she has no man whose specific responsibility towards her she can claim.

20. This situation can be different in villages with a longer history of migration, where men migrate further away and cannot return so often (North and South America), and where a larger number of men are away.

21. See Rosenfeld, 1980. While in Al-Balad in the 1930s building an extra room was somewhat cheaper than in the *mahr*, now a house usually costs at least ten times as much. Elsewhere developments might be different. For example, in areas such as the Ramallah region with a tradition of migration to the USA the *mahr* of a bride is higher if she has US citizenship (Escribano and El-Joubeth, 1981, p. 156).

22. In a sample of the marriage age of women the following shift becomes apparent: in the period 1928–1967 half of the brides were under 16, and a quarter under 14 (N = 45); in the period 1967–1981 only 10% was under 16 and none under 14 (N = 10).

## Selected Bibliography

Dalman, Gustav, 1964, *Arbeit und Sitte in Palastina*, Hildeshemim: Georg Olms.

Escribano, Marisa and El-Joubeh, Nazmi, 1981, 'Migration and change in a West Bank village: the case of Deir Dibwan', *Journal of Palestine Studies*, vol. 11, No. 1, pp. 150–61.

Granqvist, Hilma, 1931, *Marriage Conditions in a Palestinian Village*, I, Helsingfors: Akademische Buchhandlung.

_______ 1935, *Marriage Conditions in a Palestinian Village*, II, Helsingfors: Akademische Buchhandlung.

Graham-Brown, Sarah, 1982, 'The political economy of the Jabal Nablus, 1920–1948', in Roger Owen (ed.), *Studies in the Economic and Social History of Palestine in the Nineteenth and Twentieth Centuries*, London: Macmillan, pp. 88–176.

Harris, Olivia, 1981, 'Households as natural units,' in Kate Young, Carol Wolkowitz and Roslyn McCullagh (eds.), *Of Marriage and the Market: Women's Subordination in International Perspective*, London: CSE Books, pp. 109–47.

Law in the Service of Man, 1984, *Israeli Proposed Roadplan for the West Bank: A Question for the International Court of Justice*, Ramallah: Law in the Service of Man.

Rosaldo, Michelle, 1980, 'The use and abuse of anthropology: reflections on feminism and cross-cultural understanding, *Signs*, vol. 5, no. 3, pp. 389–417.

Rosenfeld, Henry, 1980, 'Men and women in Arab peasant to proletariat transformation', in Stanley Diamond (ed.), *Theory and Practice: Essays presented to Gene Weltfish*, The Hague, Paris, New York: Mouton, pp. 195–219.

Sayigh, Rosemary, 1981, 'Roles and functions of Arab women: a reappraisal', *Arab Studies Quarterly*, vol. 3, no. 3, pp. 258–74.

Tamari, Salim and Giacaman, Rita, 1980, *Zbeidat: The Social Impact of Drip Irrigation on a Palestinian Peasant Community in the Jordan Valley*, Bir Zeit: Bir Zeit University Publications.

# Index